TWITTER: THE COMIC

(THE BOOK)

TWITTER: THE COMIC

(THE BOOK)

COMICS BASED ON
THE GREATEST TWEETS
OF OUR GENERATION

Mike Rosenthal (@VectorBelly)

CHRONICLE BOOKS

SAN FRANCISCO

LIBRARY OF CONGRESS CATALOGING-IN-PUBLICATION DATA AVAILABLE.
ISBN: 978-1-4521-3513-7

MANUFACTURED IN CHINA

MIX
Paper from
responsible sources
FSC® C104723
FSC
www.fsc.org

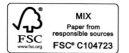

DESIGNED BY EMILY DUBIN

10 9 8 7 6 5 4 3 2 1

CHRONICLE BOOKS LLC
680 SECOND STREET
SAN FRANCISCO, CALIFORNIA 94107
WWW.CHRONICLEBOOKS.COM

ACKNOWLEDGMENTS

THANK YOU TO ALL THE FANTASTIC TWEET AUTHORS:

@2TONBUG
@ACEMAKESWORDS
@ACOMPLEXCOLLIN
@AHUJ9
@ALIEN_SUSHI
@AMELIALIKESYOU
@BBW_BFF
@BLAUDIABLOGAN
@BORING_AS_HECK
@BRANDONELZBY
@BRO_PAIR
@BROWNBOYBLUES
@BUB__BUB
@BUCKYISOTOPE
@BURGERKRANG
@CAKETENDO64
@CEEJOYNER
@CHEESEBOY22
@CHUCHUGOOGOO
@COOLBABYRAT
@CRIMEGOLEM
@CRUSHINGBORT
@CRYLENOL
@DANKHERBMULLET
@DAVEDITTELL
@DEBBIE_HAIRY
@DIAPER_WOLF
@DIESELCHEESE
@DOCTOR_ASS

@DOGBONER
@DONG_PARTY
@DRUGLEAF
@DUBSTEP4DADS
@DUCKPUPPET
@DVOTED_HUSBAND
@DVSBLAST
@ELECTROLEMON
@FAMOUSCRAB
@FAMOUSHORSE
@FART
@FART_BRINGER
@FECKLESSWASTER
@FRED_DELICIOUS
@FUCPK
@GØM
@GOODNAPS
@GRAEYALIEN
@HAPPYINVENTOR
@HELL_HOMER
@HRTBPS
@IAMENIDCOLESLAW
@IDIOT_TEEN
@INGMARBIRDMAN
@INITFO
@INMYNEWSKIN
@JENNAMARIECAREY
@JEVENSTEAKOBSON
@JONBRUH

@JONNY_WAGS
@JONNYSUN
@KELLANBC
@KYLE_LIPPERT
@LAWBLOB
@LAZY_JOE_
@LENNOXTRUMAN
@LOSTCATDOG
@MEAN_CROW
@MEEPISMURDER
@MOUTHEATERS
@MRSJOHNGOODMAN
@MXRK
@NICE_MUSTARD
@NOOG
@OBIIIEEEE
@PAINTED_EEL
@PAJAMABEN_
@PISS_WIZARD
@PISSCOP
@PISSRIFLE
@POSH
@PUPPY_EGGS
@RACHELMILLMAN
@RAD_MILK
@RAD_MOUSE
@RADSTUNTS
@RICH_MCCARTHY
@ROBFEE

@RUBEN_FERDINAND
@SADDESTTIGER
@SATANSTONGUE
@SCREWCUMBER
@SEX_COLUM
@SHANUSMCANUS
@SHRUGLORD
@SHY_BONER
@TARASHOE
@TASTEFACTORY
@THEMINDTWEAK
@THYNEBEAR
@TINYDOGE
@TORMNY_PICKEALS
@TRASH_EATER_DOG
@TWELVEYEARSOLD
@URFAVORITEJOEL
@VERY_TALL_MAN
@VINCENESS
@VLADCHOC
@WAELWULF
@WEBBEDSPACE
@WEEDCOFFIN
@WIMPSICLE
@WOODMUFFIN
@YOGURTPYRAMID

AND A VERY SPECIAL THANK YOU TO @KANYEWEST.

INTRODUCTION

I STARTED COLLECTING TWEETS IN 2012.
SPECIAL TWEETS.
MAGICAL TWEETS.

THEY CAPTURED EVERYTHING
WONDERFUL AND
TERRIBLE AND
WONDERFULLY TERRIBLE
ABOUT OUR GENERATION.

HOW COULD I NOT DRAW THEM
AS LITTLE COMICS?
SO I DID.
THEN DUMPED 'EM ON
TWITTERTHECOMIC.TUMBLR.COM.

I THINK WE'RE
ALL COMPELLED TO
REIMAGINE GREAT THINGS.
WHY ELSE WOULD THERE BE
SO MANY REMIXES OF
THE *SPACE JAM* SONG?

LOOK IT UP.

ANYWAY, THE TUMBLR GOT A MILLION FOLLOWERS OR WHATEVER.

PEOPLE LIKED THEM. PEOPLE SHARED THEM. PEOPLE RIOTED IN THE STREETS BECAUSE I DIDN'T EDIT THE TYPOS OUT OF THEM.

BUT YOU KNOW WHAT? MISTAKES AREN'T ILLEGAL.
LIFE ISN'T EDITED. AN EDITOR DIDN'T CORRECT THAT TIME YOU MADE
OUT WITH YOUR EX IN THE BATHROOM AT THE PASADENA CHIPOTLE.
AND A WEEK LATER, AN EDITOR DIDN'T WARN YOU AGAINST
TAKING THAT RASH CREAM ORALLY.
SO THE FOLLOWING COMICS WILL REMAIN FLAWED AND WEIRD AND ITCHY.
THAT'S WHAT MAKES THEM BEUATIFUL.

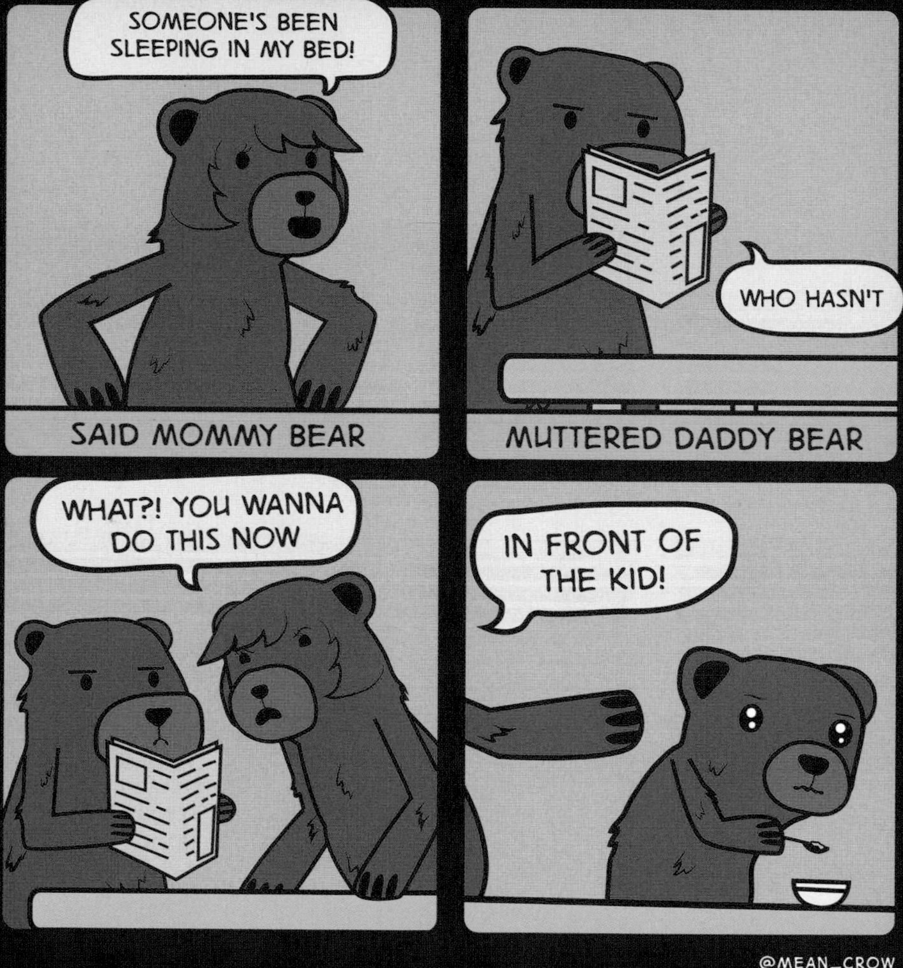

SOMEONE'S BEEN SLEEPING IN MY BED!
SAID MOMMY BEAR
WHO HASN'T
MUTTERED DADDY BEAR
WHAT?! YOU WANNA DO THIS NOW
IN FRONT OF THE KID!
@MEAN_CROW

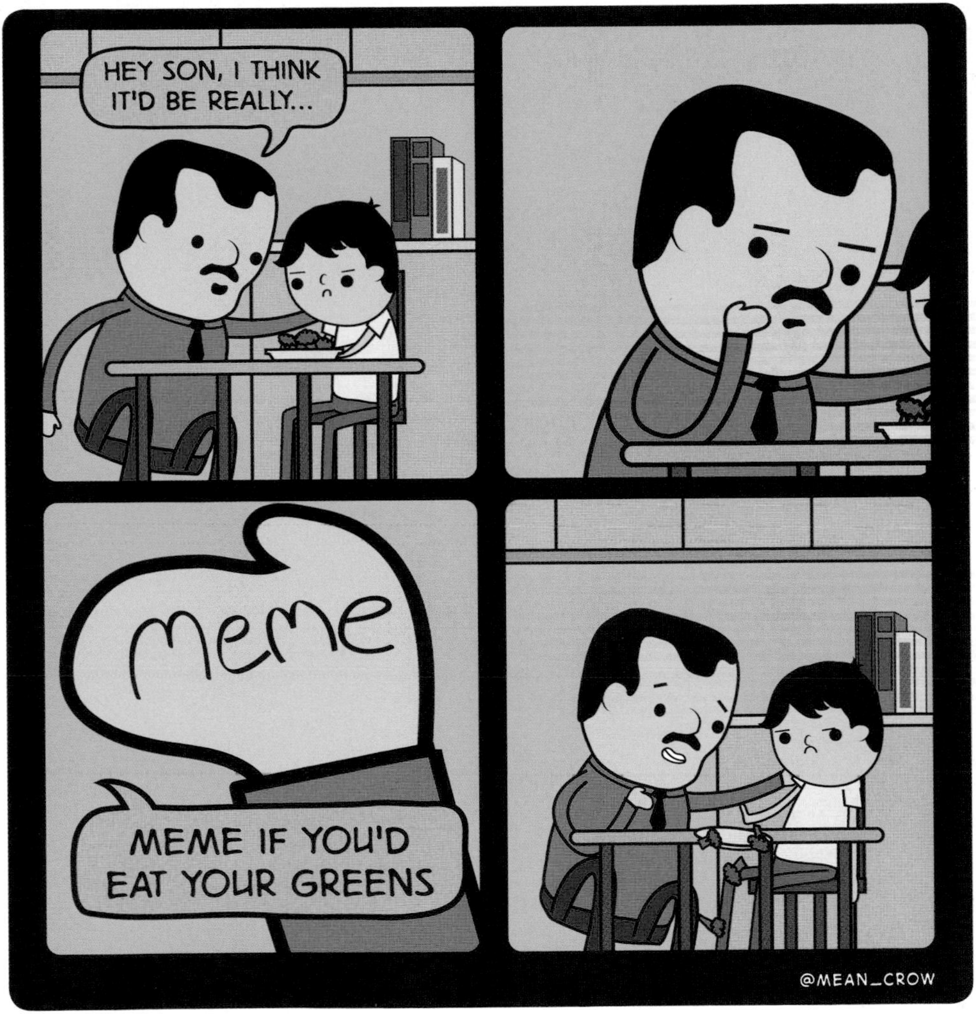
HEY SON, I THINK IT'D BE REALLY...
meme
MEME IF YOU'D EAT YOUR GREENS
@MEAN_CROW

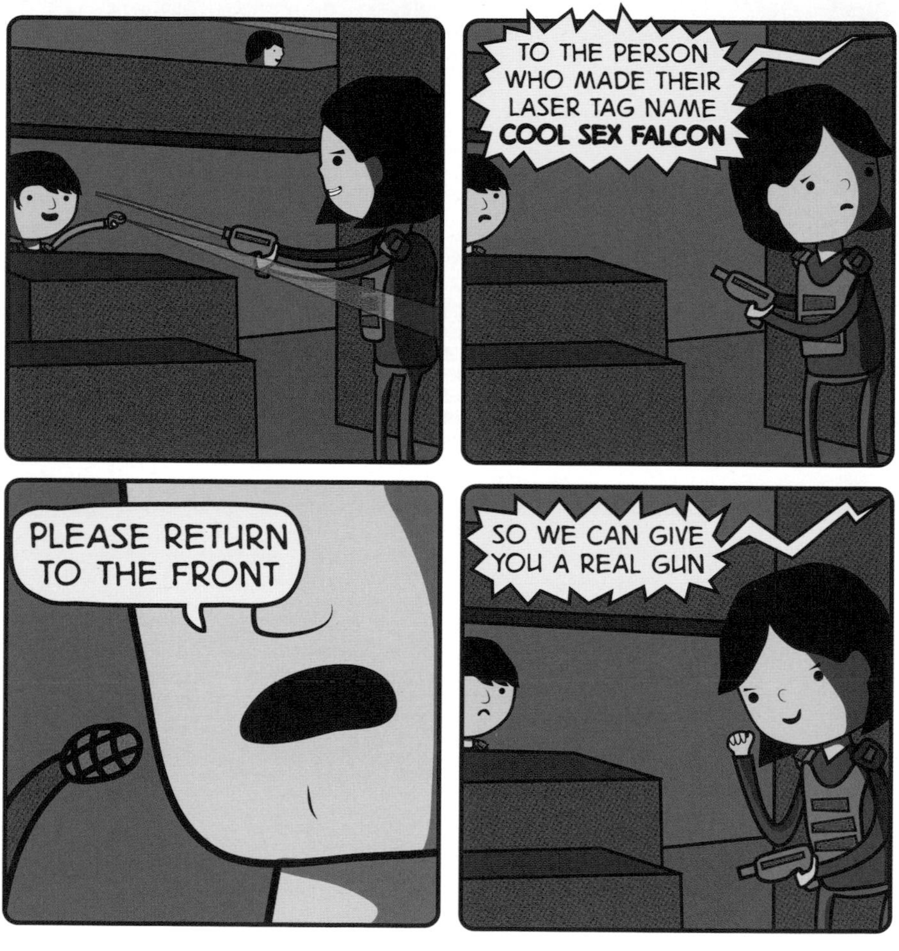
TO THE PERSON WHO MADE THEIR LASER TAG NAME **COOL SEX FALCON**
PLEASE RETURN TO THE FRONT
SO WE CAN GIVE YOU A REAL GUN

@BORING_AS_HECK

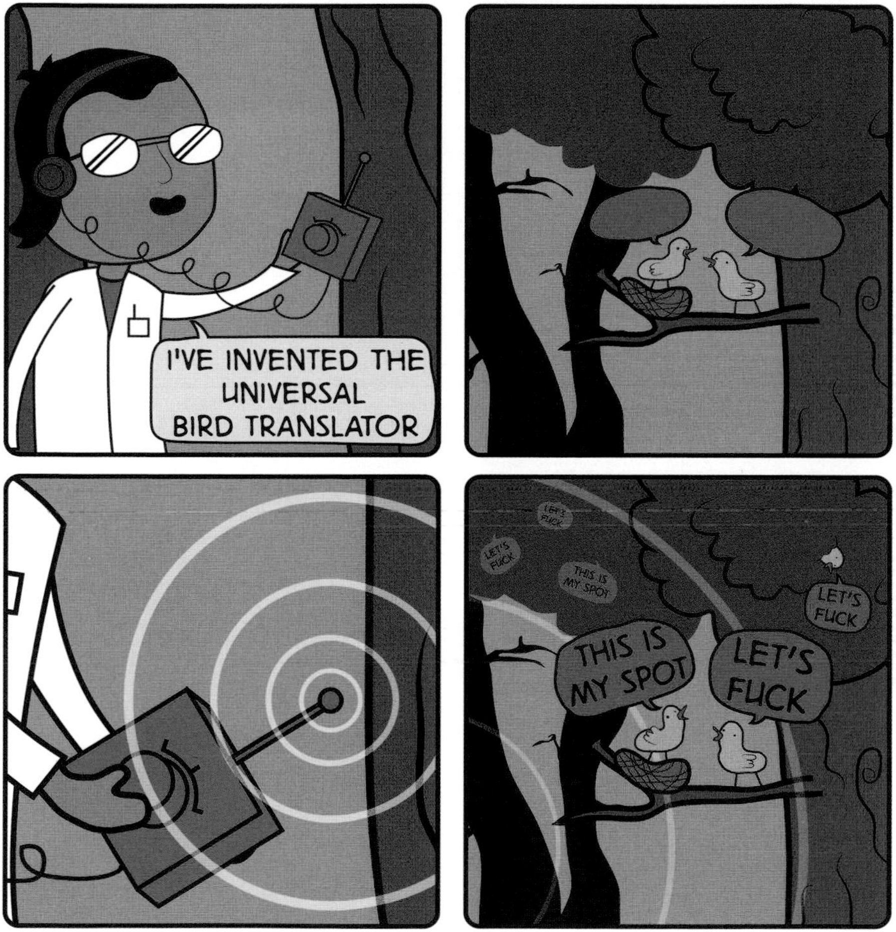
I'VE INVENTED THE UNIVERSAL BIRD TRANSLATOR
LET'S FUCK
THIS IS MY SPOT
LET'S FUCK
THIS IS MY SPOT
LET'S FUCK

@WOODMUFFIN

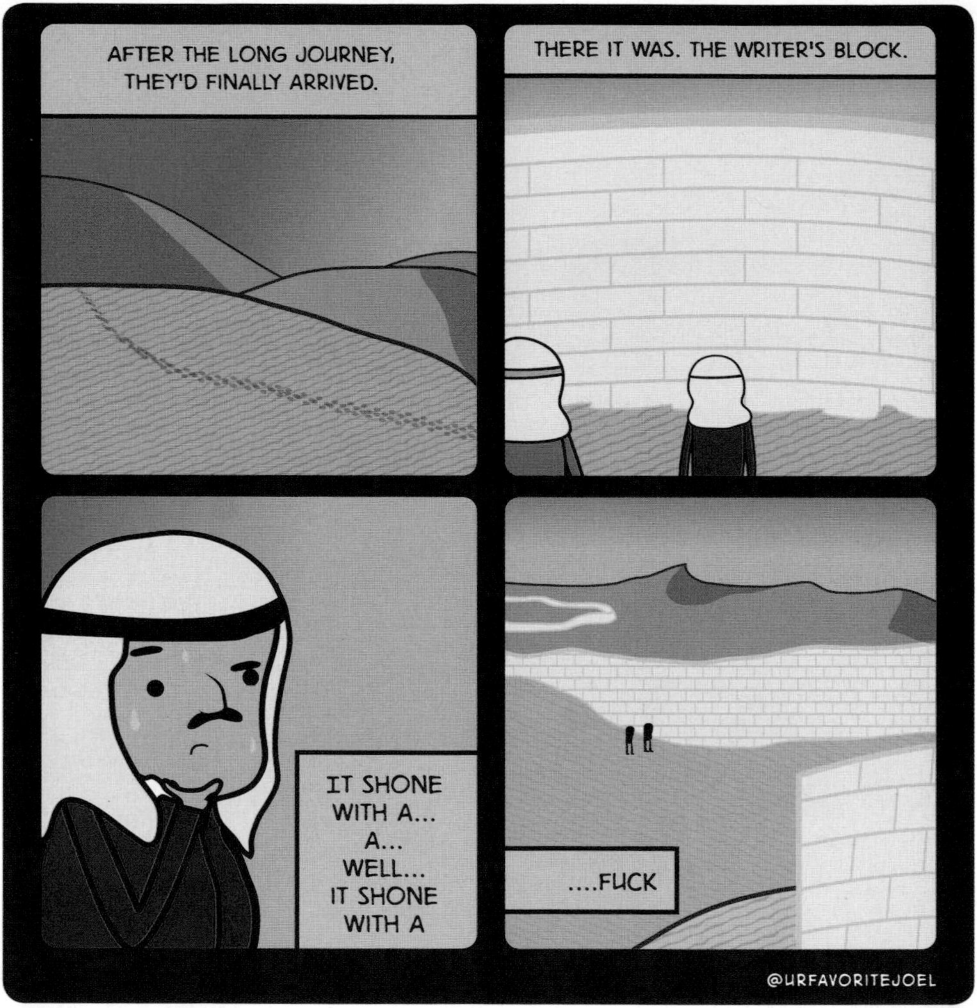
AFTER THE LONG JOURNEY, THEY'D FINALLY ARRIVED.
THERE IT WAS. THE WRITER'S BLOCK.
IT SHONE WITH A... A... WELL... IT SHONE WITH A
....FUCK
@URFAVORITEJOEL

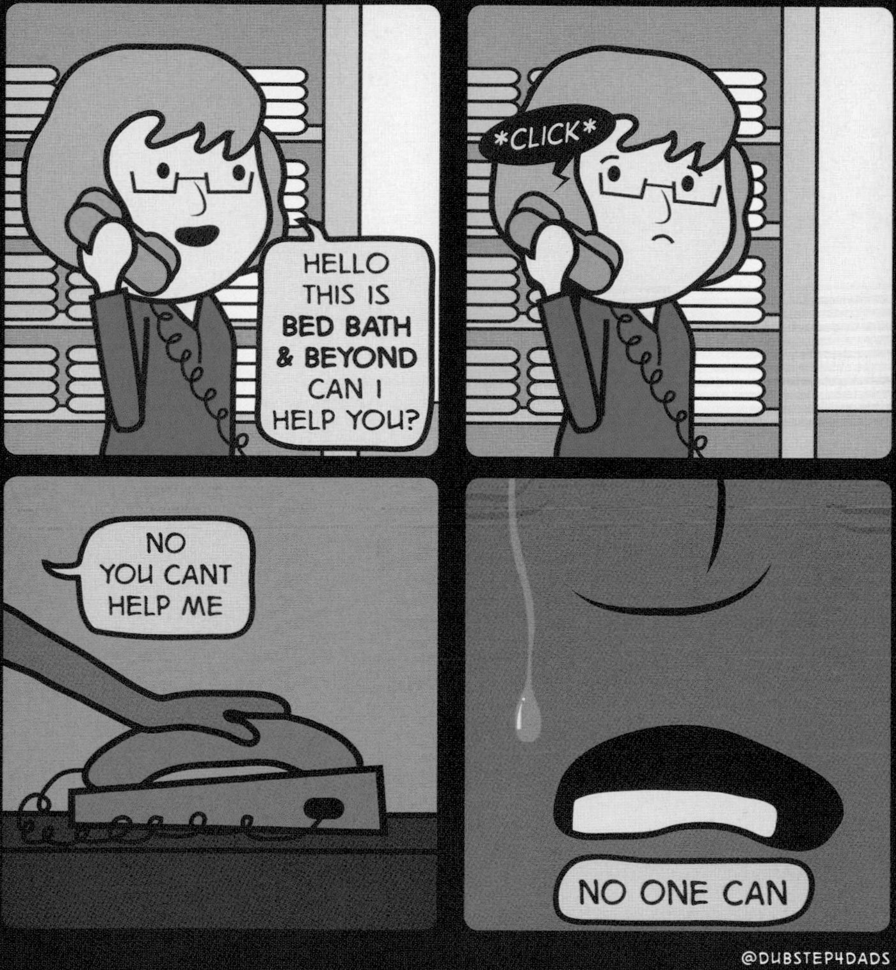
HELLO THIS IS BED BATH & BEYOND CAN I HELP YOU?
CLICK
NO YOU CANT HELP ME
NO ONE CAN
@DUBSTEP4DADS

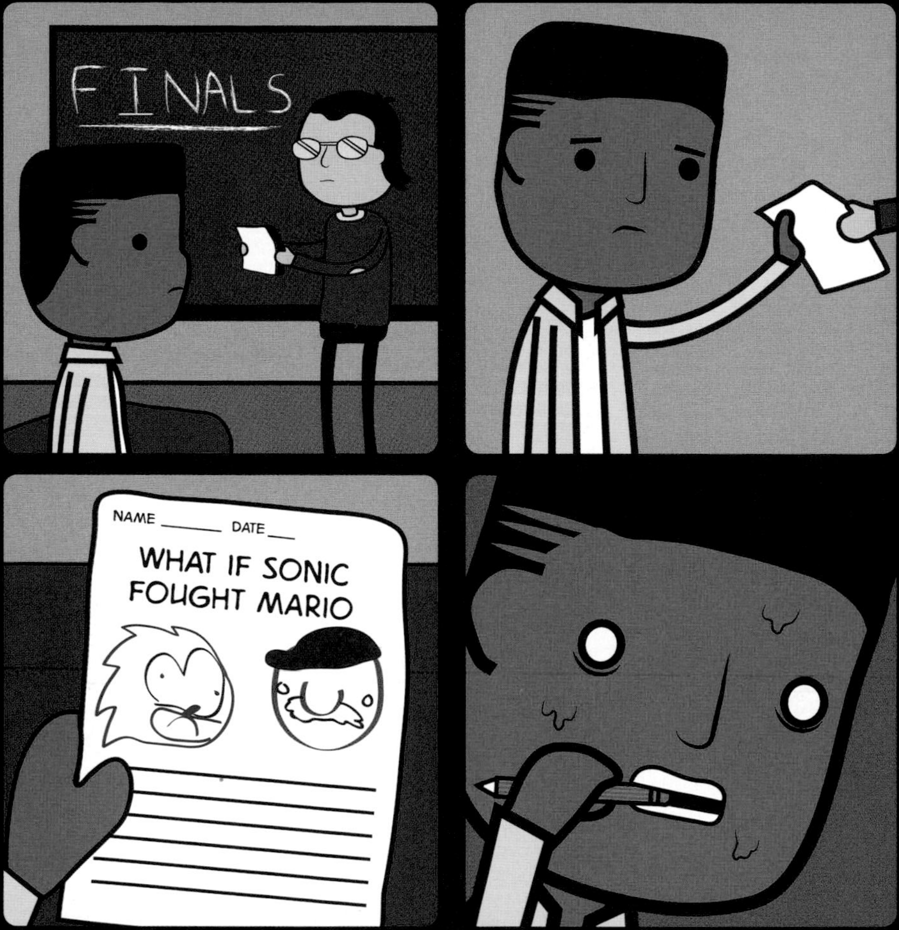
FINALS
NAME ______ DATE ___
WHAT IF SONIC FOUGHT MARIO

@TINYDOGE

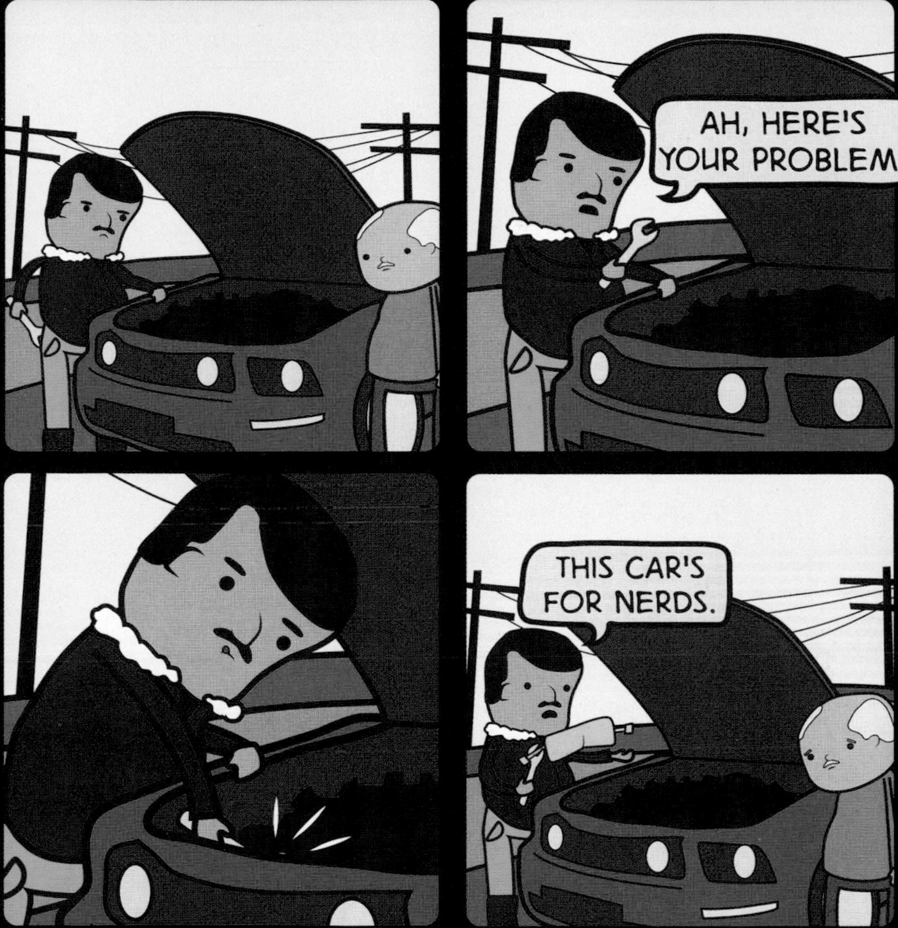
AH, HERE'S YOUR PROBLEM.
THIS CAR'S FOR NERDS.
@AHUJ9

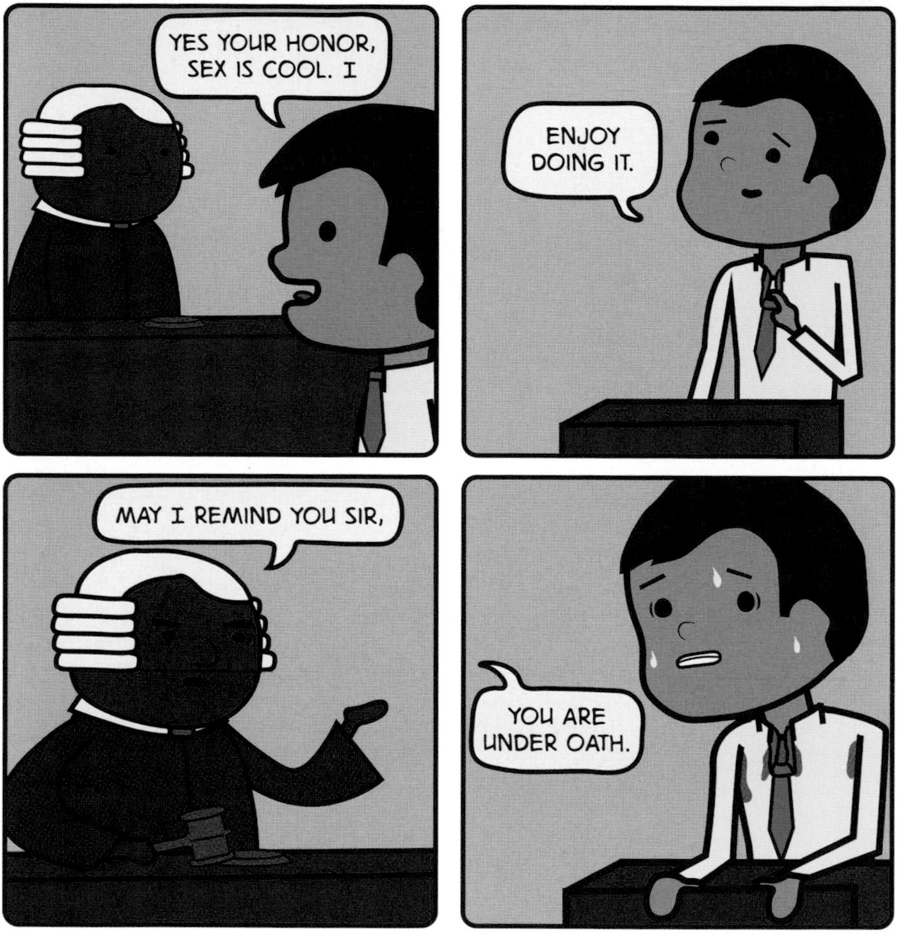
YES YOUR HONOR, SEX IS COOL. I
ENJOY DOING IT.
MAY I REMIND YOU SIR,
YOU ARE UNDER OATH.

@VERY_TALL_MAN

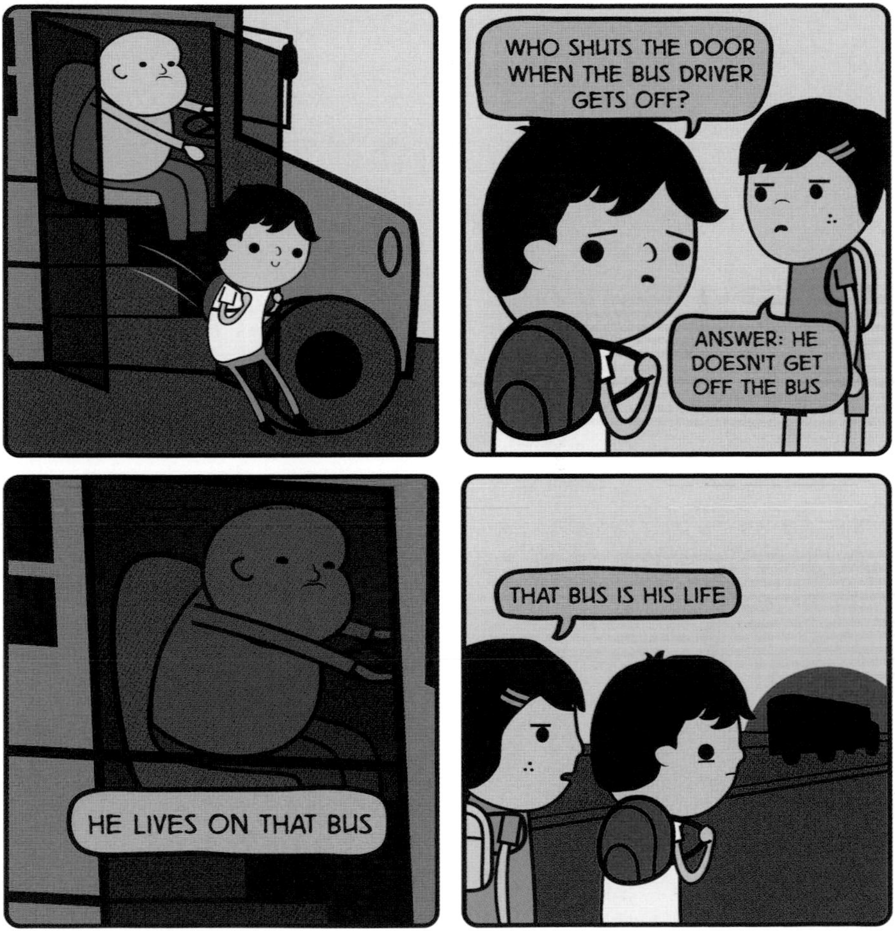
WHO SHUTS THE DOOR WHEN THE BUS DRIVER GETS OFF?
ANSWER: HE DOESN'T GET OFF THE BUS
HE LIVES ON THAT BUS
THAT BUS IS HIS LIFE

@YOGURTPYRAMID

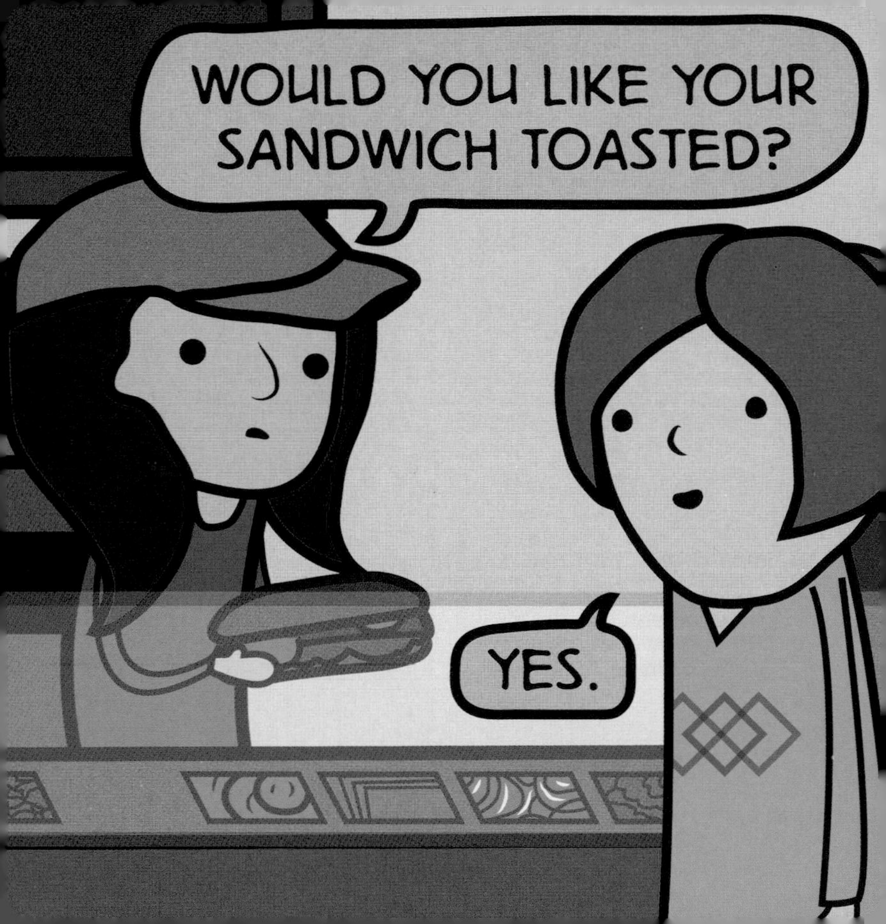
WOULD YOU LIKE YOUR SANDWICH TOASTED?
YES.

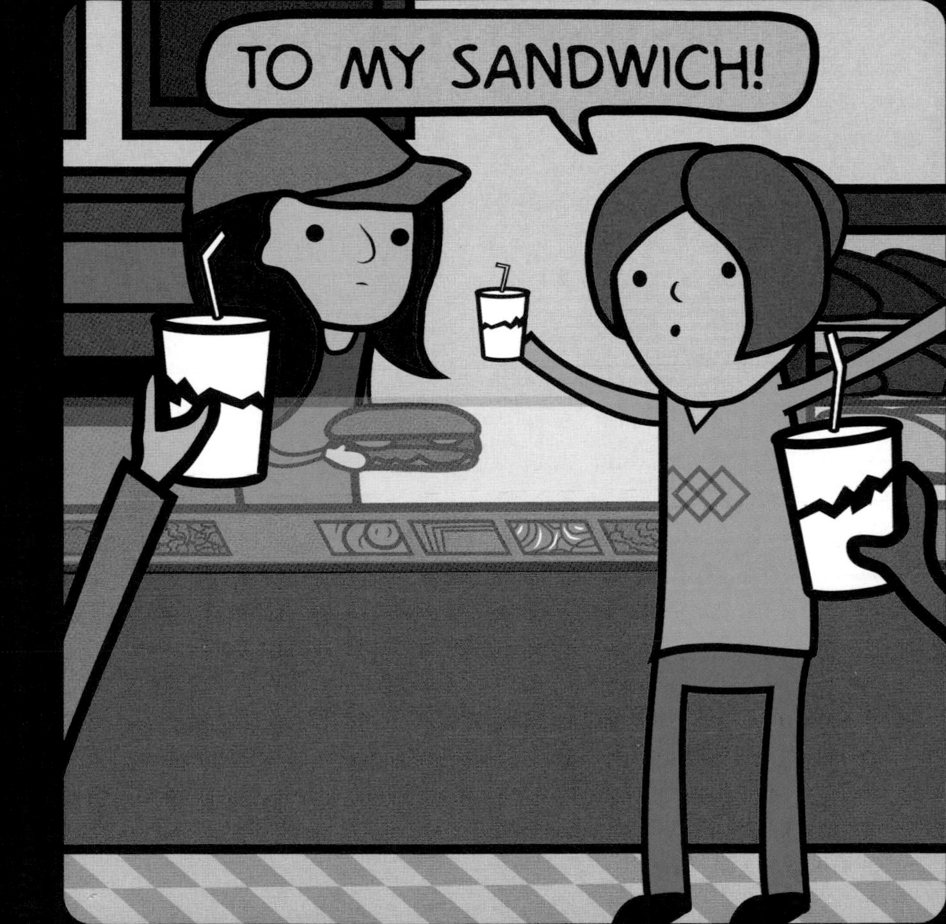
TO MY SANDWICH!

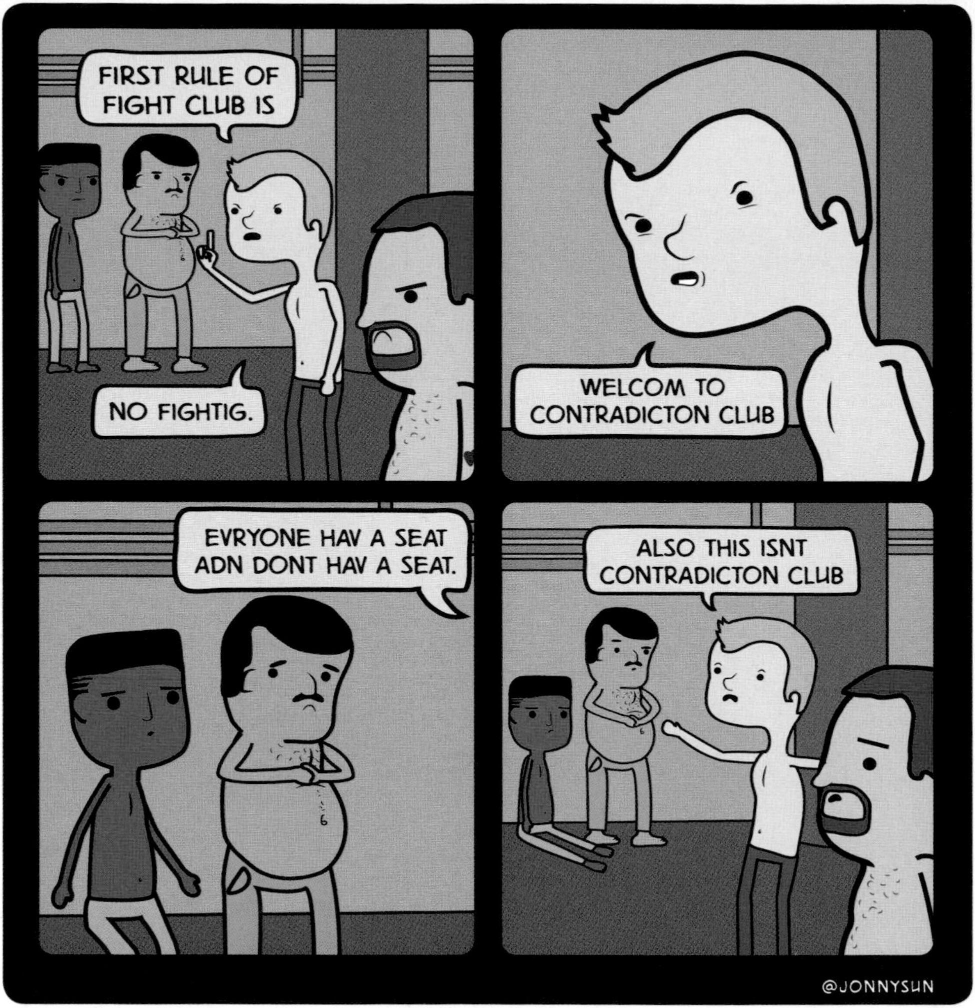
FIRST RULE OF FIGHT CLUB IS
NO FIGHTIG.
WELCOM TO CONTRADICTON CLUB
EVRYONE HAV A SEAT ADN DONT HAV A SEAT.
ALSO THIS ISNT CONTRADICTON CLUB
@JONNYSUN

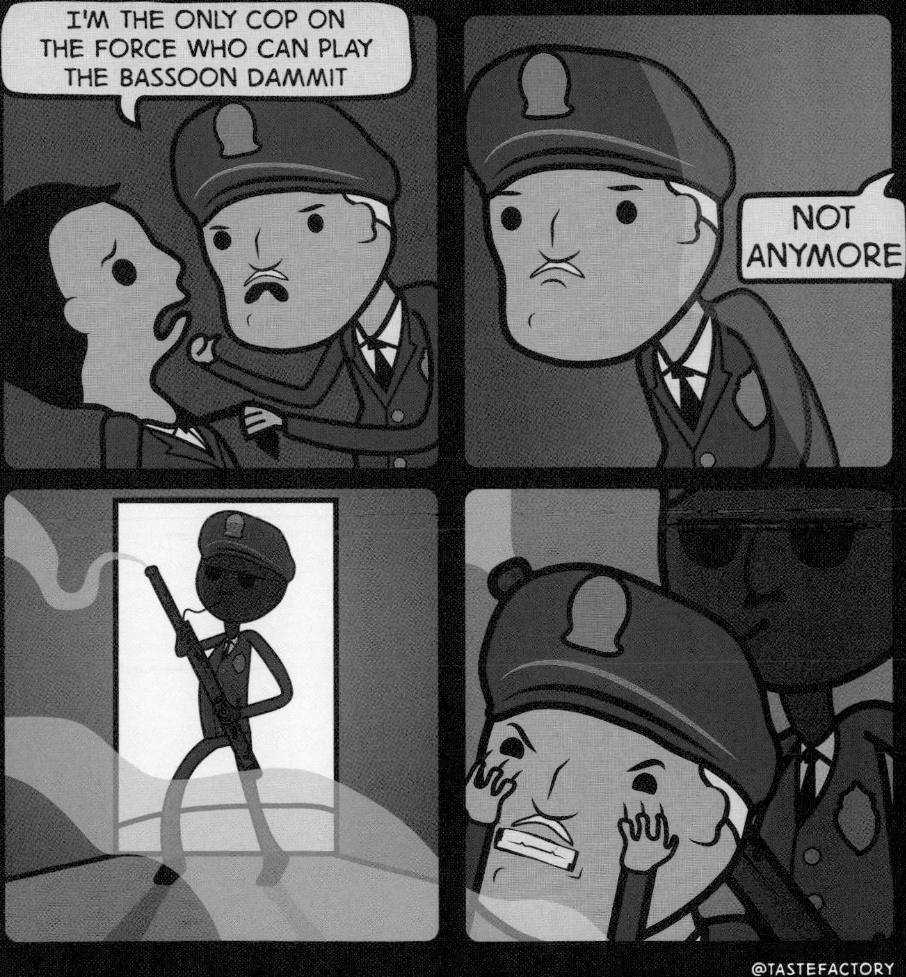
I'M THE ONLY COP ON THE FORCE WHO CAN PLAY THE BASSOON DAMMIT
NOT ANYMORE
@TASTEFACTORY

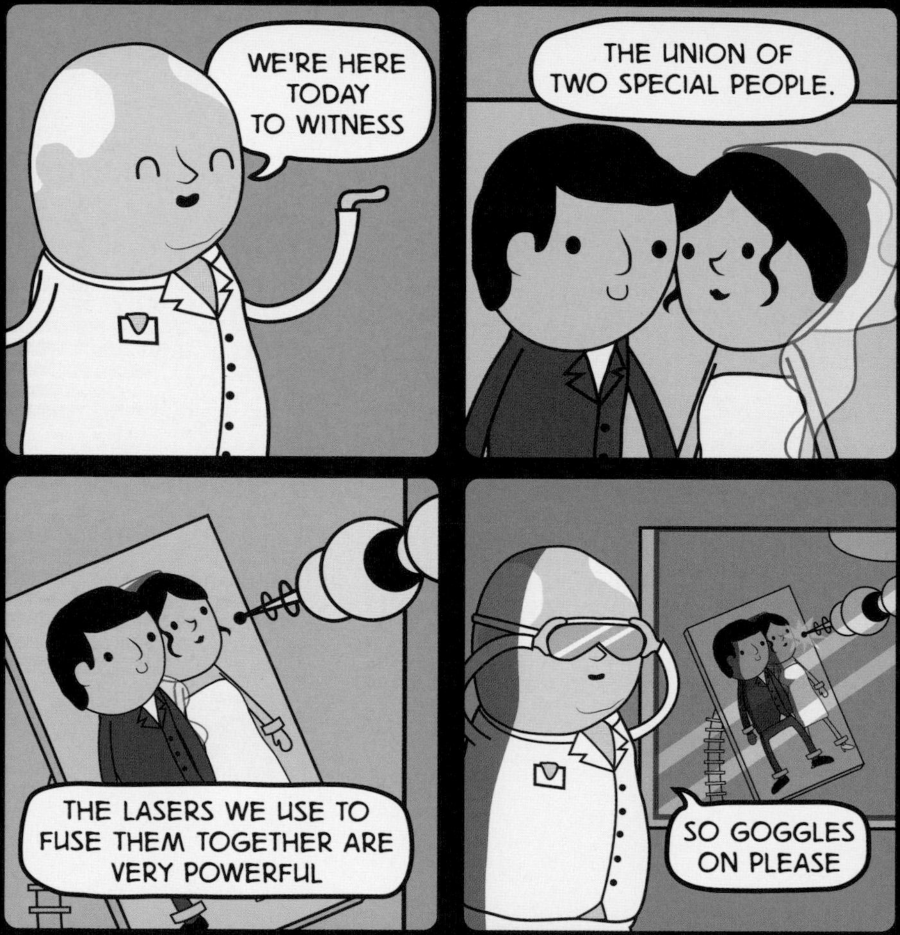
WE'RE HERE TODAY TO WITNESS
THE UNION OF TWO SPECIAL PEOPLE.
THE LASERS WE USE TO FUSE THEM TOGETHER ARE VERY POWERFUL
SO GOGGLES ON PLEASE
@CHUCHUGOOGOO

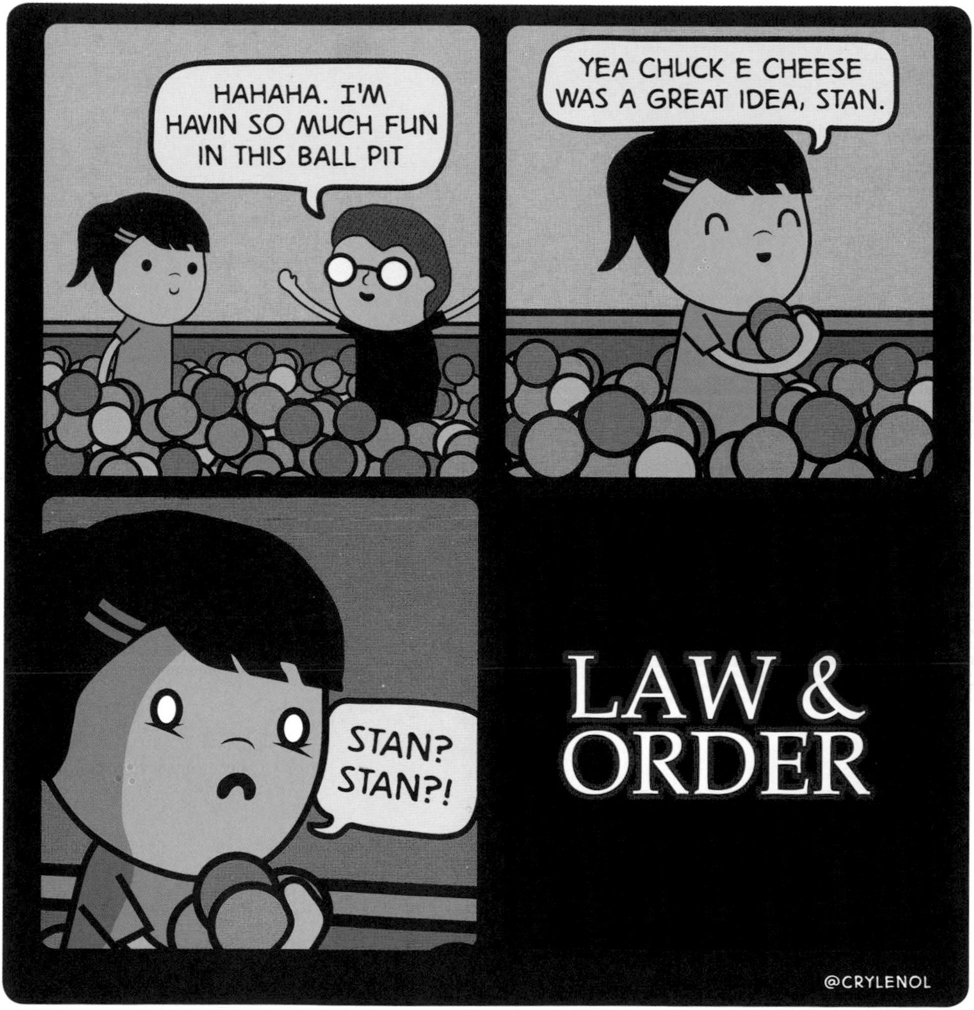
HAHAHA. I'M HAVIN SO MUCH FUN IN THIS BALL PIT
YEA CHUCK E CHEESE WAS A GREAT IDEA, STAN.
STAN? STAN?!
LAW & ORDER
@CRYLENOL

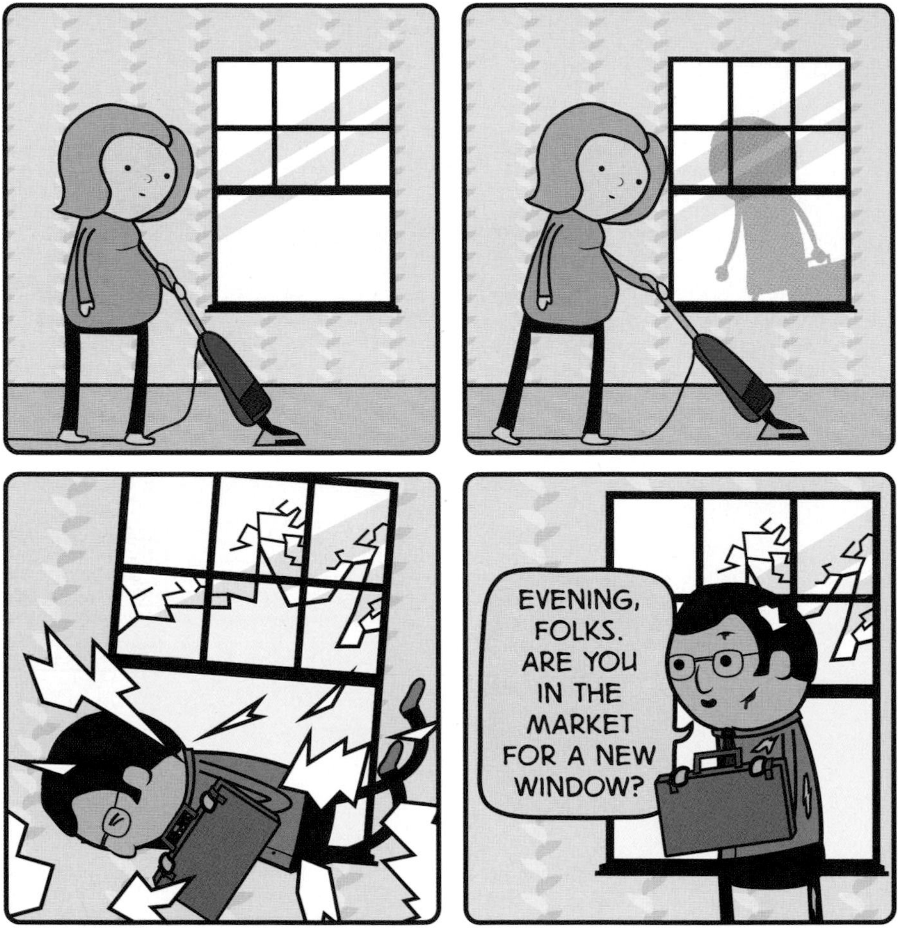
EVENING, FOLKS. ARE YOU IN THE MARKET FOR A NEW WINDOW?

@RICH_MCCARTHY

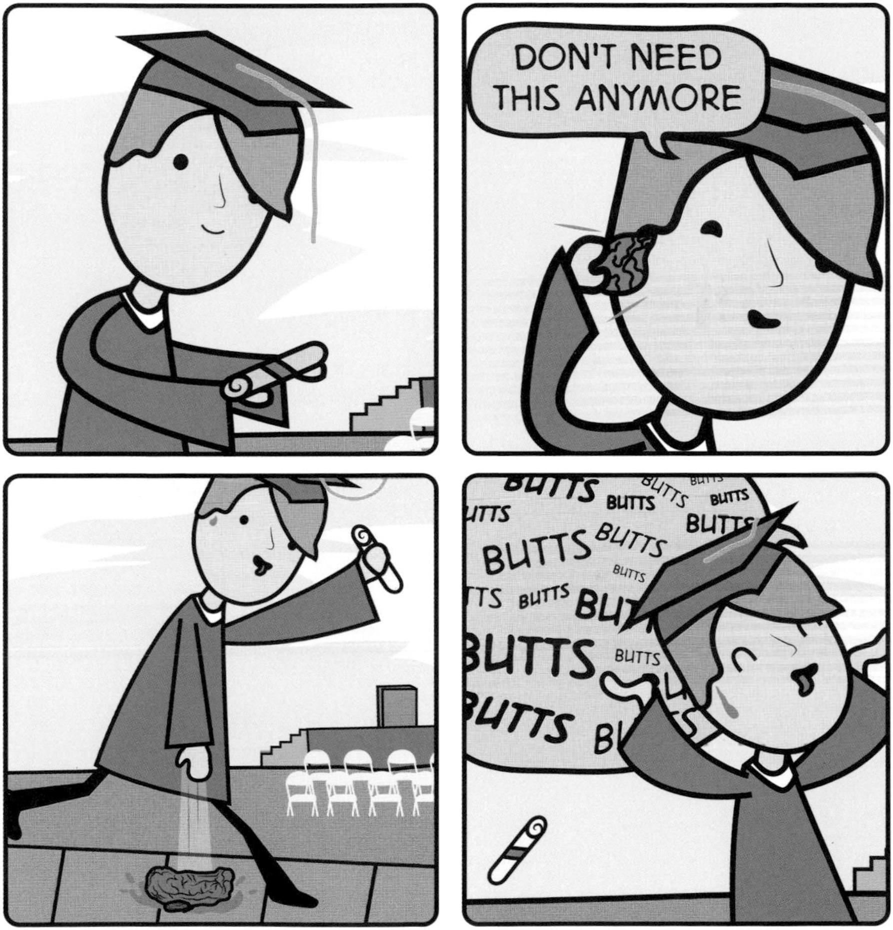
DON'T NEED THIS ANYMORE
BUTTS
BUTTS
BUTTS
BUTTS
BUTTS
BUTTS
BUTTS
BUTTS
BUTTS
BUTTS

@WIMPSICLE

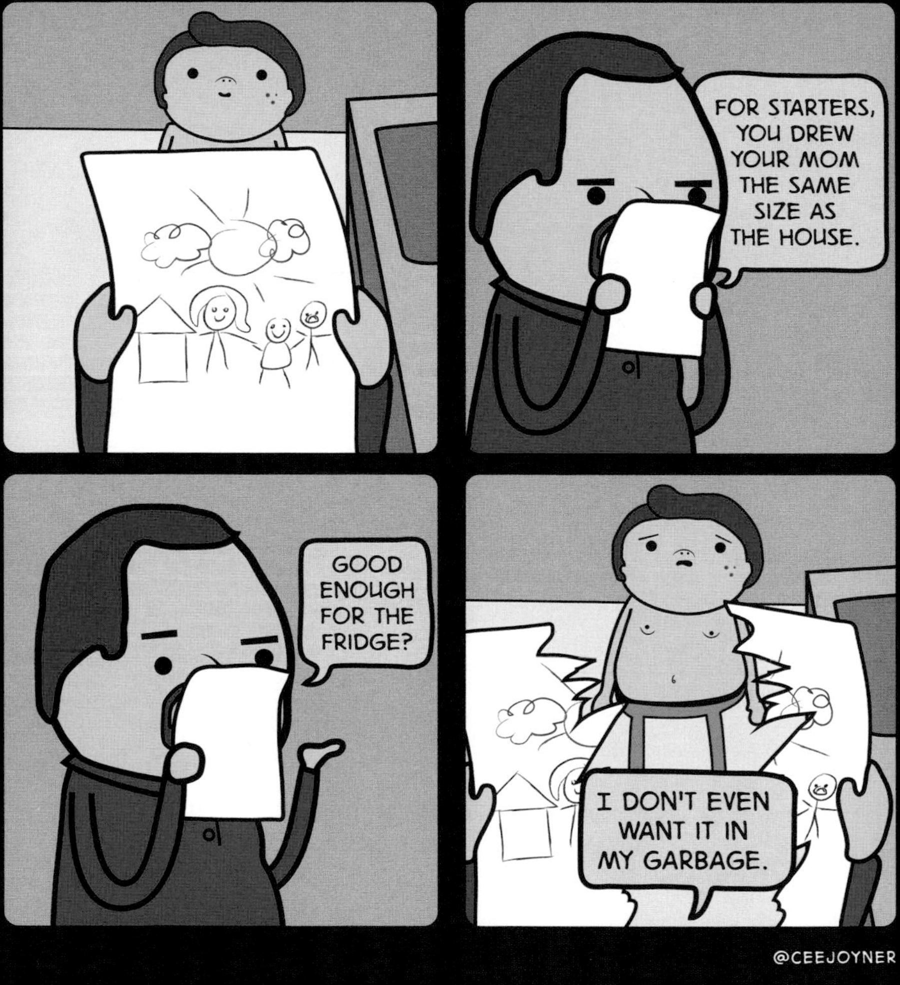
FOR STARTERS, YOU DREW YOUR MOM THE SAME SIZE AS THE HOUSE.
GOOD ENOUGH FOR THE FRIDGE?
I DON'T EVEN WANT IT IN MY GARBAGE.
@CEEJOYNER

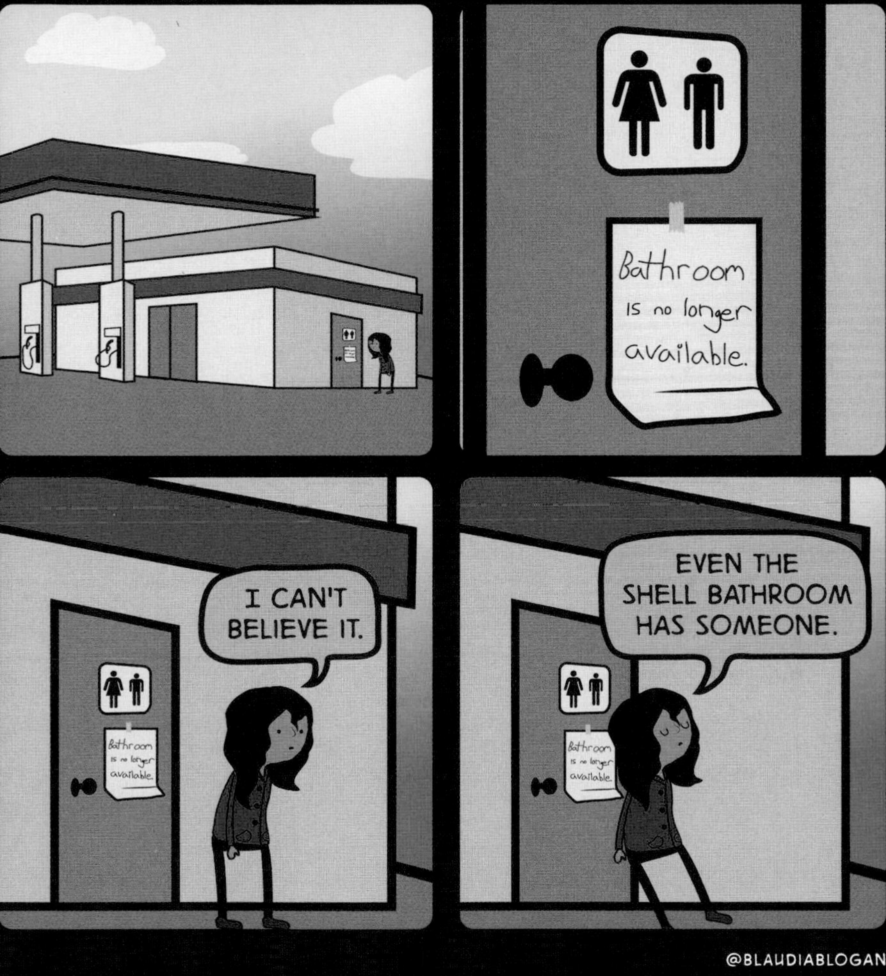
Bathroom is no longer available.
I CAN'T BELIEVE IT.
EVEN THE SHELL BATHROOM HAS SOMEONE.
@BLAUDIABLOGAN

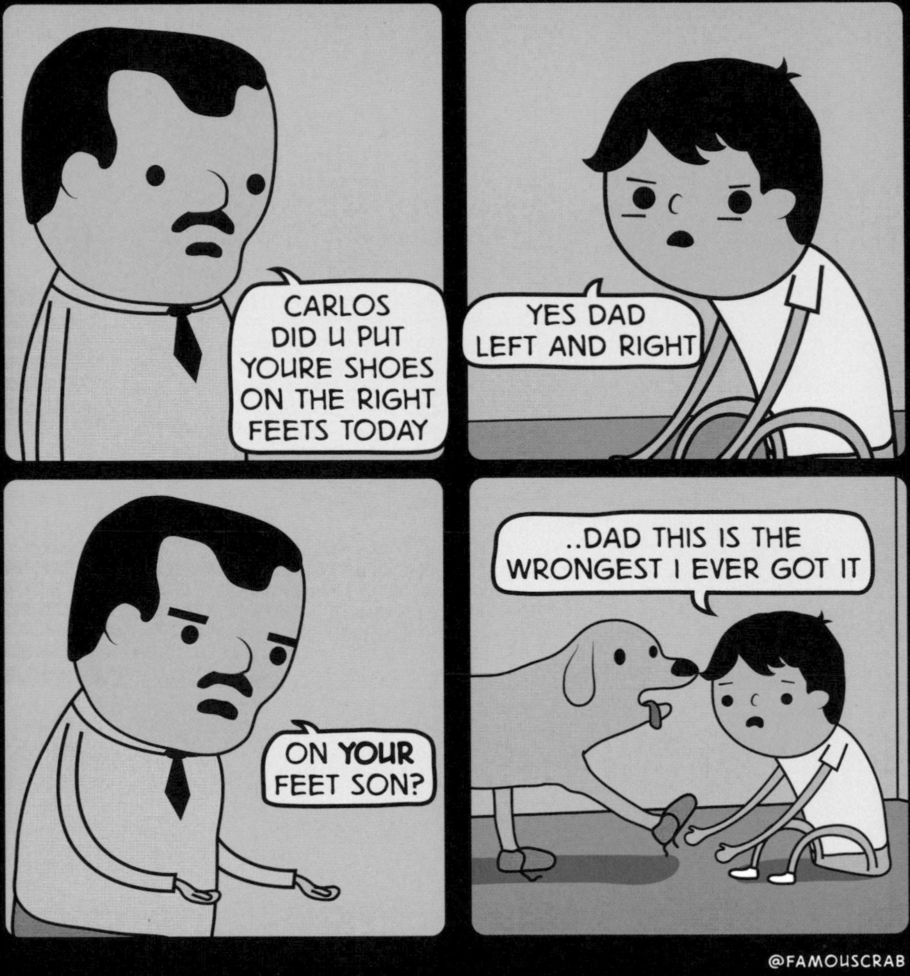
CARLOS DID U PUT YOURE SHOES ON THE RIGHT FEETS TODAY
YES DAD LEFT AND RIGHT
ON **YOUR** FEET SON?
..DAD THIS IS THE WRONGEST I EVER GOT IT
@FAMOUSCRAB

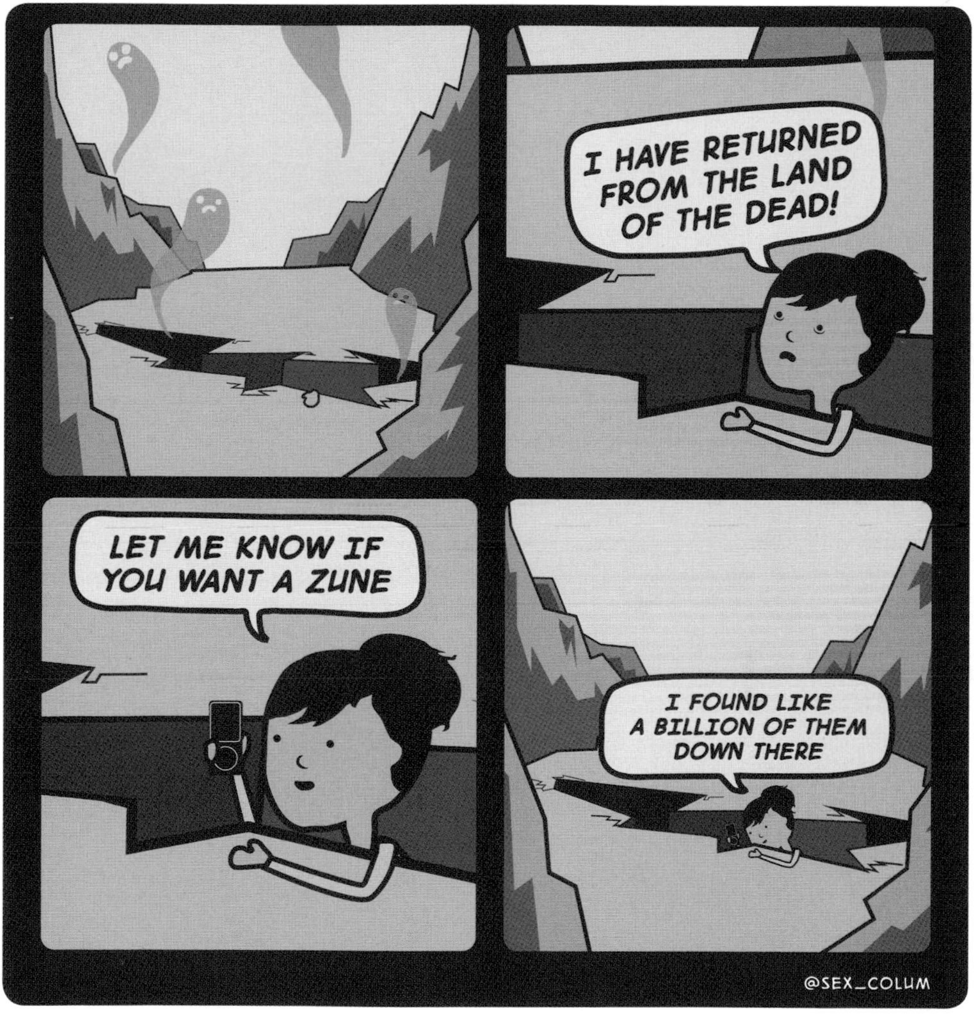
I HAVE RETURNED FROM THE LAND OF THE DEAD!
LET ME KNOW IF YOU WANT A ZUNE
I FOUND LIKE A BILLION OF THEM DOWN THERE
@SEX_COLUM

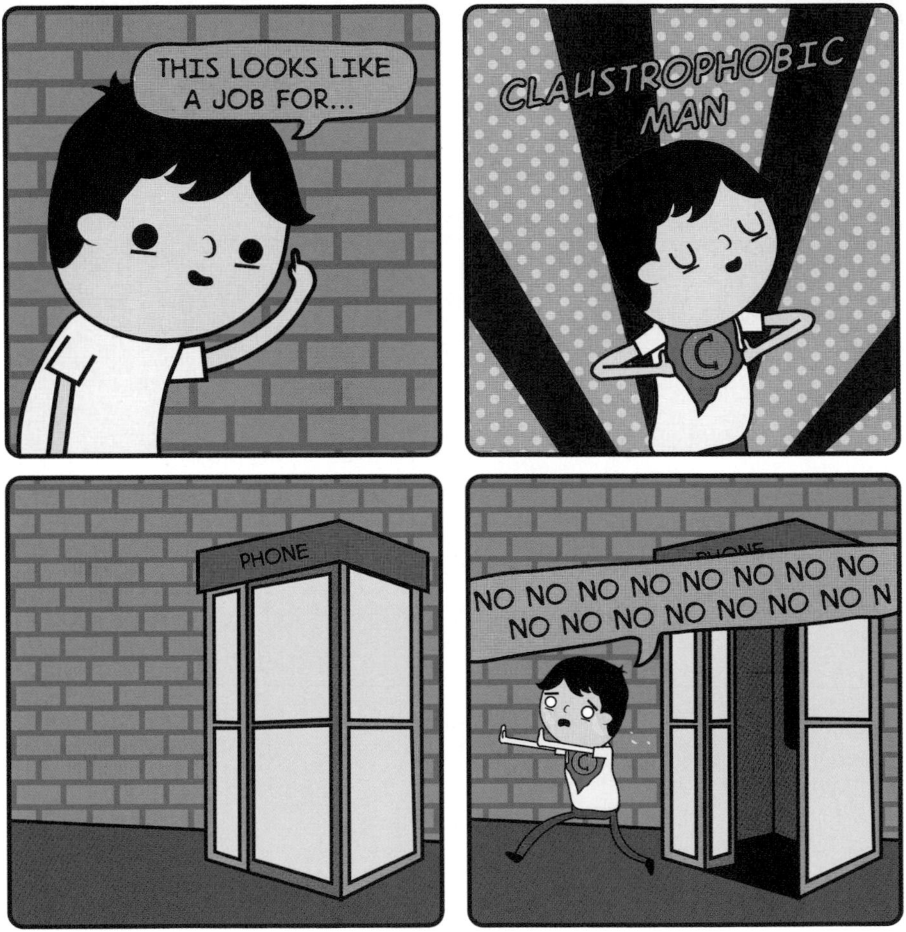
THIS LOOKS LIKE A JOB FOR...
CLAUSTROPHOBIC MAN
C
PHONE
NO NO NO NO NO NO NO NO
NO NO NO NO NO NO NO NO N
NO NO NO NO NO NO NO
C

@ACEMAKESWORDS

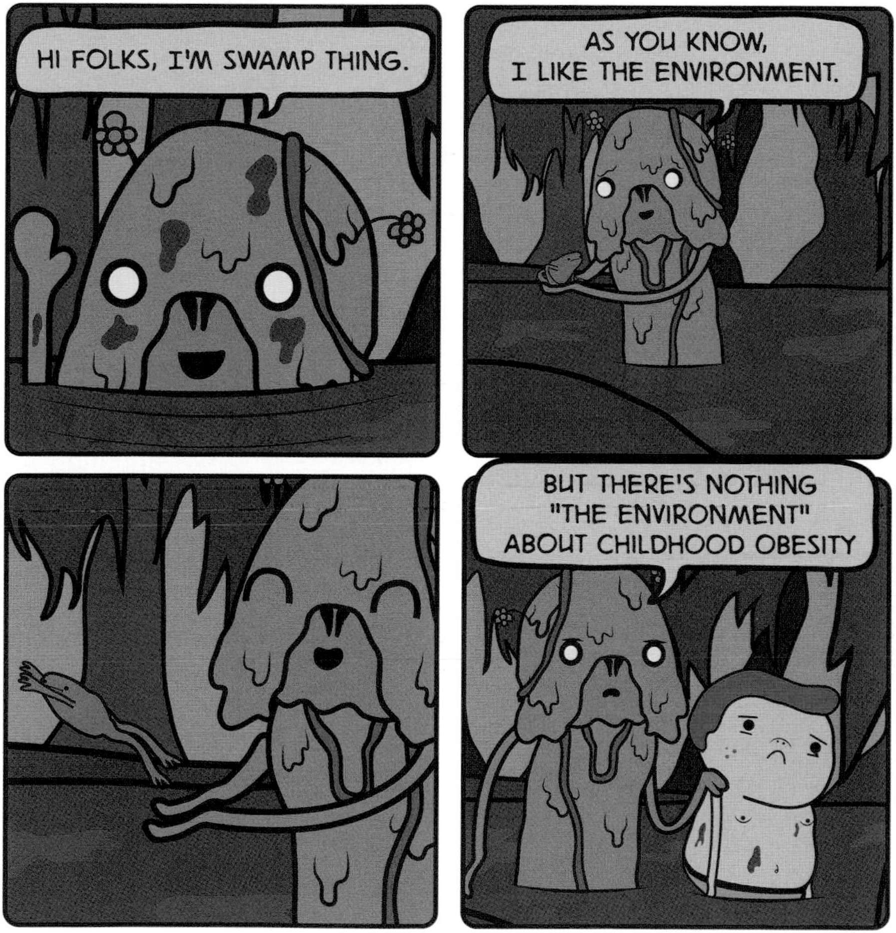
HI FOLKS, I'M SWAMP THING.
AS YOU KNOW, I LIKE THE ENVIRONMENT.
BUT THERE'S NOTHING "THE ENVIRONMENT" ABOUT CHILDHOOD OBESITY

@DVSBLAST

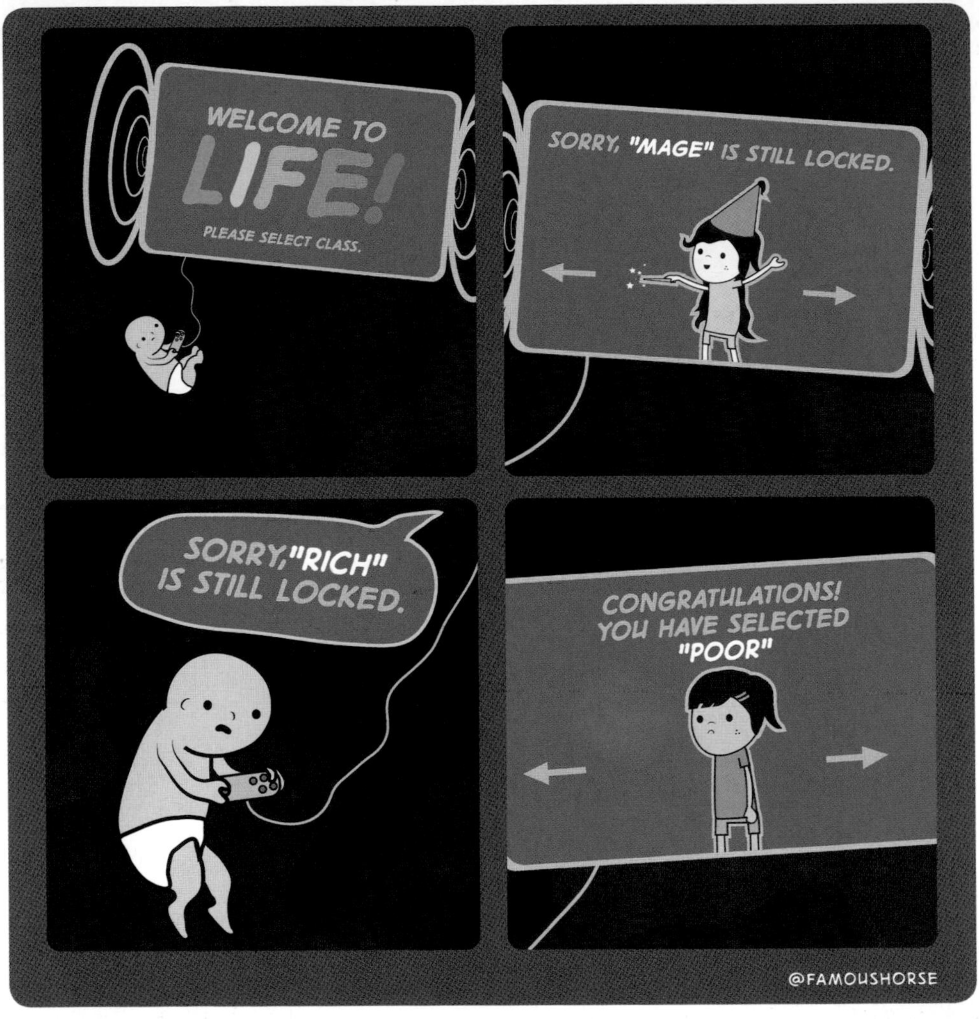
WELCOME TO
LIFE!
PLEASE SELECT CLASS.
SORRY, "MAGE" IS STILL LOCKED.
SORRY, "RICH" IS STILL LOCKED.
CONGRATULATIONS! YOU HAVE SELECTED "POOR"
@FAMOUSHORSE

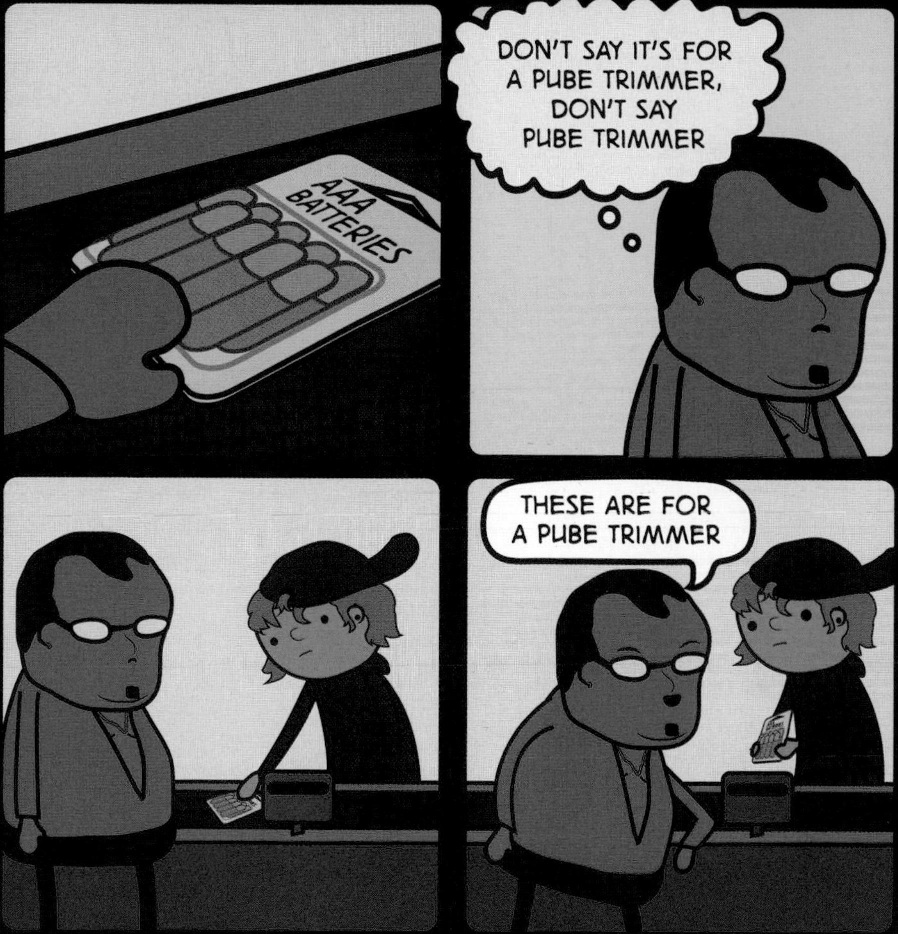
AAA BATTERIES
DON'T SAY IT'S FOR A PUBE TRIMMER, DON'T SAY PUBE TRIMMER
THESE ARE FOR A PUBE TRIMMER

@FART

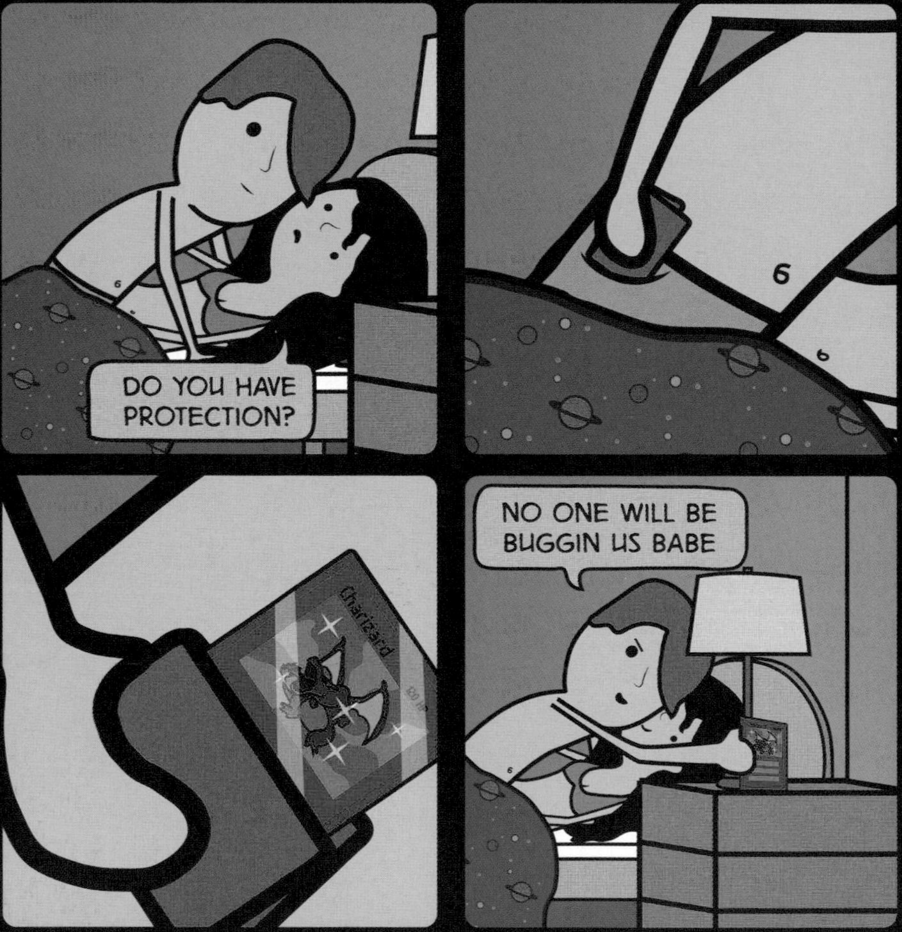
DO YOU HAVE PROTECTION?
Charizard
NO ONE WILL BE BUGGIN US BABE

@DONG_PARTY

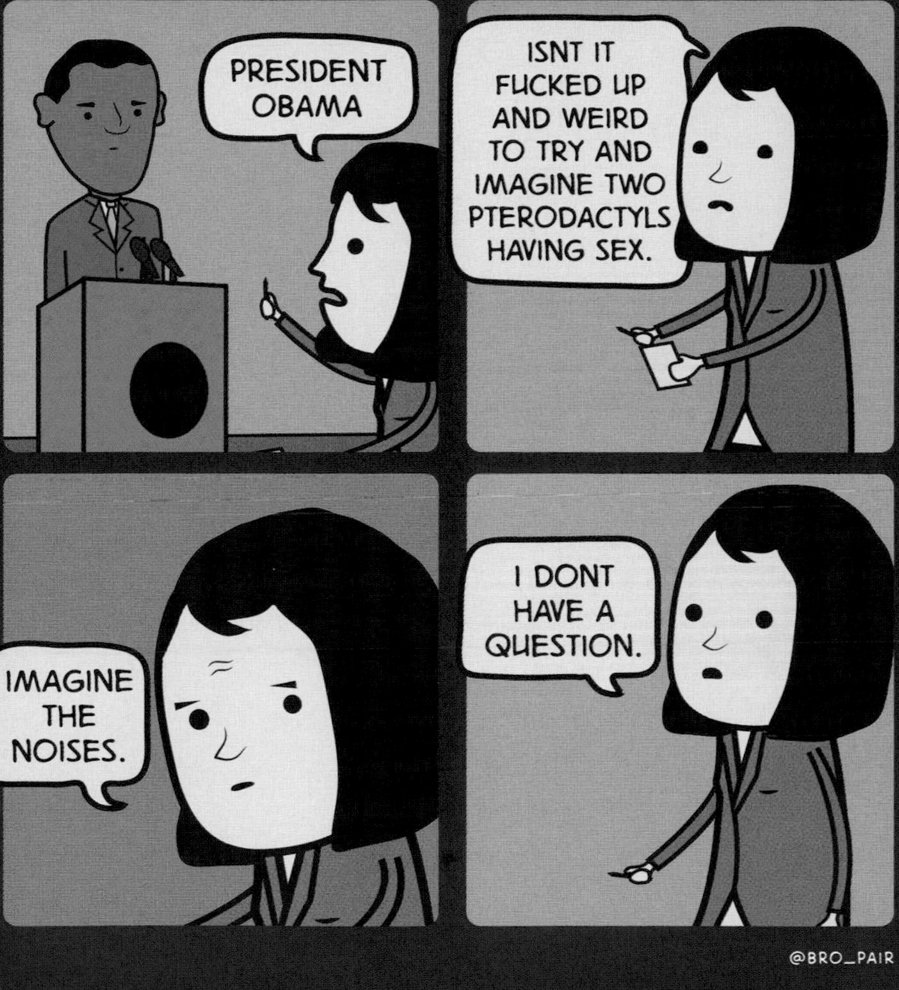
PRESIDENT OBAMA
ISNT IT FUCKED UP AND WEIRD TO TRY AND IMAGINE TWO PTERODACTYLS HAVING SEX.
IMAGINE THE NOISES.
I DONT HAVE A QUESTION.
@BRO_PAIR

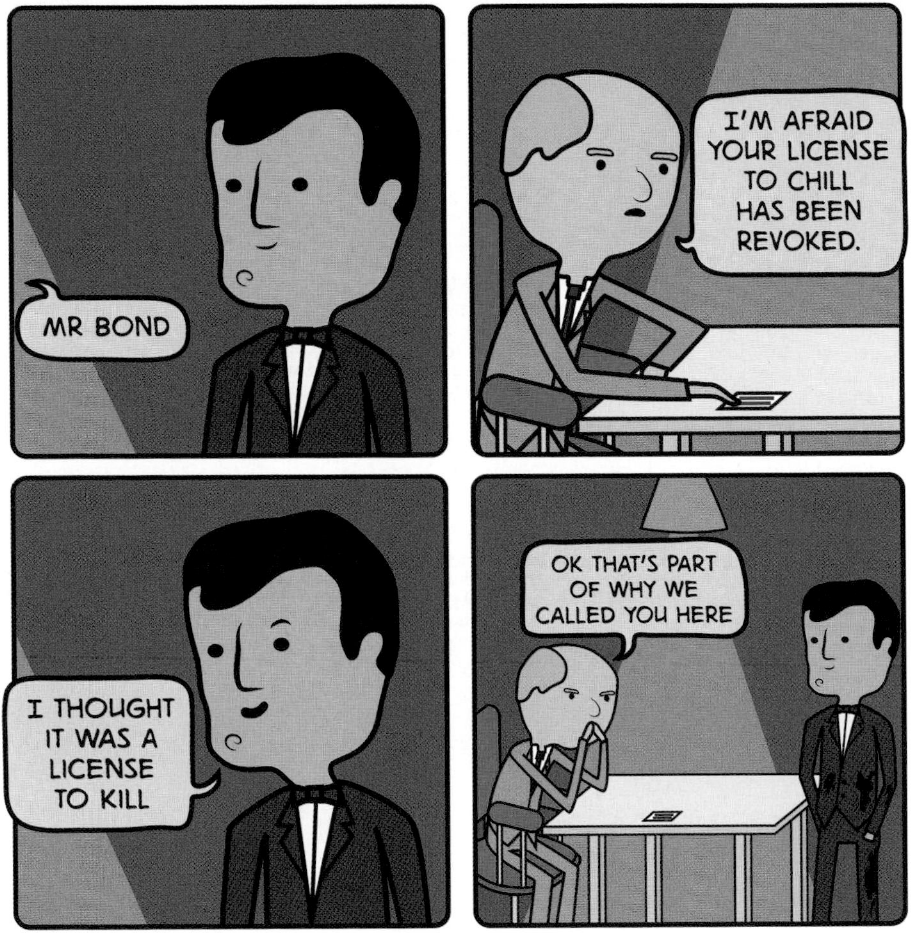
MR BOND
I'M AFRAID YOUR LICENSE TO CHILL HAS BEEN REVOKED.
I THOUGHT IT WAS A LICENSE TO KILL
OK THAT'S PART OF WHY WE CALLED YOU HERE

@MXRK

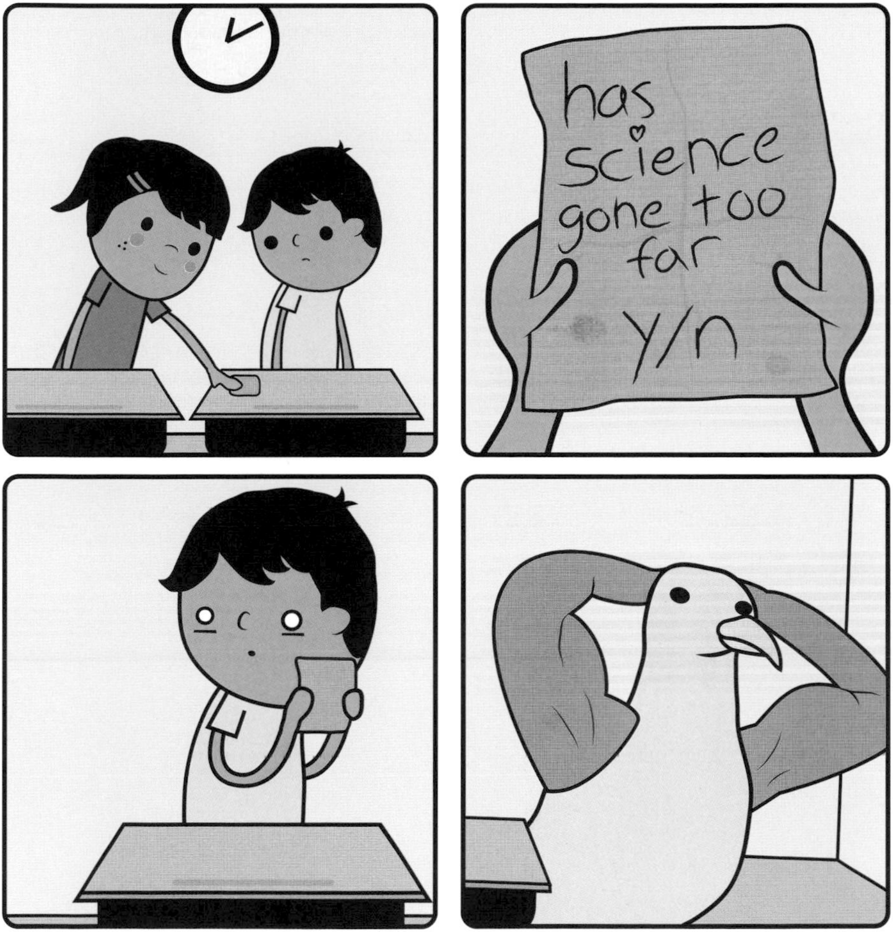
has
science
gone too
far
y/n

@IDIOT_TEEN

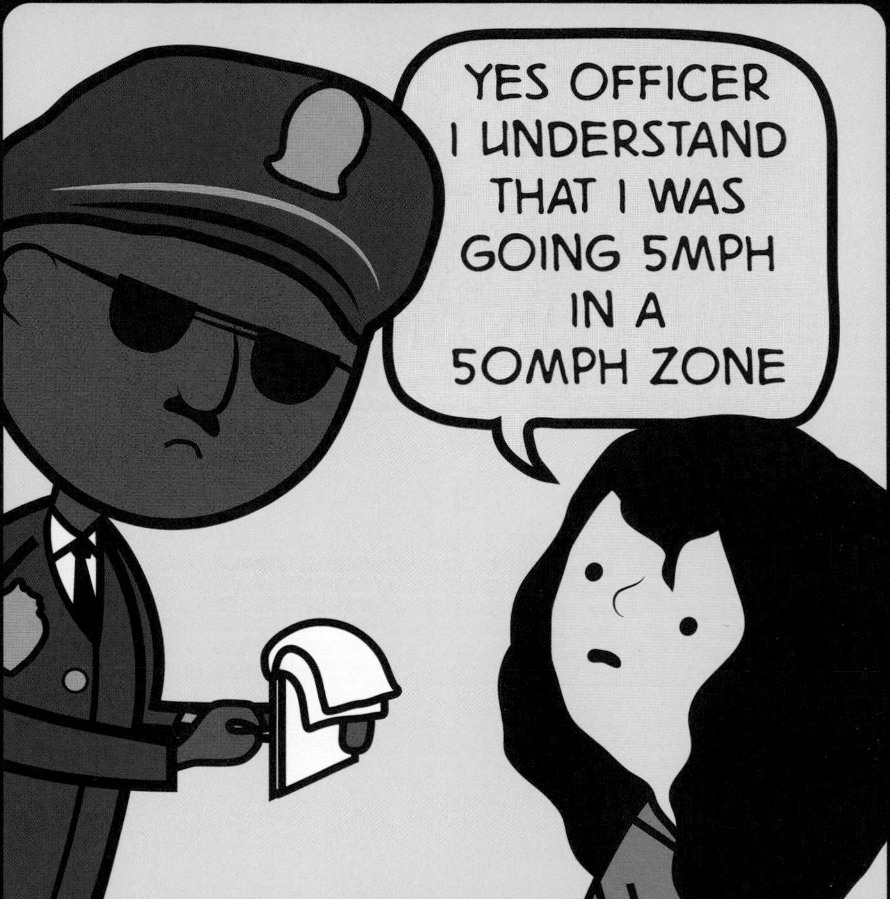
YES OFFICER I UNDERSTAND THAT I WAS GOING 5MPH IN A 50MPH ZONE

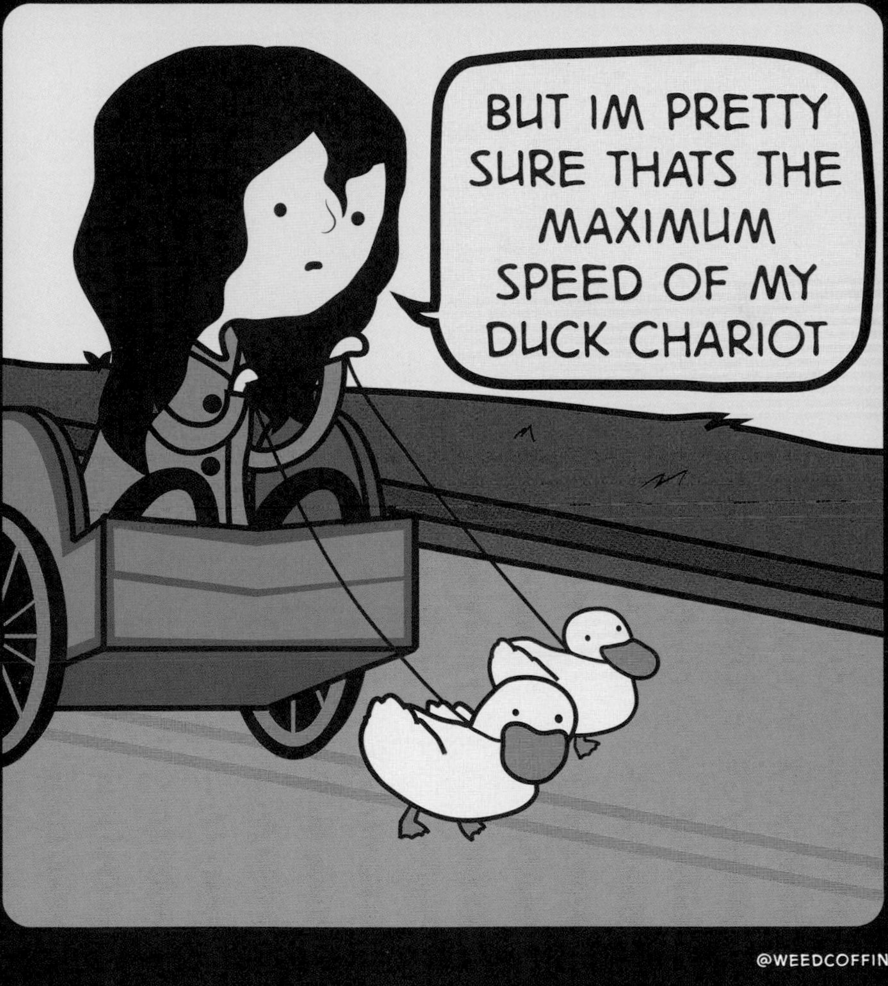
BUT IM PRETTY SURE THATS THE MAXIMUM SPEED OF MY DUCK CHARIOT

@WEEDCOFFIN

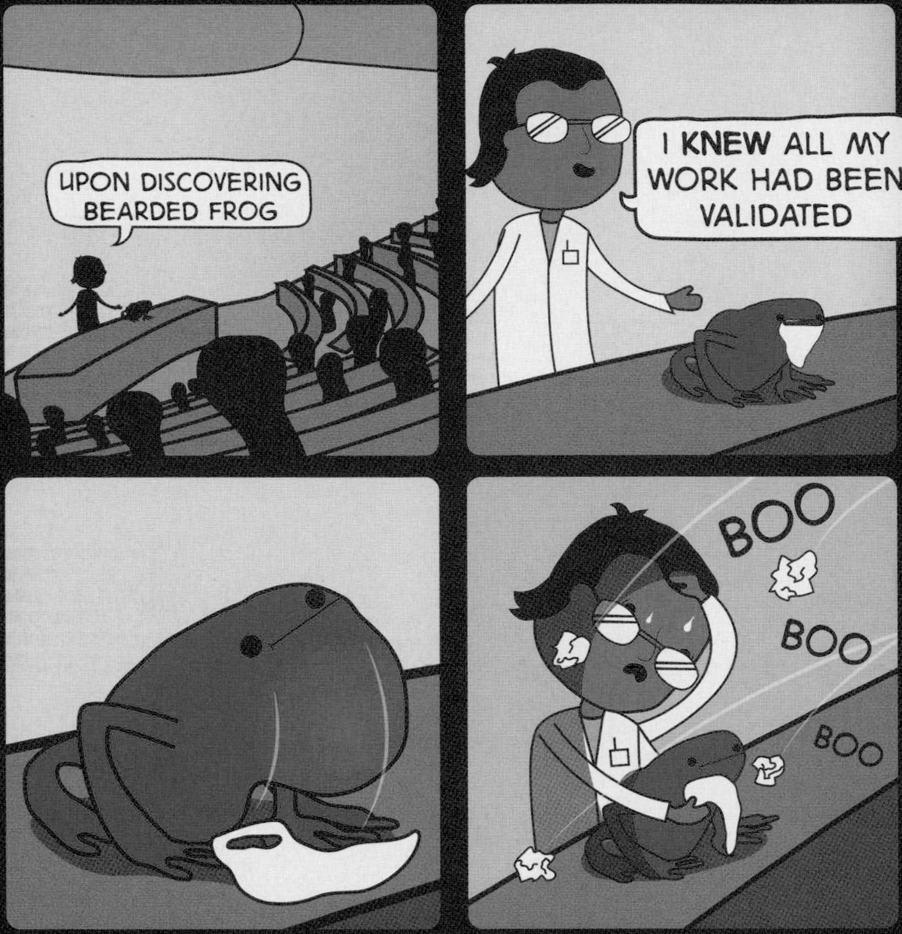
UPON DISCOVERING BEARDED FROG
I KNEW ALL MY WORK HAD BEEN VALIDATED
BOO
BOO
BOO

@GRAEYALIEN

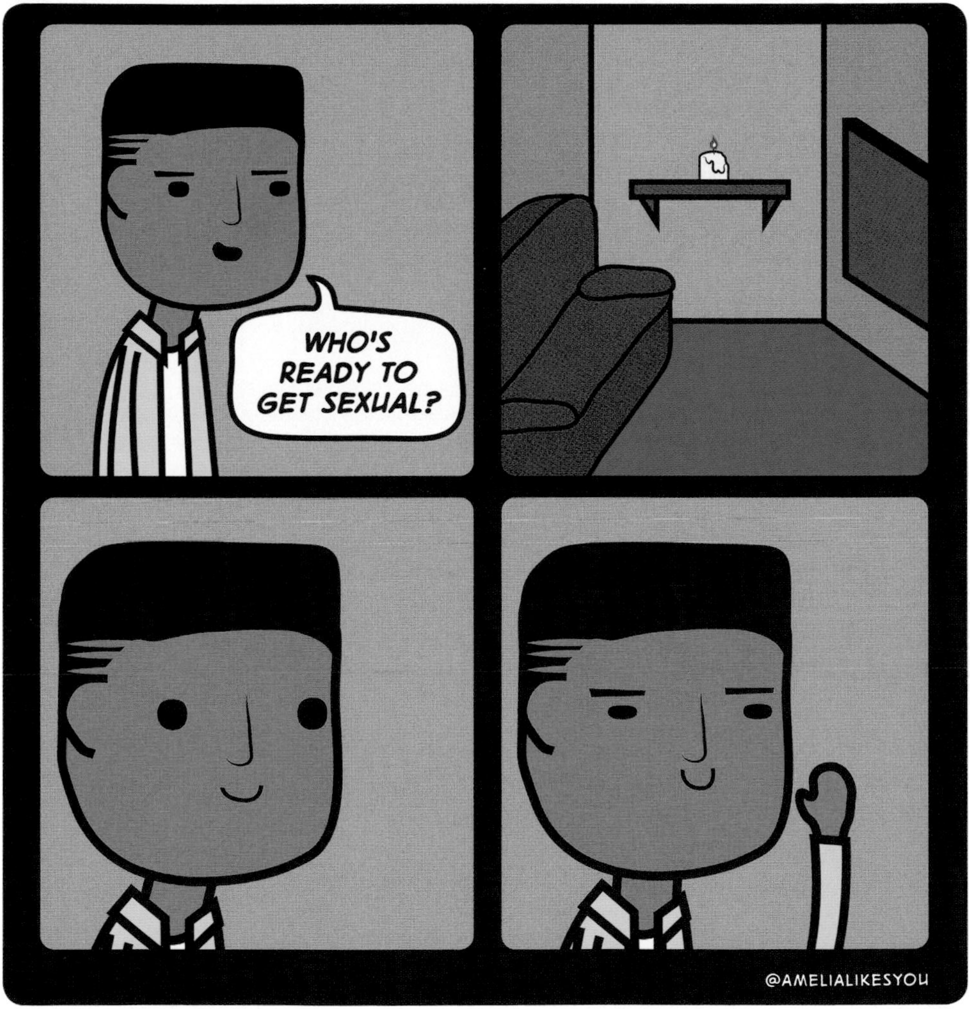
WHO'S READY TO GET SEXUAL?
@AMELIALIKESYOU

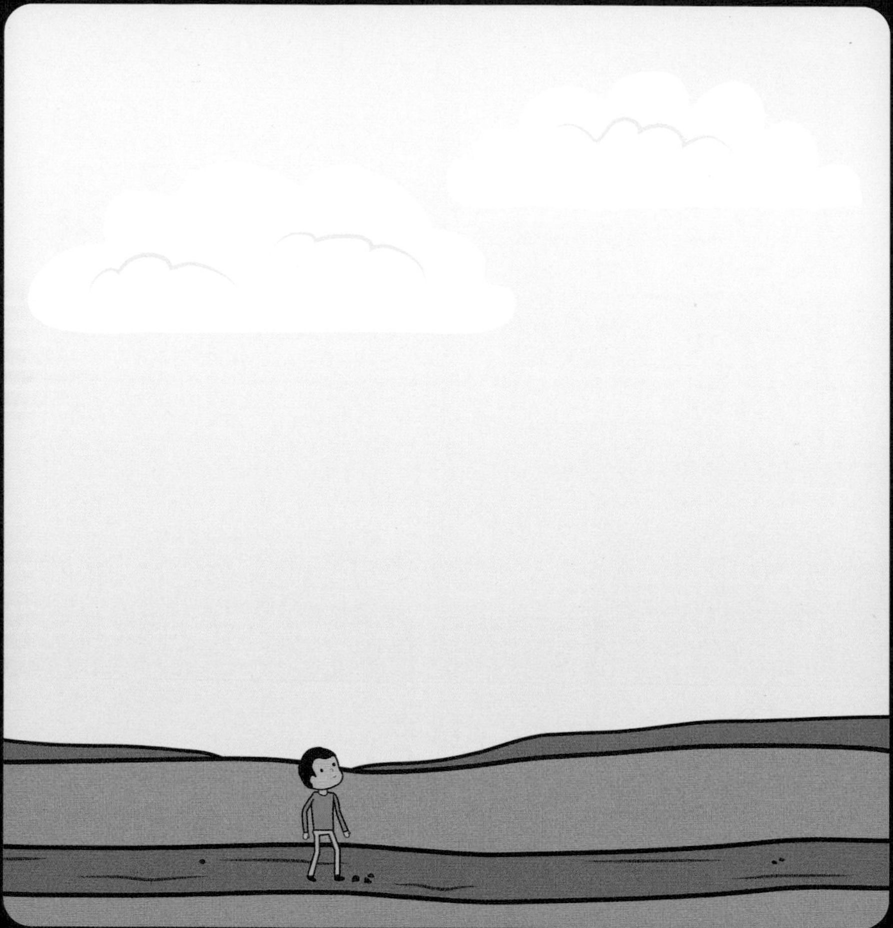

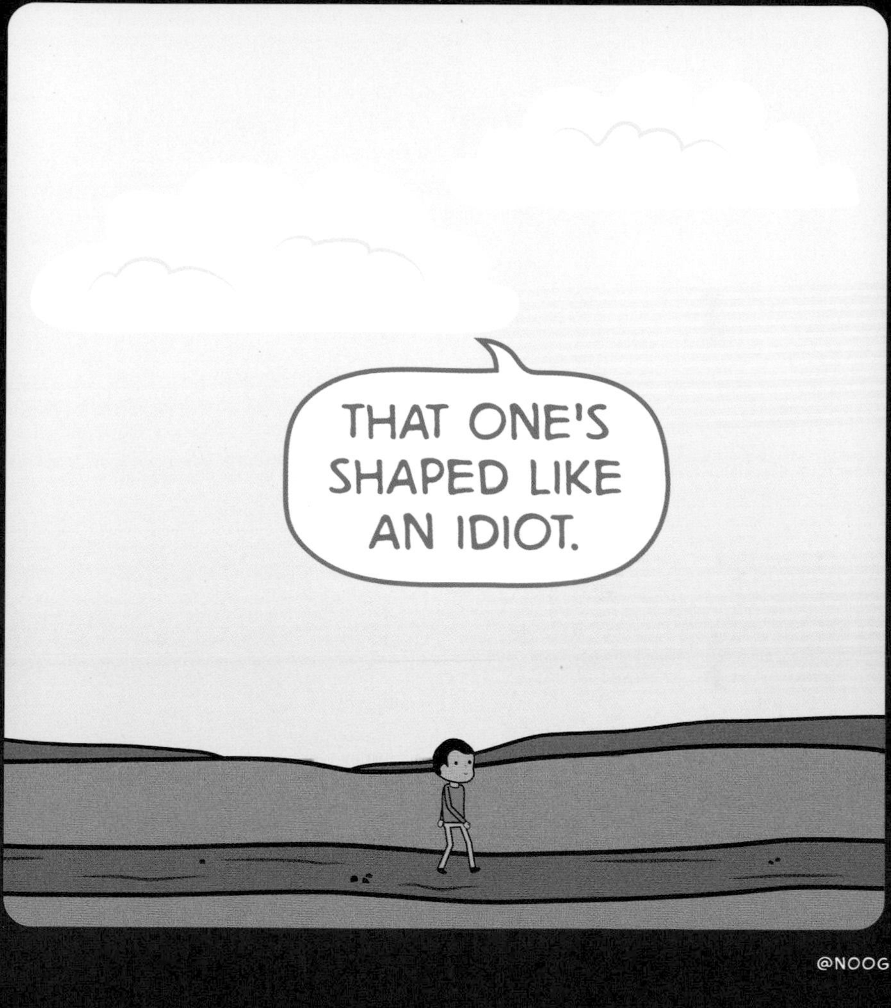
THAT ONE'S SHAPED LIKE AN IDIOT.

@NOOG

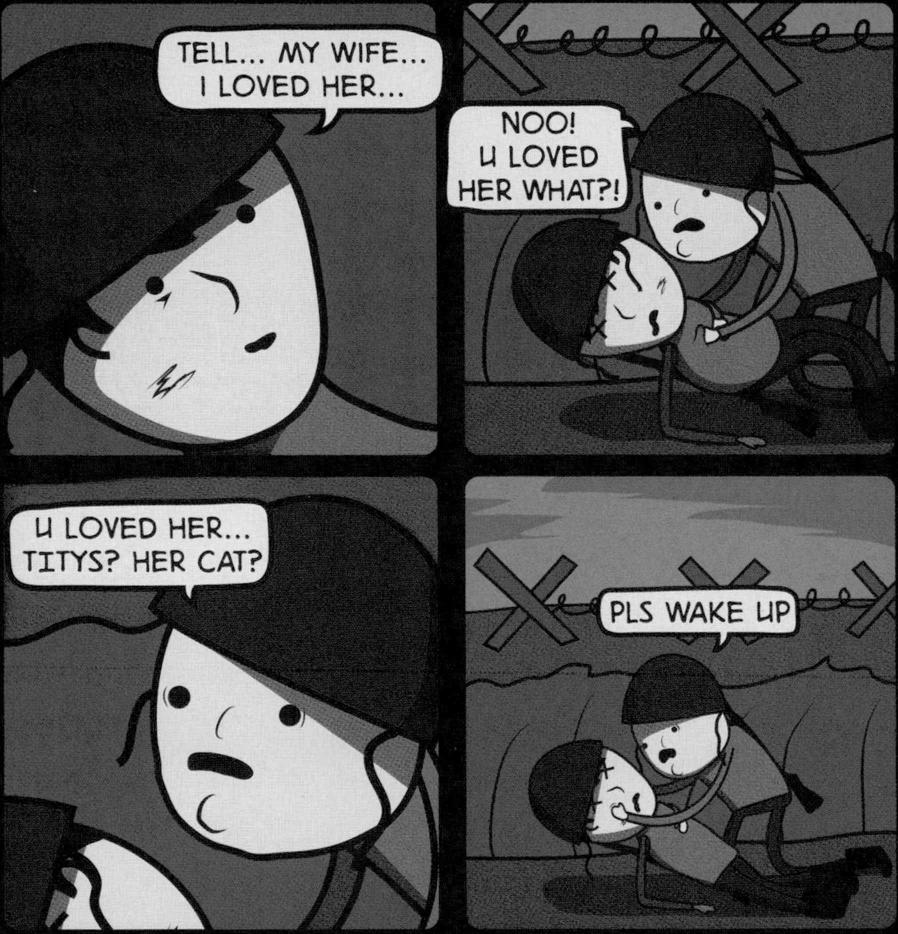
TELL... MY WIFE...
I LOVED HER...
NOO!
U LOVED
HER WHAT?!
U LOVED HER...
TITYS? HER CAT?
PLS WAKE UP

@TORMNY_PICKEALS

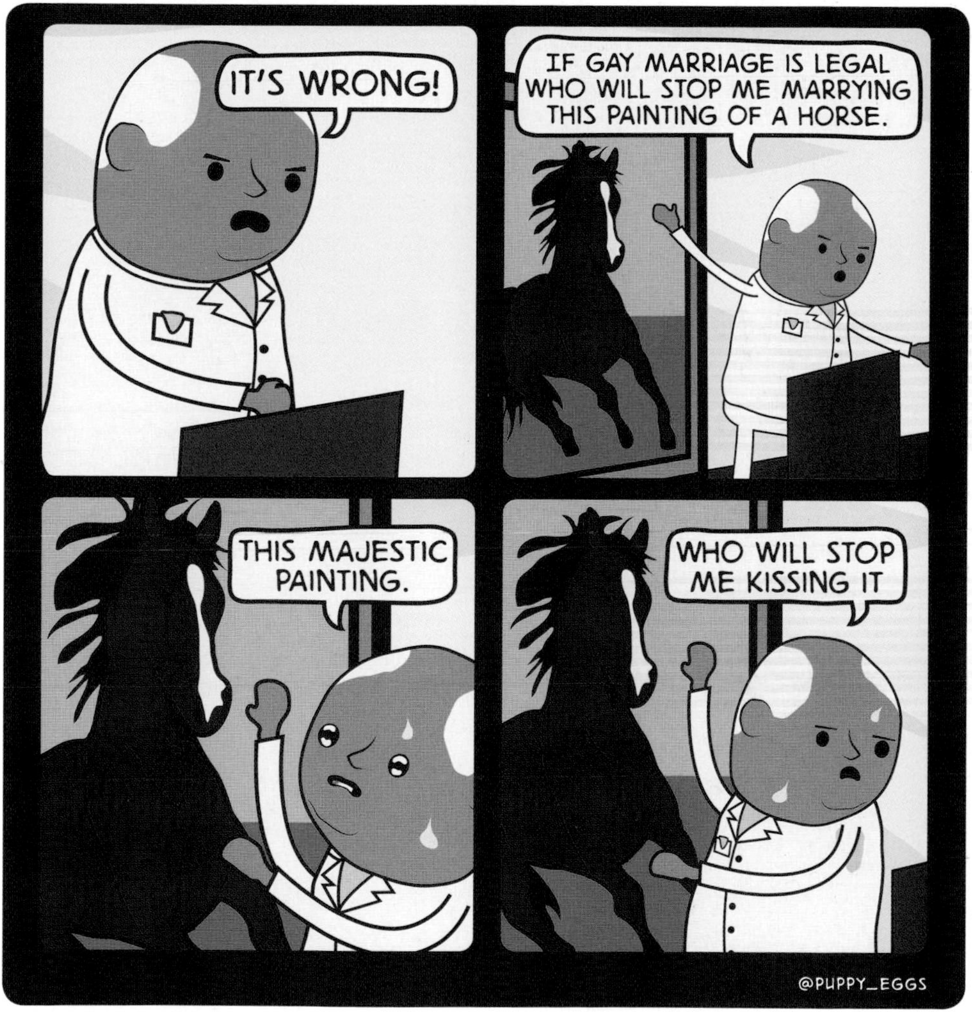
IT'S WRONG!
IF GAY MARRIAGE IS LEGAL WHO WILL STOP ME MARRYING THIS PAINTING OF A HORSE.
THIS MAJESTIC PAINTING.
WHO WILL STOP ME KISSING IT
@PUPPY_EGGS

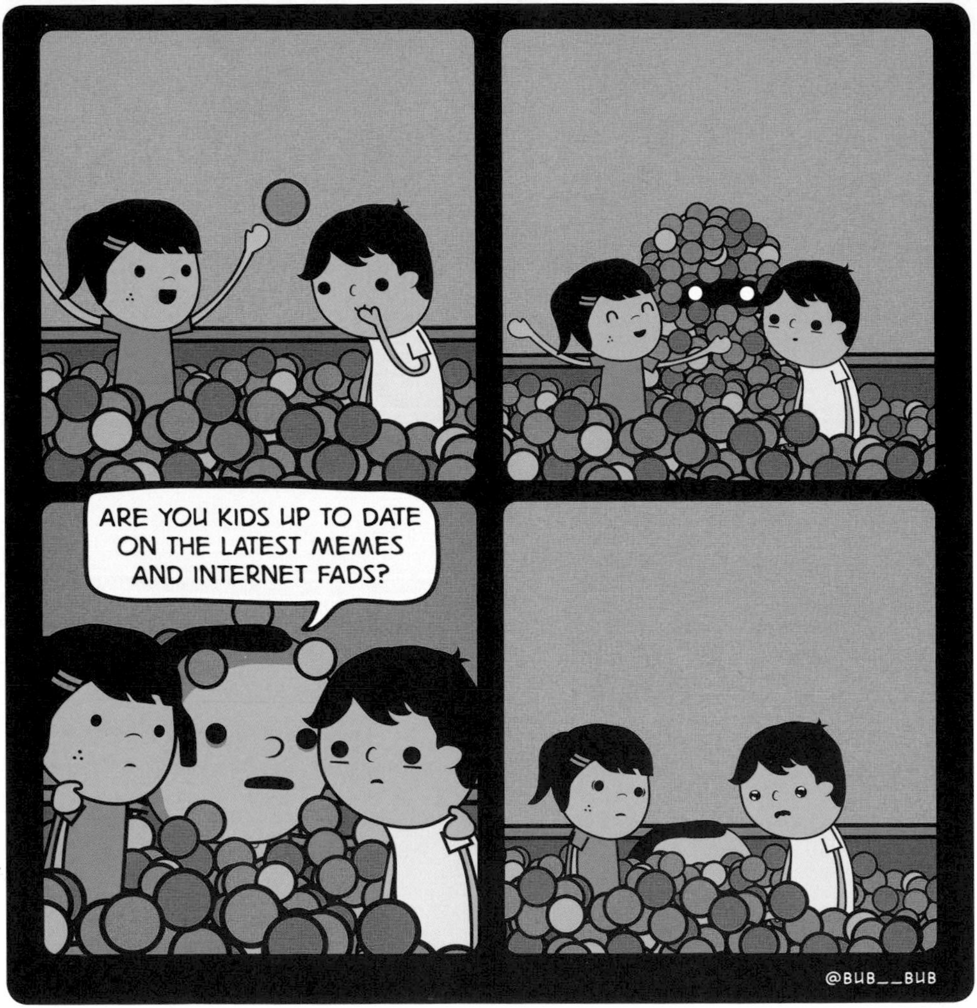
ARE YOU KIDS UP TO DATE ON THE LATEST MEMES AND INTERNET FADS?
@BUB__BUB

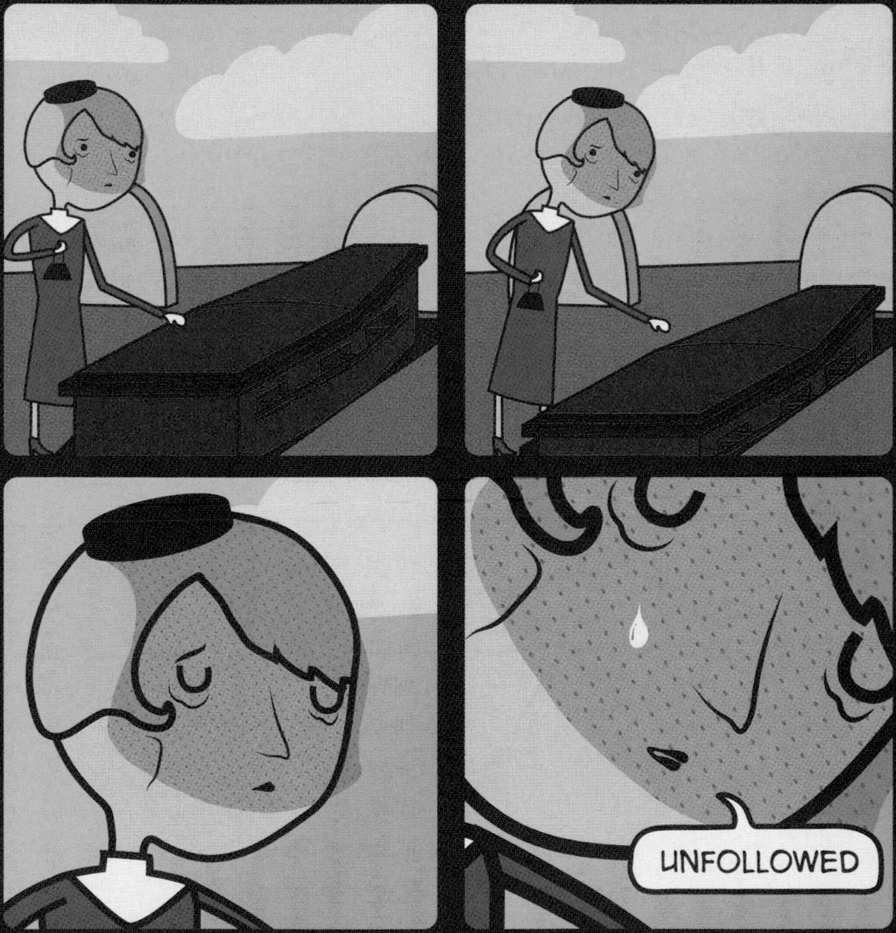
UNFOLLOWED

@DIAPER_WOLF

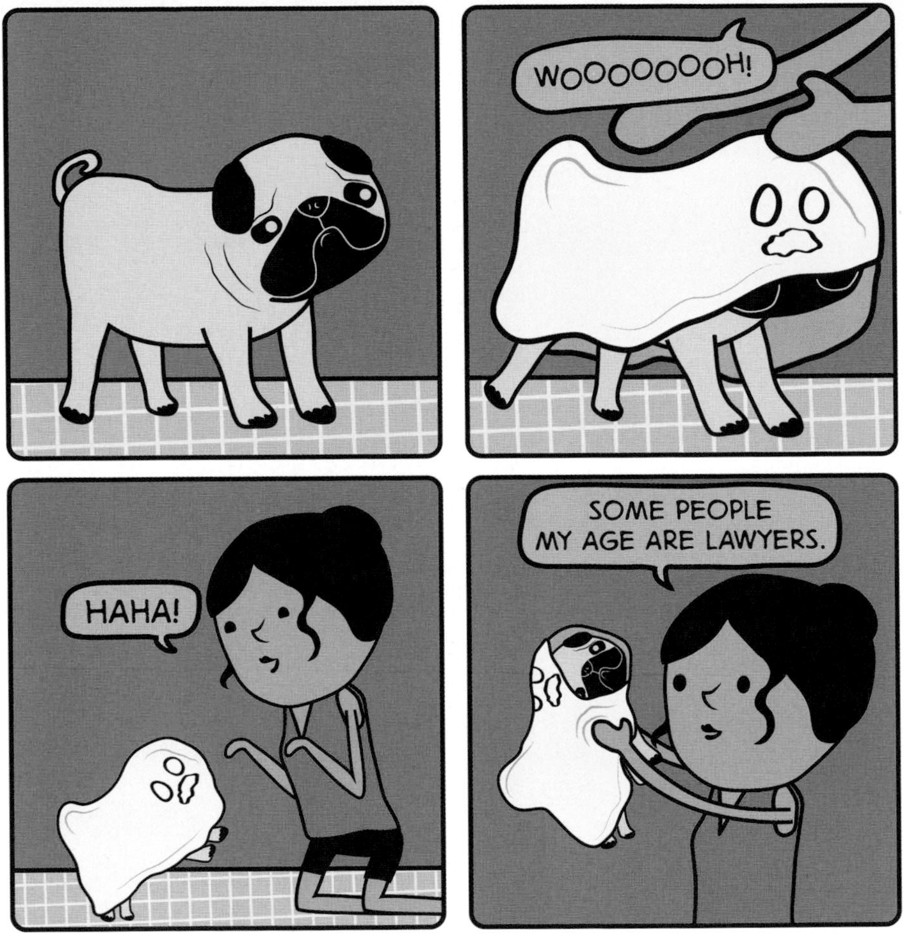
WOOOOOOOOH!
HAHA!
SOME PEOPLE MY AGE ARE LAWYERS.

@MRSJOHNGOODMAN

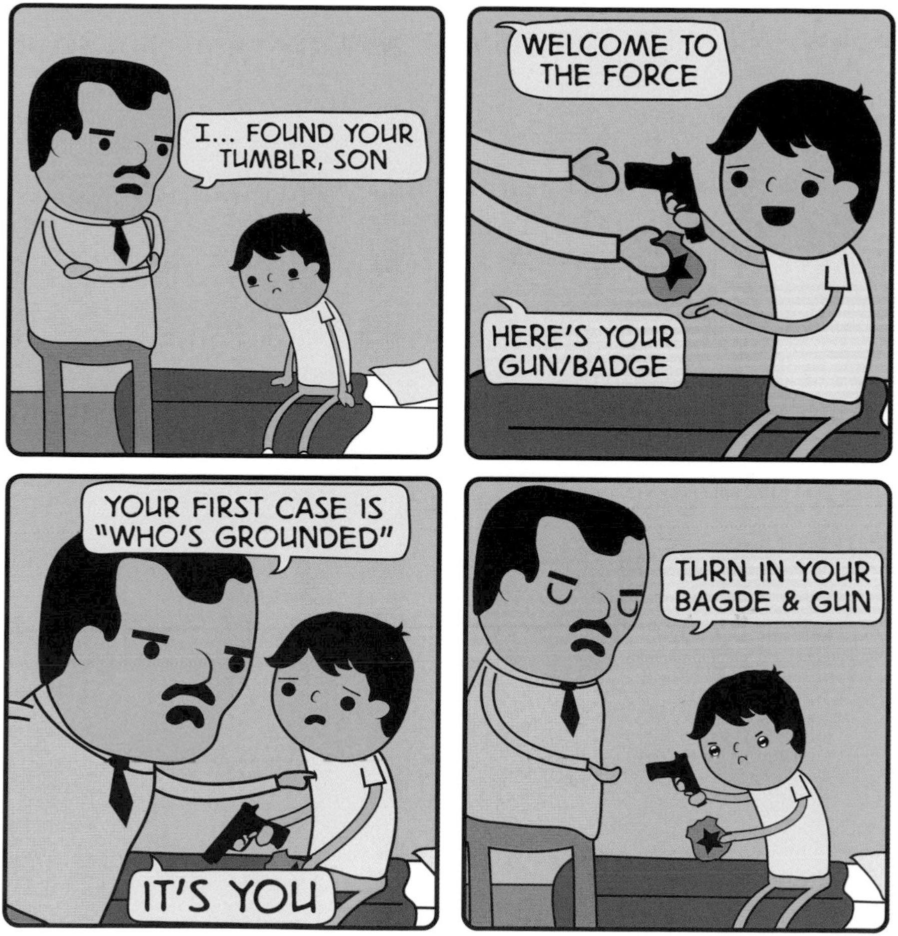
I... FOUND YOUR TUMBLR, SON
WELCOME TO THE FORCE
HERE'S YOUR GUN/BADGE
YOUR FIRST CASE IS "WHO'S GROUNDED"
IT'S YOU
TURN IN YOUR BAGDE & GUN

@DRUGLEAF

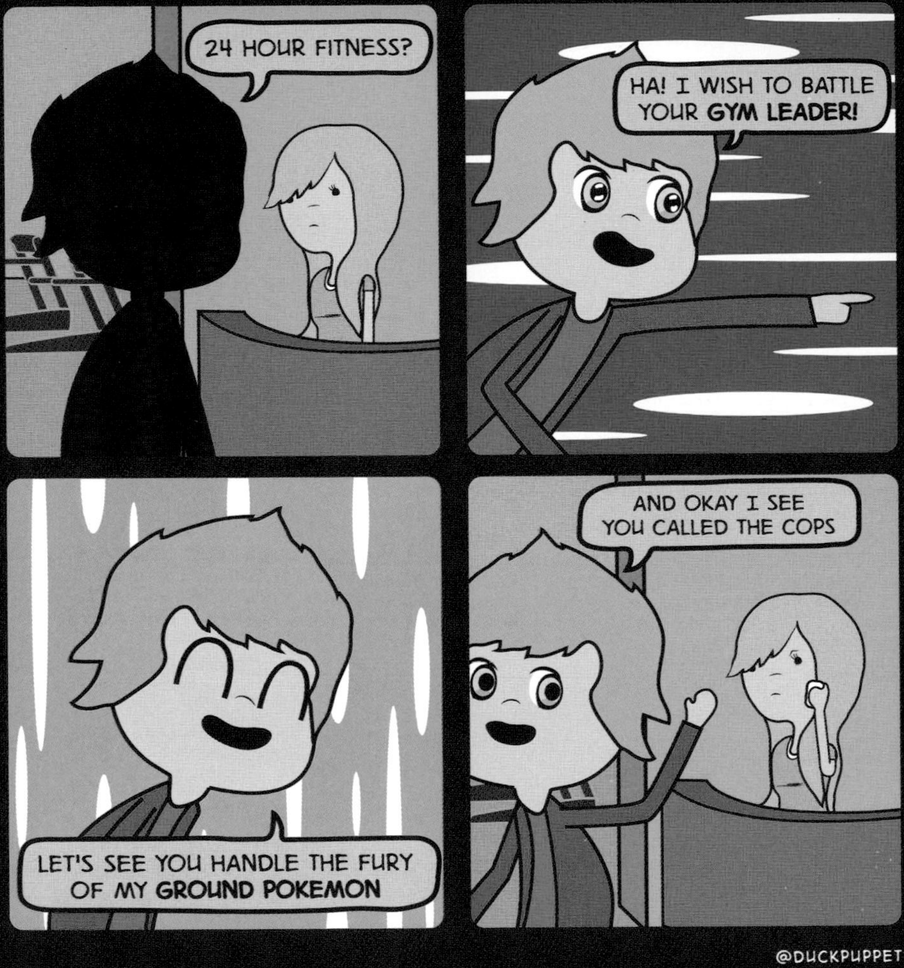
24 HOUR FITNESS?
HA! I WISH TO BATTLE YOUR **GYM LEADER!**
LET'S SEE YOU HANDLE THE FURY OF MY **GROUND POKEMON**
AND OKAY I SEE YOU CALLED THE COPS
@DUCKPUPPET

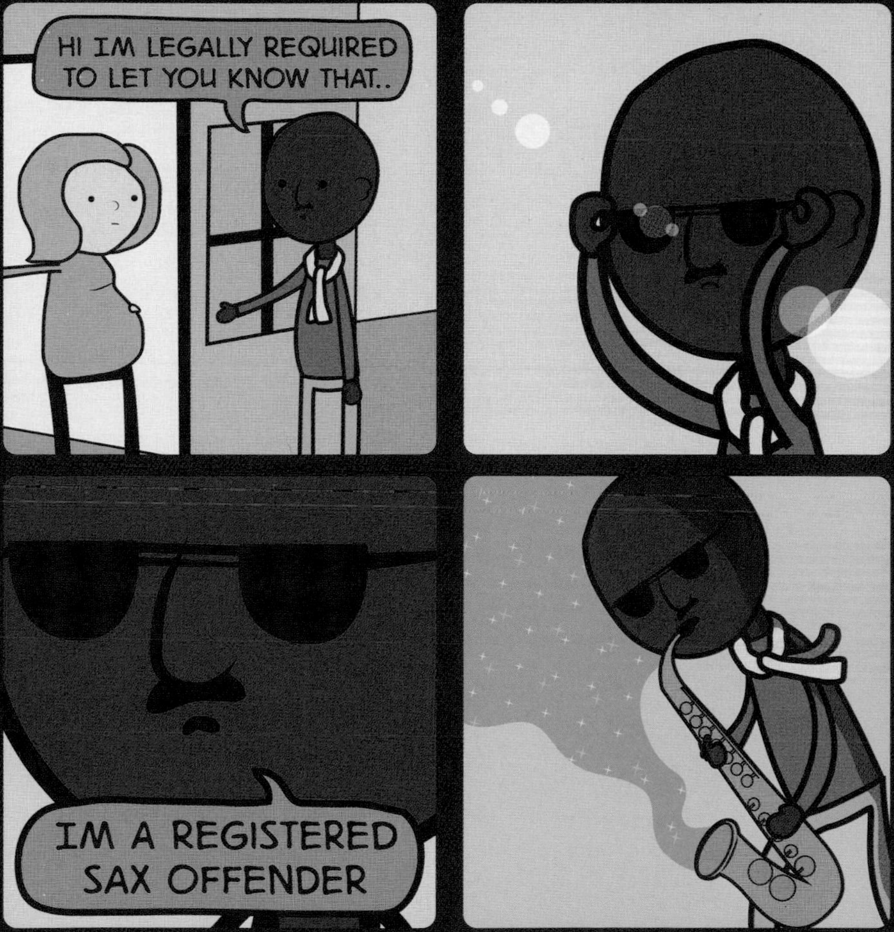
HI IM LEGALLY REQUIRED TO LET YOU KNOW THAT..
IM A REGISTERED SAX OFFENDER
@ROBFEE

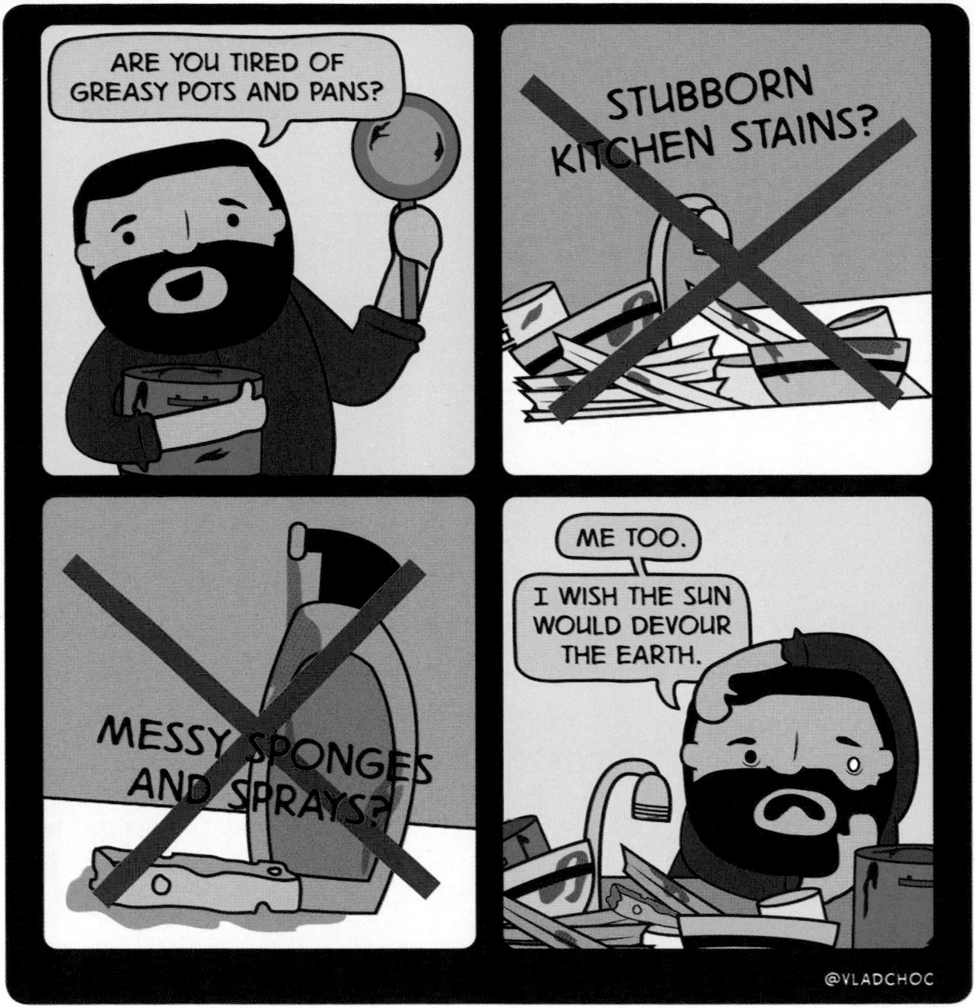
ARE YOU TIRED OF GREASY POTS AND PANS?
STUBBORN KITCHEN STAINS?
MESSY SPONGES AND SPRAYS?
ME TOO.
I WISH THE SUN WOULD DEVOUR THE EARTH.
@VLADCHOC

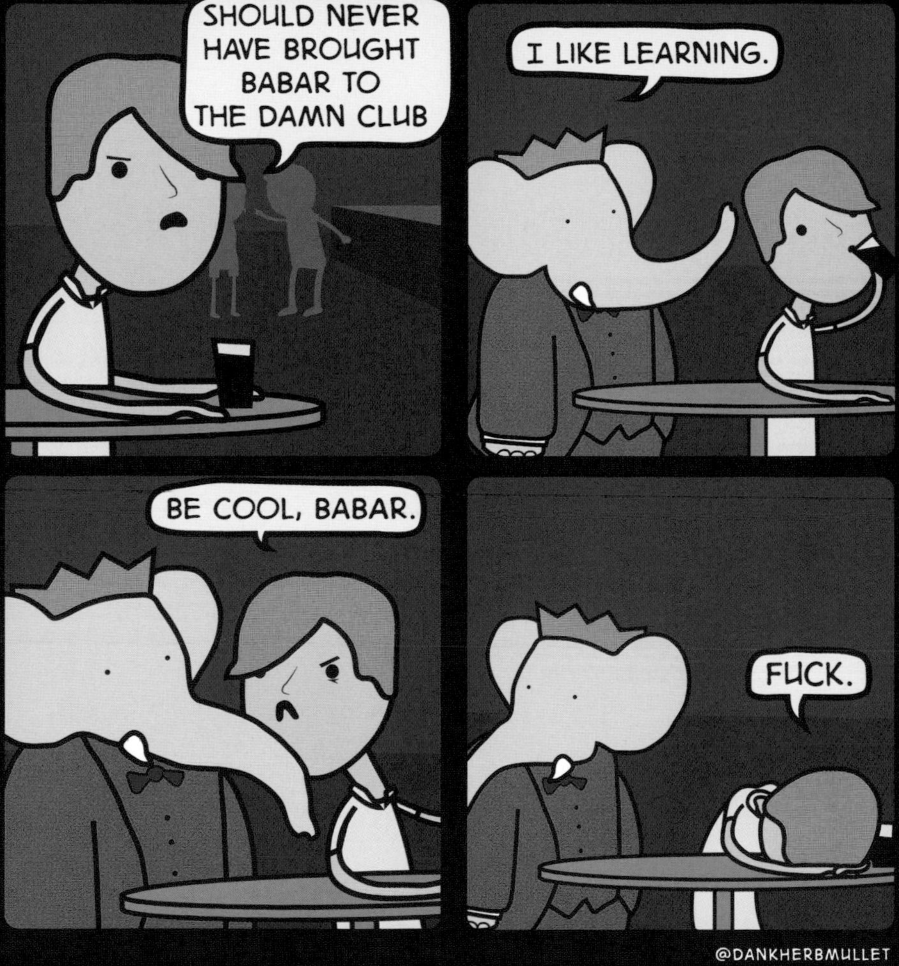
SHOULD NEVER HAVE BROUGHT BABAR TO THE DAMN CLUB
I LIKE LEARNING.
BE COOL, BABAR.
FUCK.
@DANKHERBMULLET

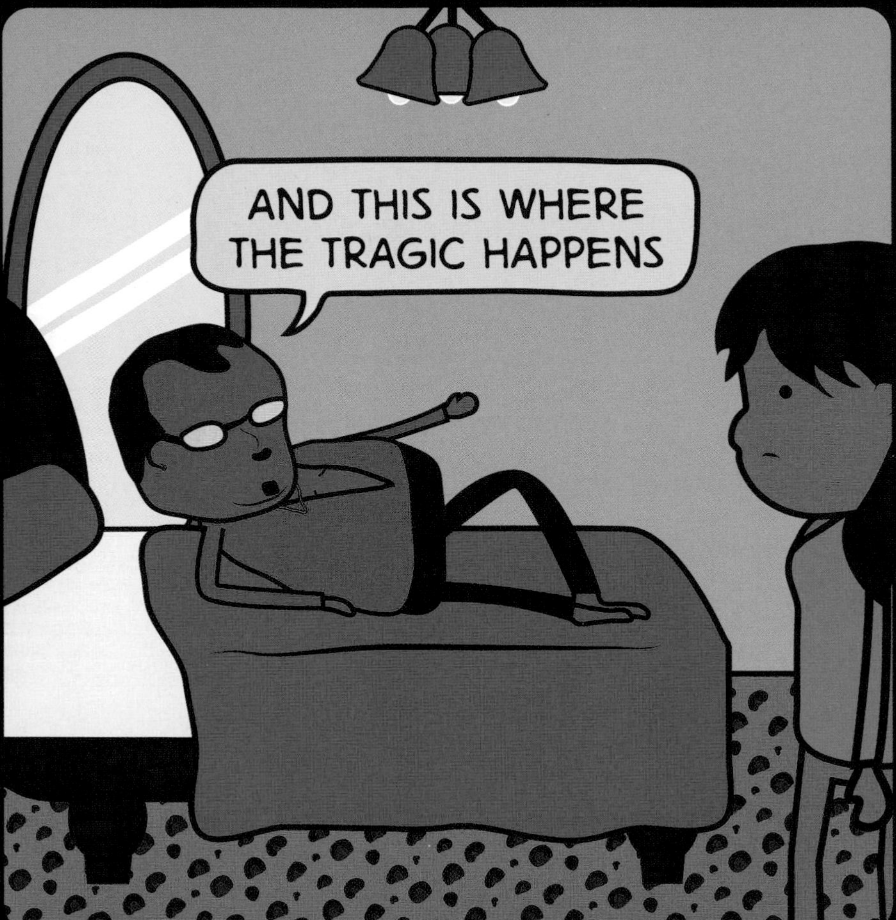
AND THIS IS WHERE THE TRAGIC HAPPENS

@JENNAMARIECAREY

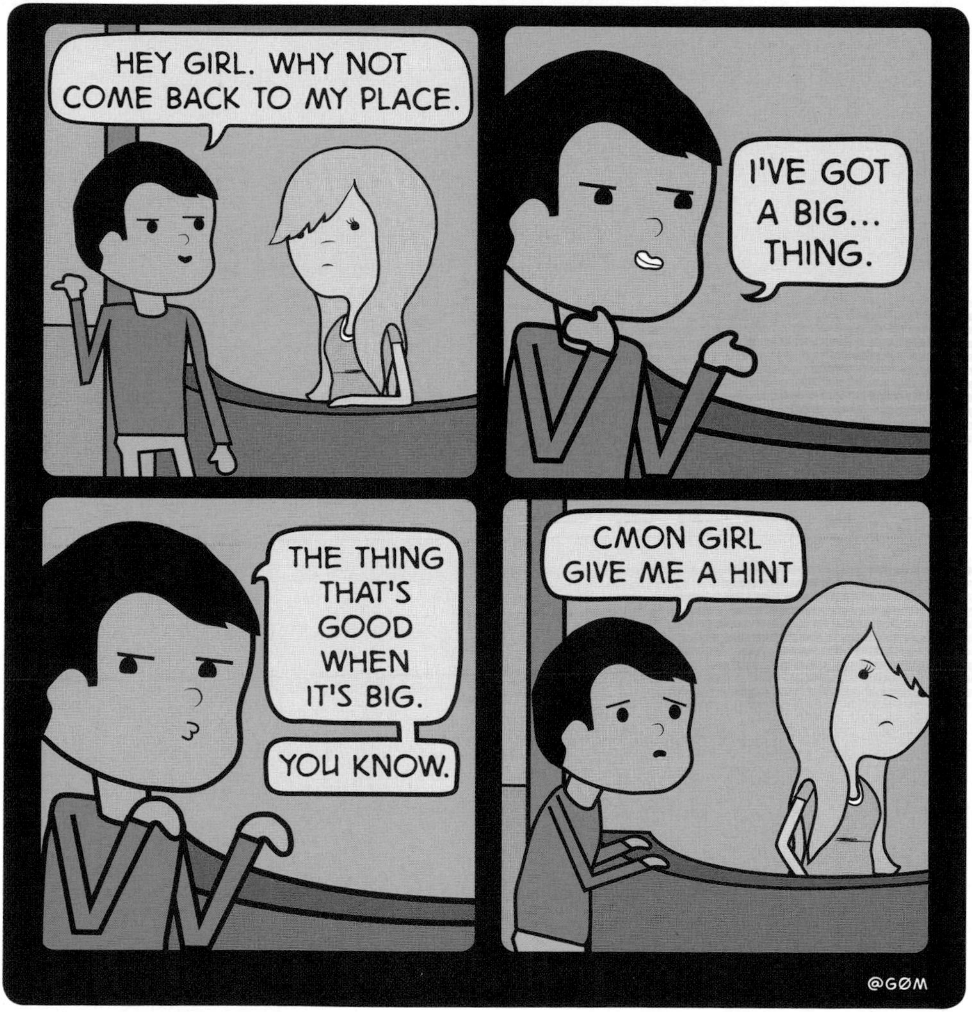
HEY GIRL. WHY NOT COME BACK TO MY PLACE.
I'VE GOT A BIG... THING.
THE THING THAT'S GOOD WHEN IT'S BIG.
YOU KNOW.
CMON GIRL GIVE ME A HINT
@GØM

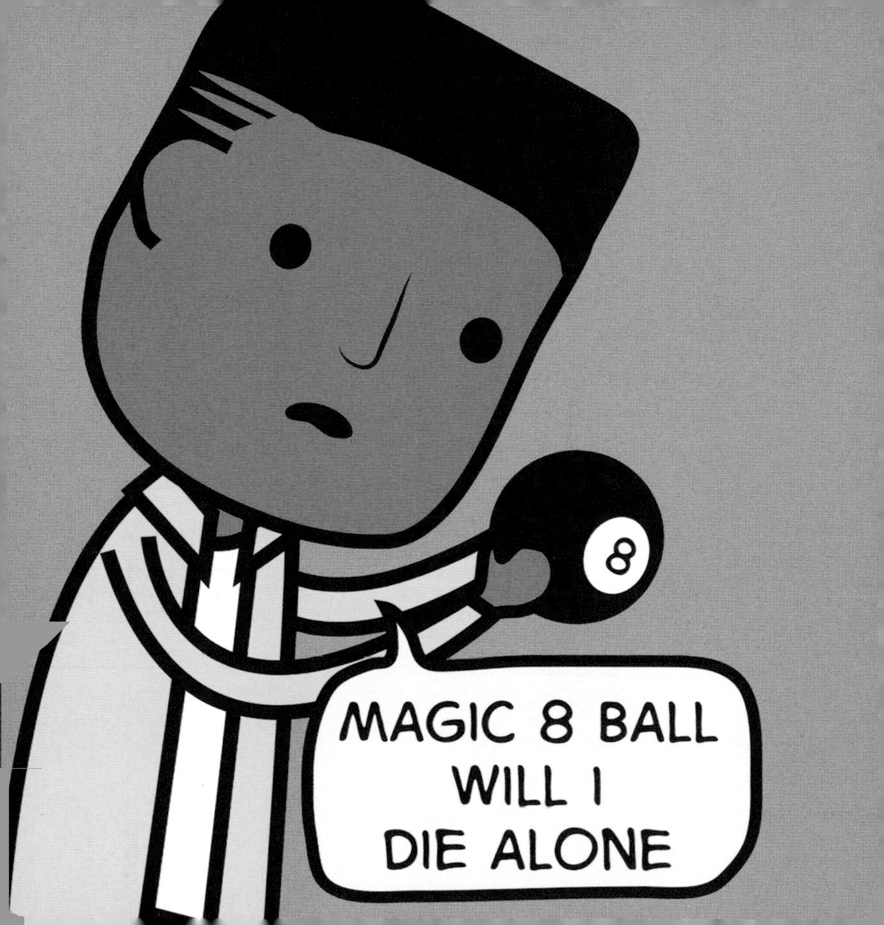
MAGIC 8 BALL
WILL I
DIE ALONE
8

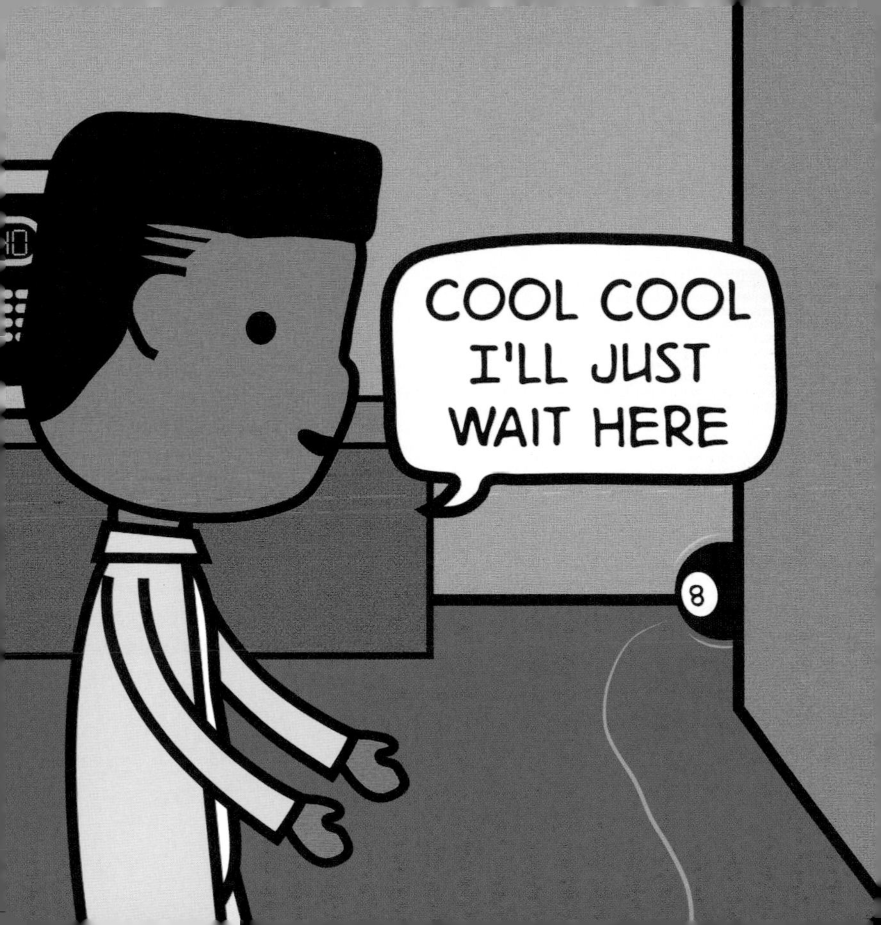
COOL COOL I'LL JUST WAIT HERE

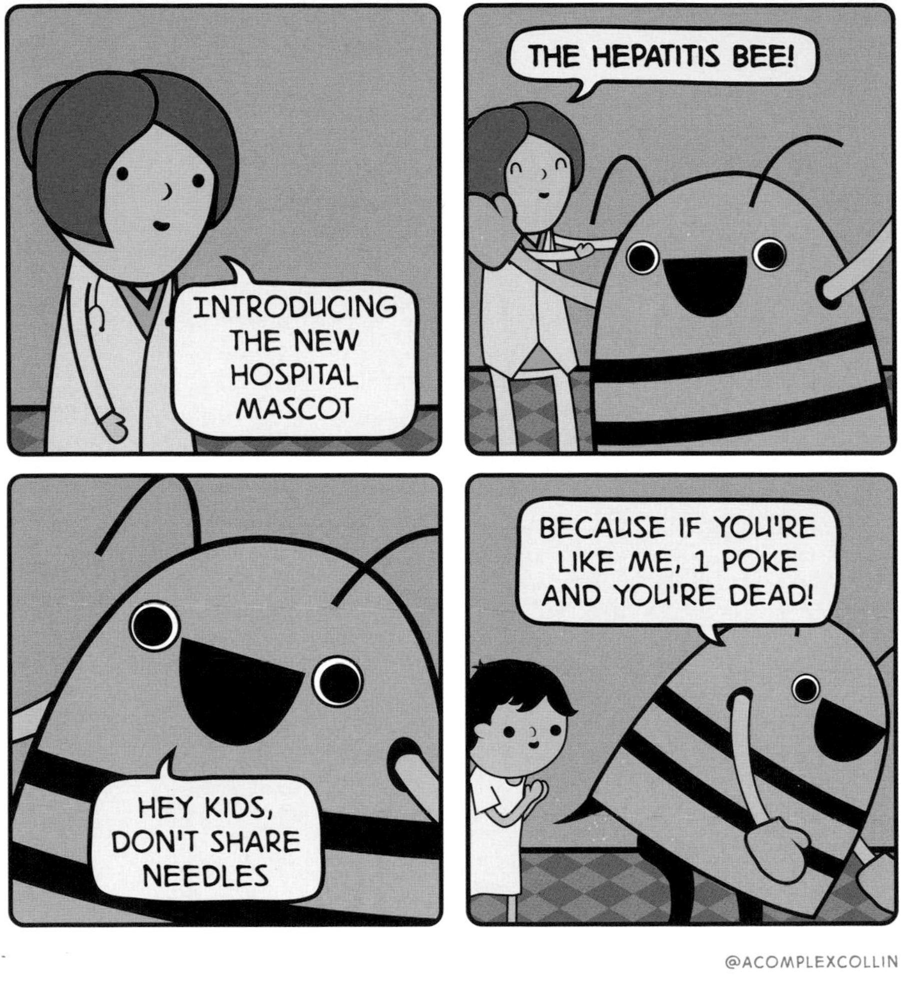
INTRODUCING THE NEW HOSPITAL MASCOT
THE HEPATITIS BEE!
HEY KIDS, DON'T SHARE NEEDLES
BECAUSE IF YOU'RE LIKE ME, 1 POKE AND YOU'RE DEAD!
@ACOMPLEXCOLLIN

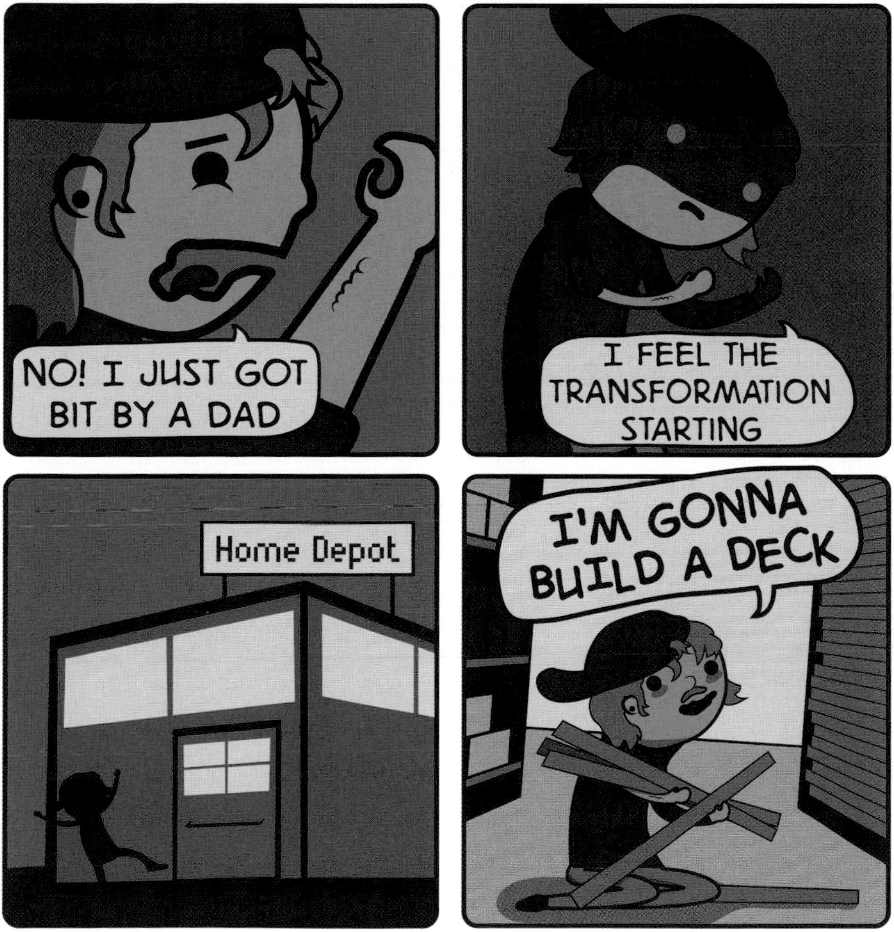
NO! I JUST GOT BIT BY A DAD
I FEEL THE TRANSFORMATION STARTING
Home Depot
I'M GONNA BUILD A DECK

@JONNY_WAGS

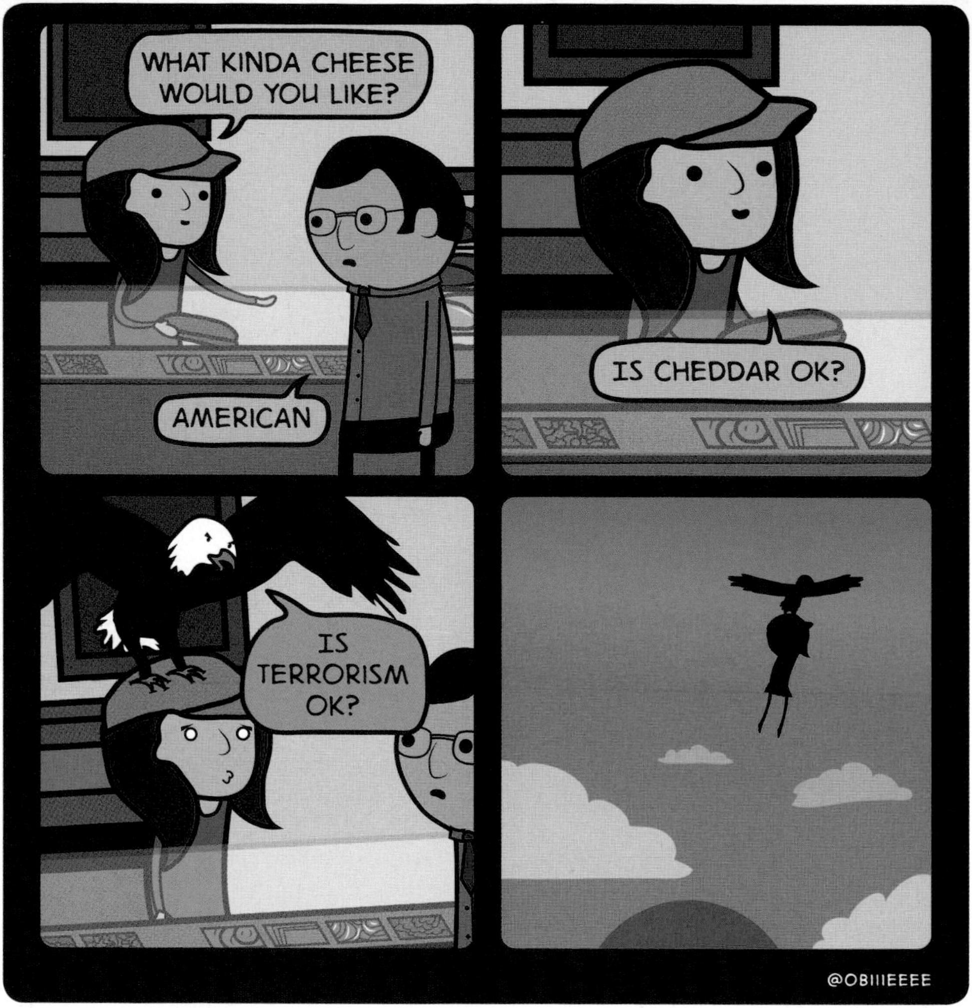
WHAT KINDA CHEESE WOULD YOU LIKE?
AMERICAN
IS CHEDDAR OK?
IS TERRORISM OK?
@OBIIIEEEE

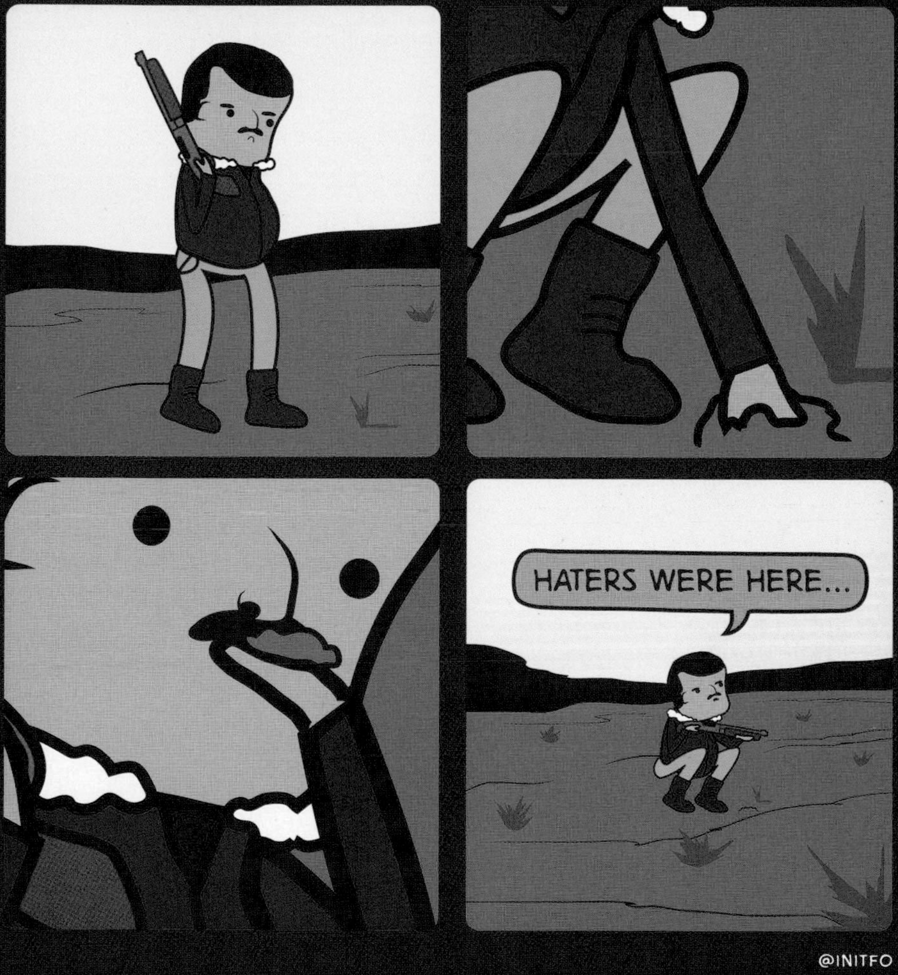
HATERS WERE HERE...
@INITFO

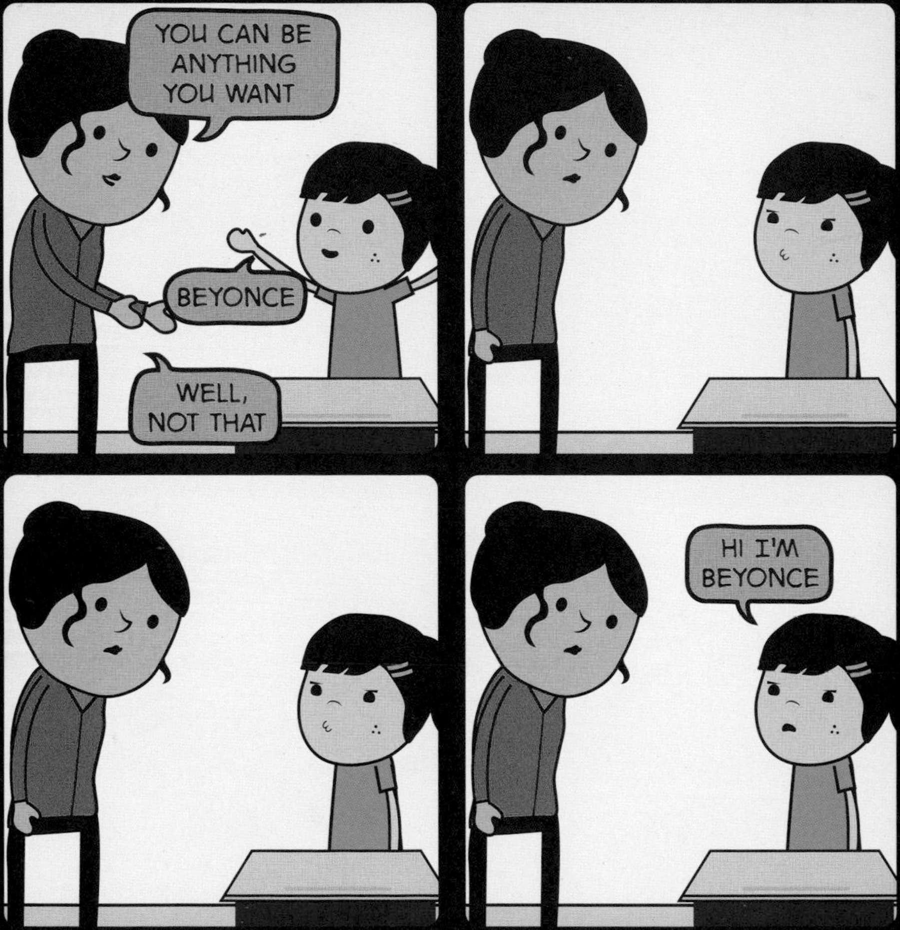
YOU CAN BE ANYTHING YOU WANT
BEYONCE
WELL, NOT THAT
HI I'M BEYONCE

@INMYNEWSKIN

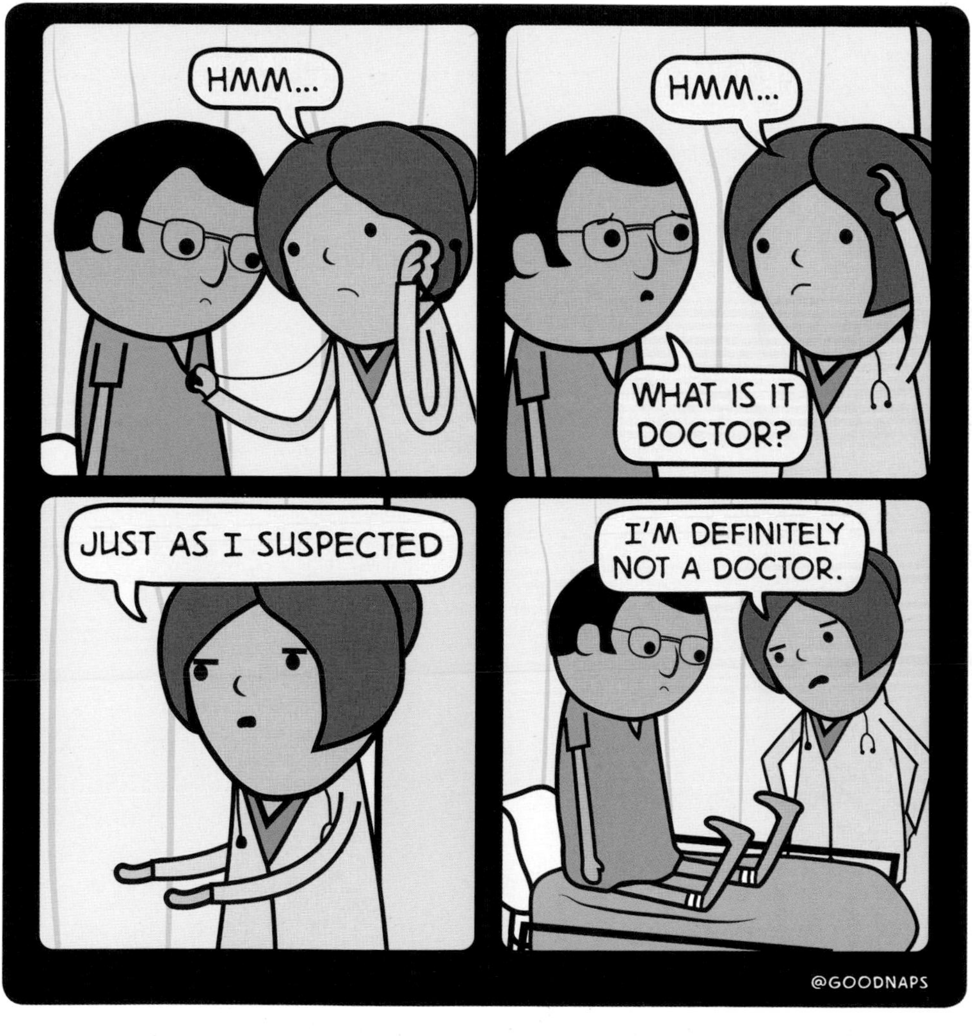
HMM...
HMM...
WHAT IS IT DOCTOR?
JUST AS I SUSPECTED
I'M DEFINITELY NOT A DOCTOR.
@GOODNAPS

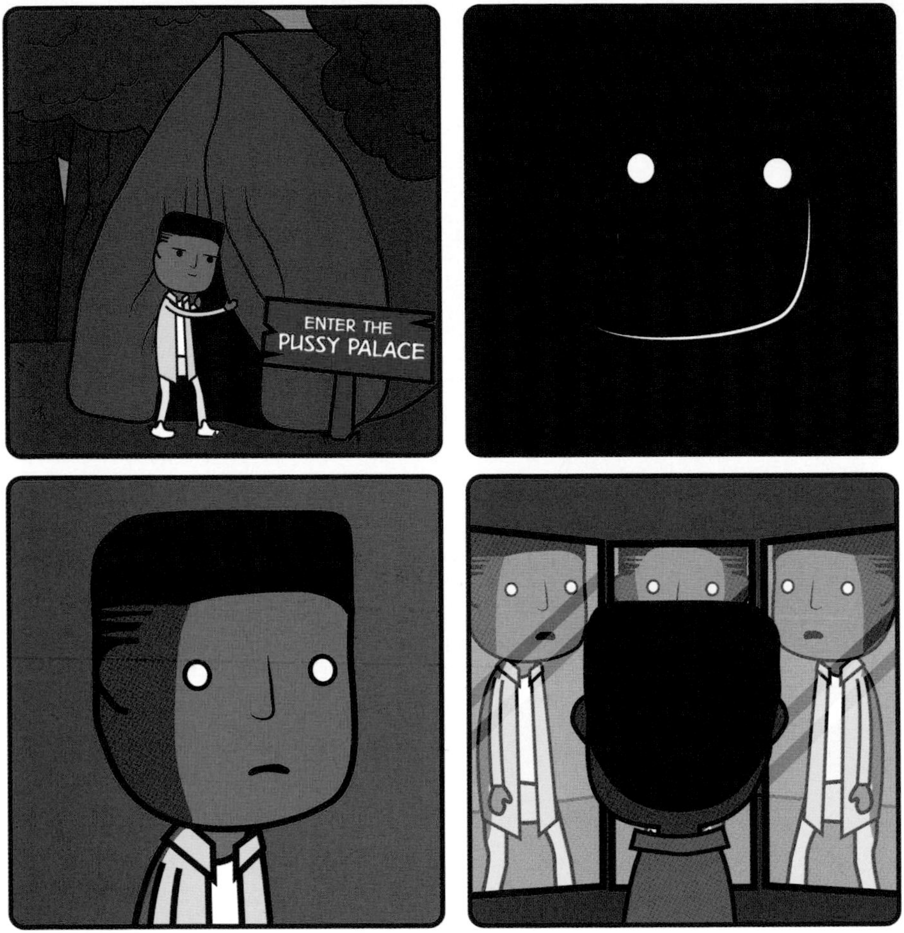
ENTER THE
PUSSY PALACE

@TRASH_EATER_DOG

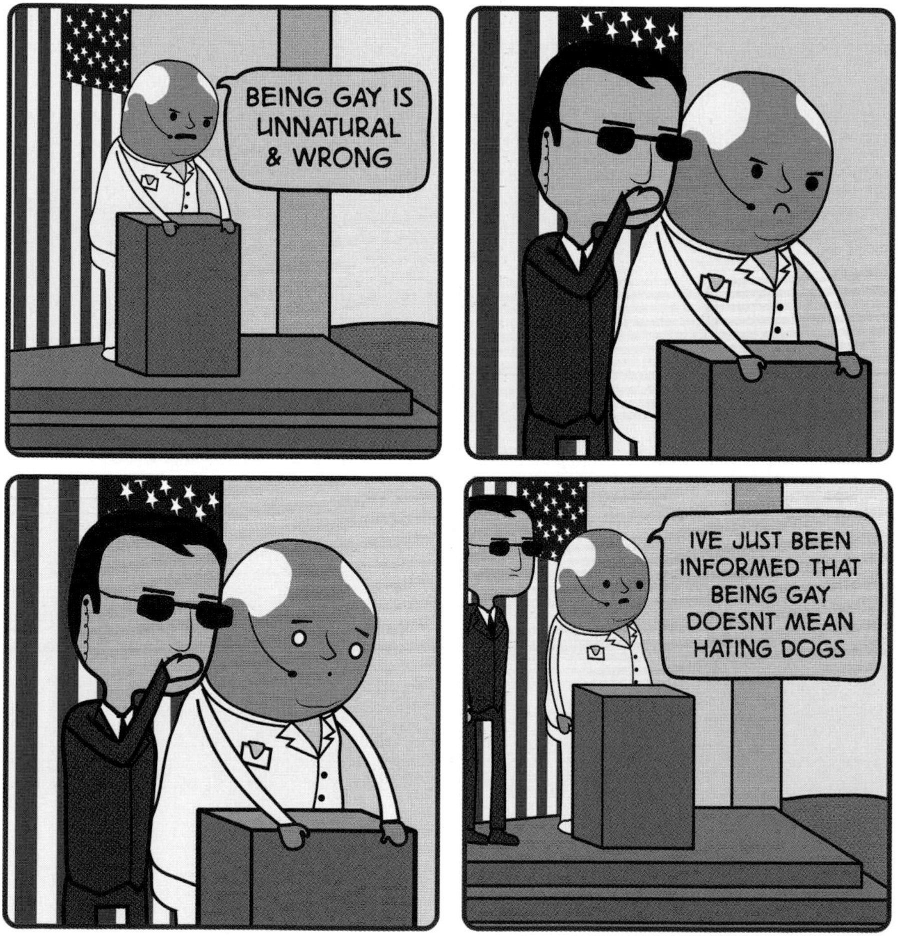
BEING GAY IS UNNATURAL & WRONG
IVE JUST BEEN INFORMED THAT BEING GAY DOESNT MEAN HATING DOGS

@JEVENSTEAKOBSON

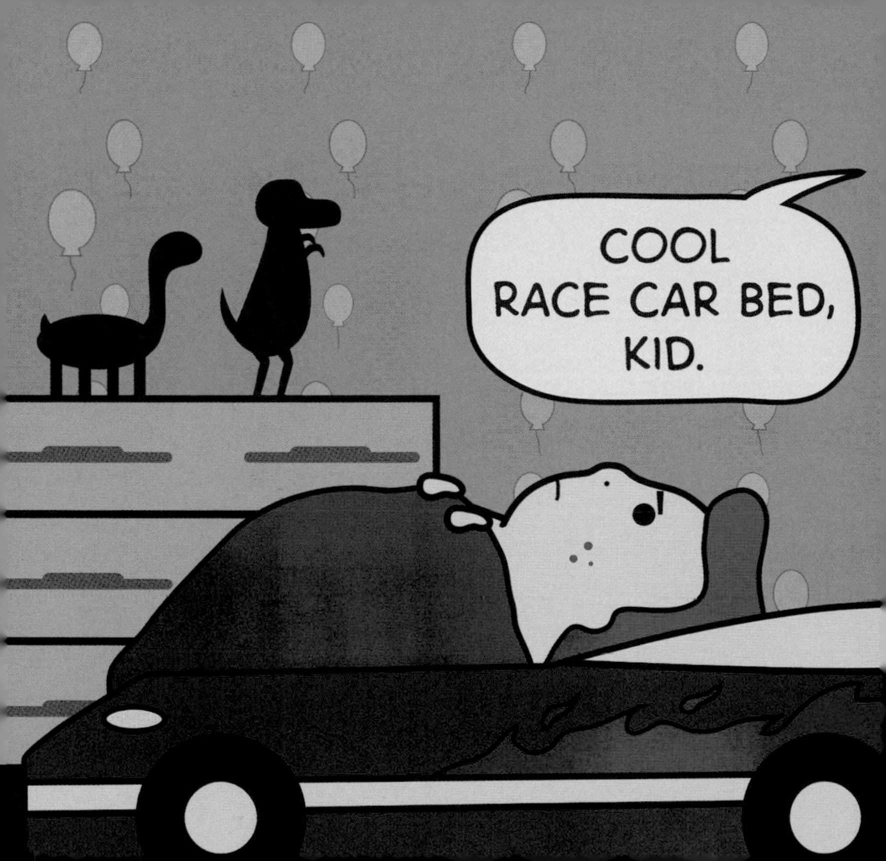
COOL RACE CAR BED, KID.

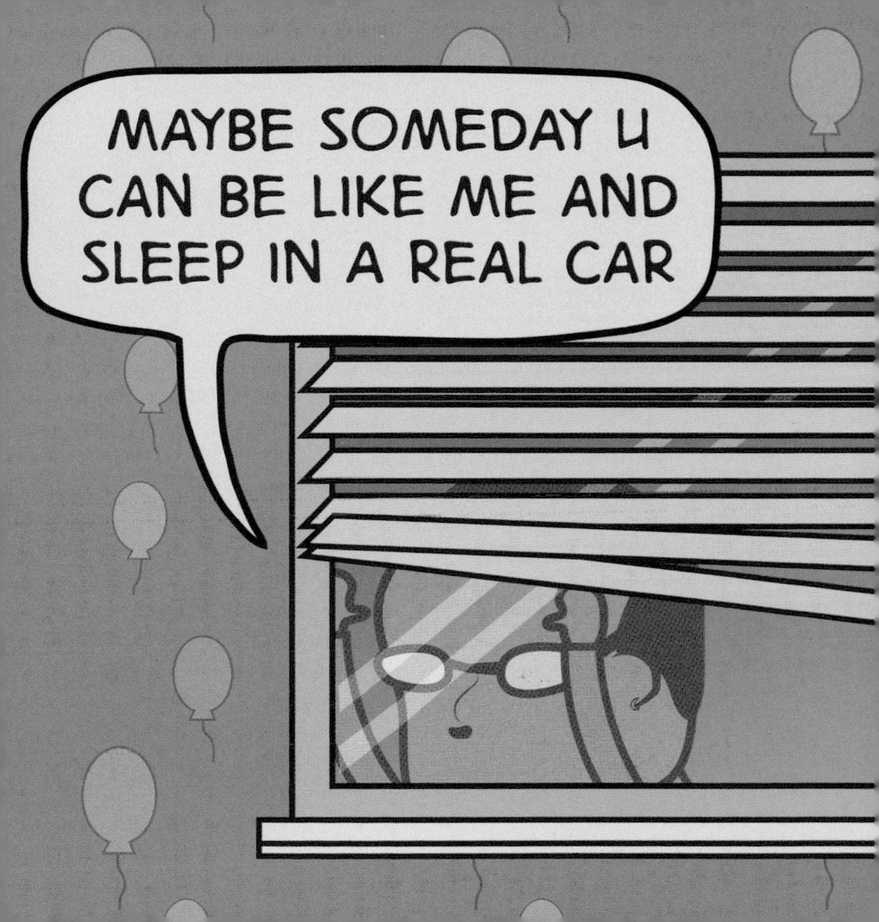
MAYBE SOMEDAY U CAN BE LIKE ME AND SLEEP IN A REAL CAR

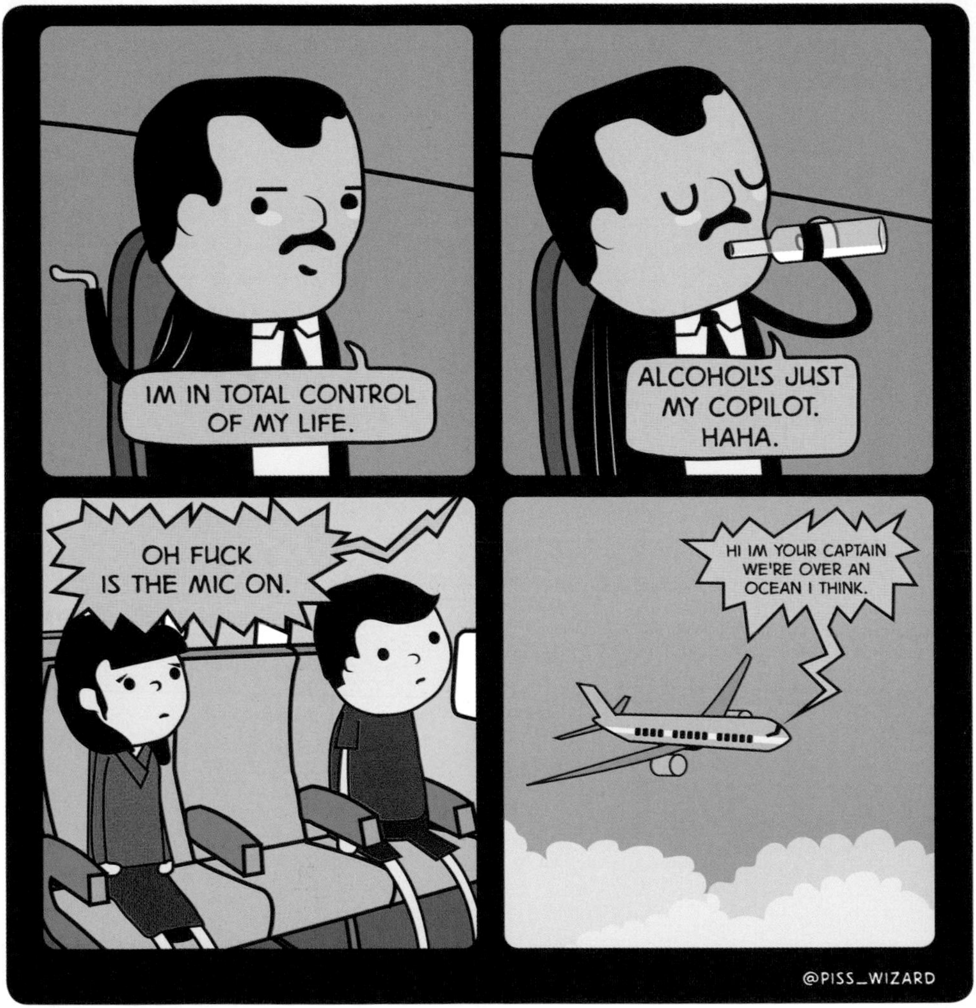
IM IN TOTAL CONTROL OF MY LIFE.
ALCOHOL'S JUST MY COPILOT. HAHA.
OH FUCK IS THE MIC ON.
HI IM YOUR CAPTAIN WE'RE OVER AN OCEAN I THINK.
@PISS_WIZARD

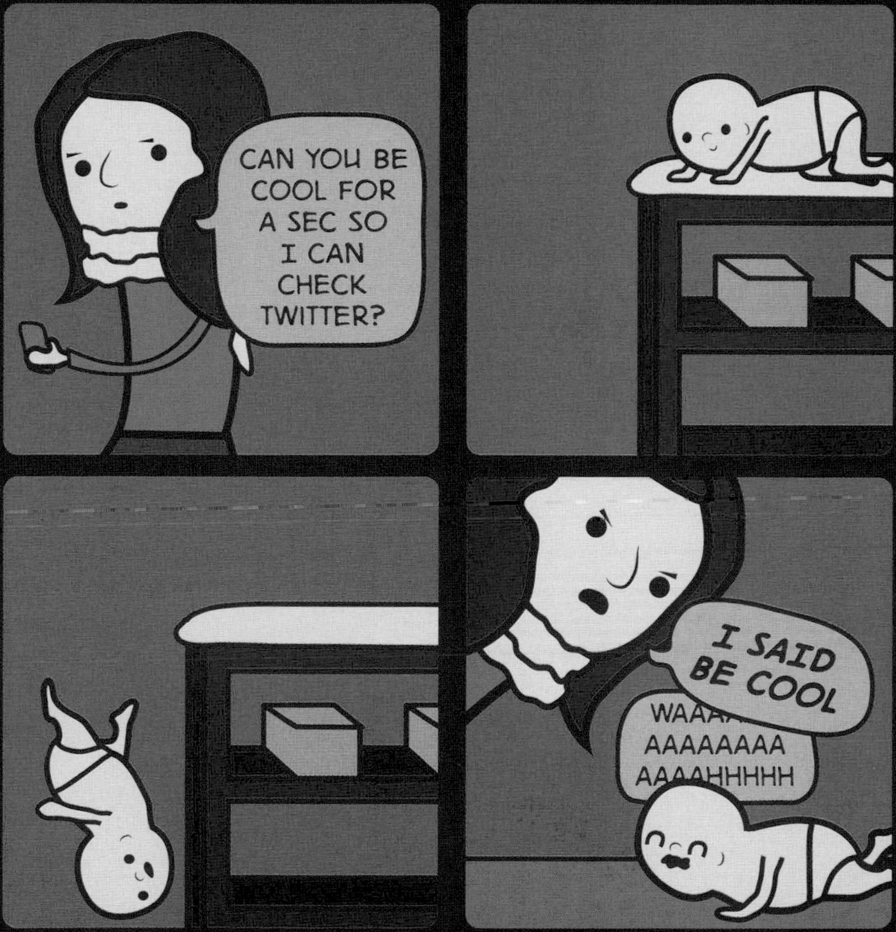
CAN YOU BE COOL FOR A SEC SO I CAN CHECK TWITTER?
I SAID BE COOL
WAAAAAAAAAAAAAAAAHHHHH
@LOSTCATDOG

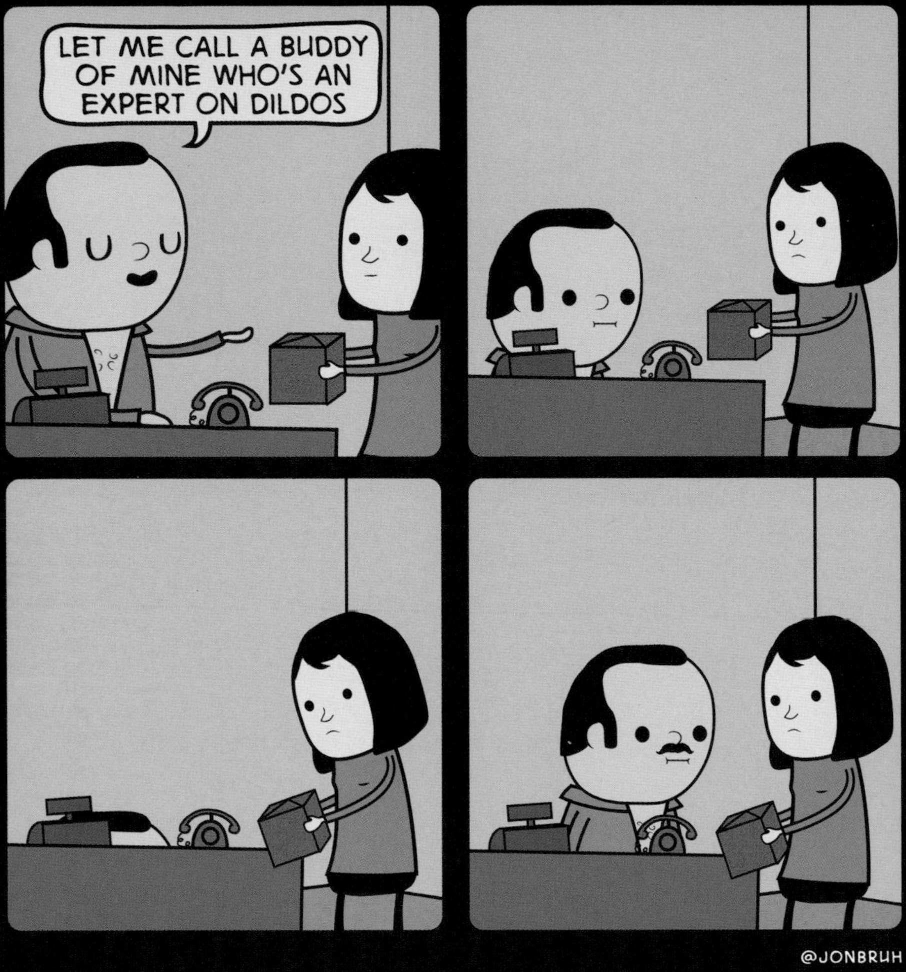
LET ME CALL A BUDDY OF MINE WHO'S AN EXPERT ON DILDOS
@JONBRUH

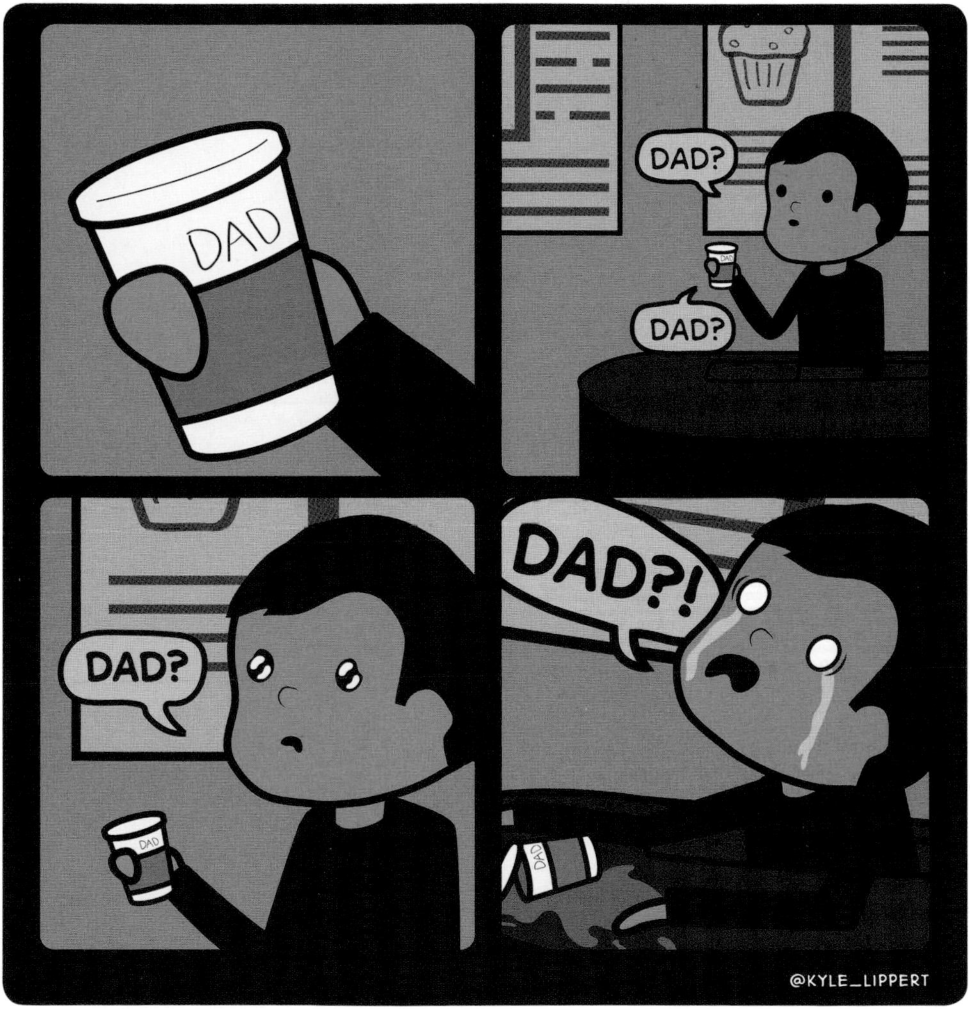
DAD
DAD?
DAD?
DAD?
DAD?!
@KYLE_LIPPERT

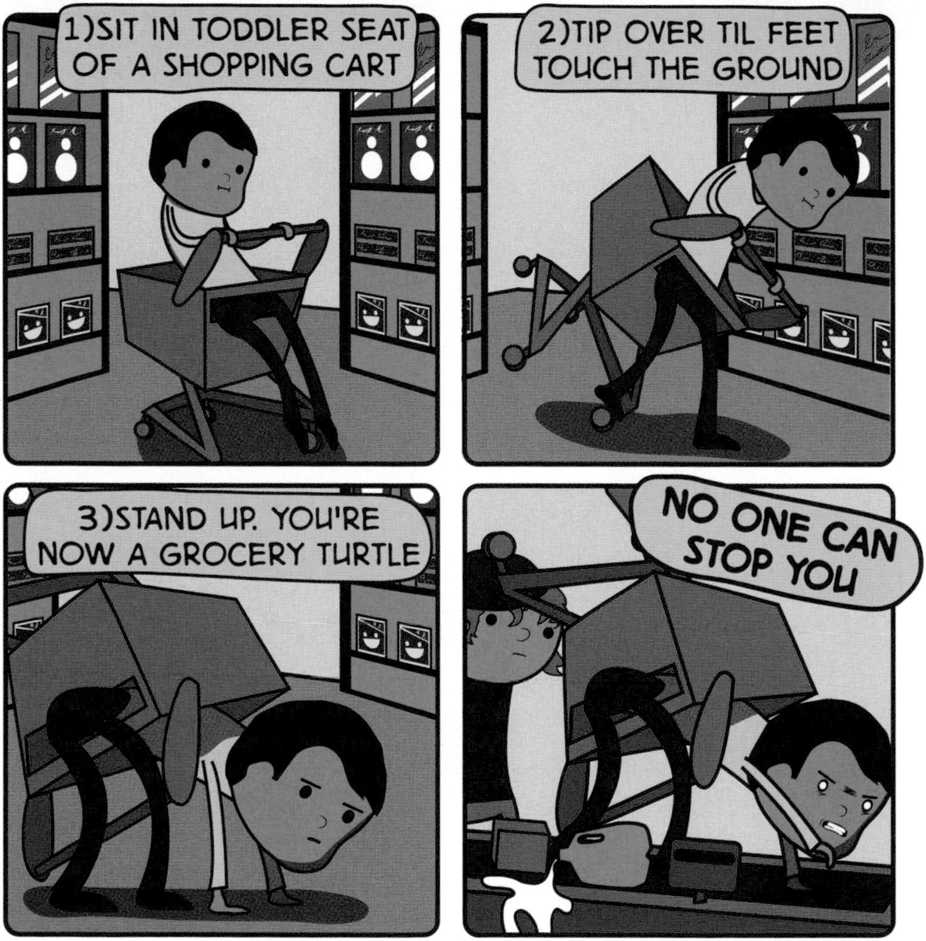
1)SIT IN TODDLER SEAT OF A SHOPPING CART
2)TIP OVER TIL FEET TOUCH THE GROUND
3)STAND UP. YOU'RE NOW A GROCERY TURTLE
NO ONE CAN STOP YOU

@HELL_HOMER

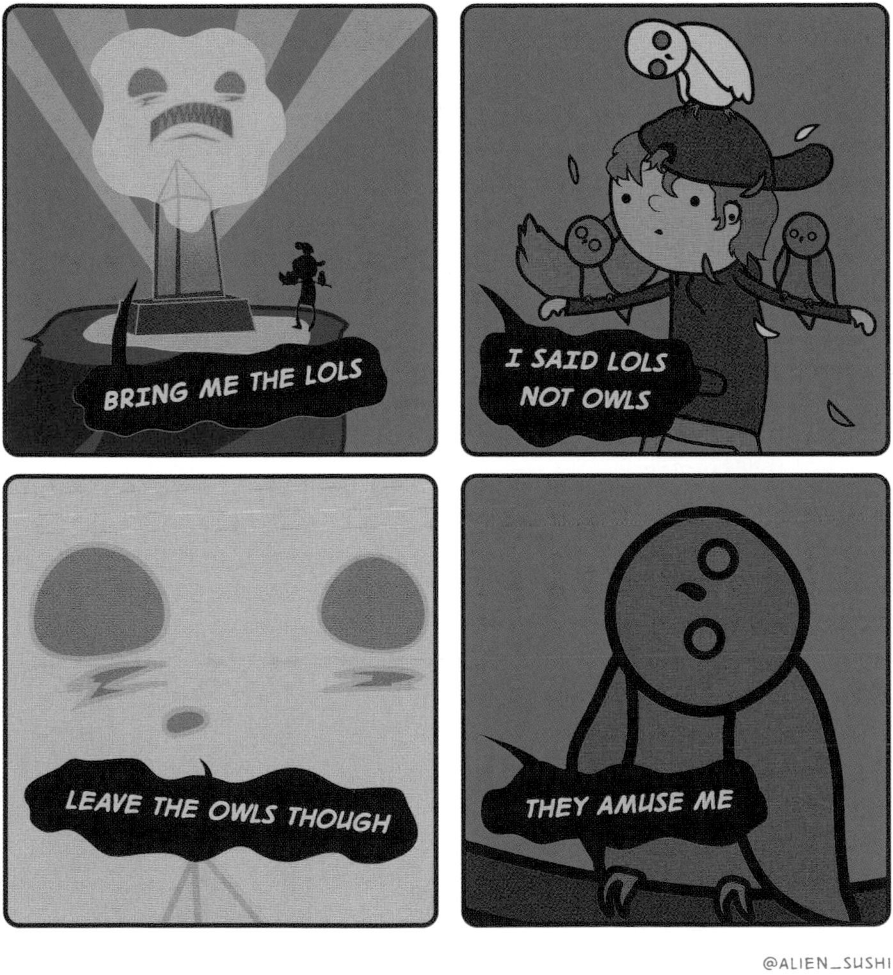
BRING ME THE LOLS
I SAID LOLS NOT OWLS
LEAVE THE OWLS THOUGH
THEY AMUSE ME

@ALIEN_SUSHI

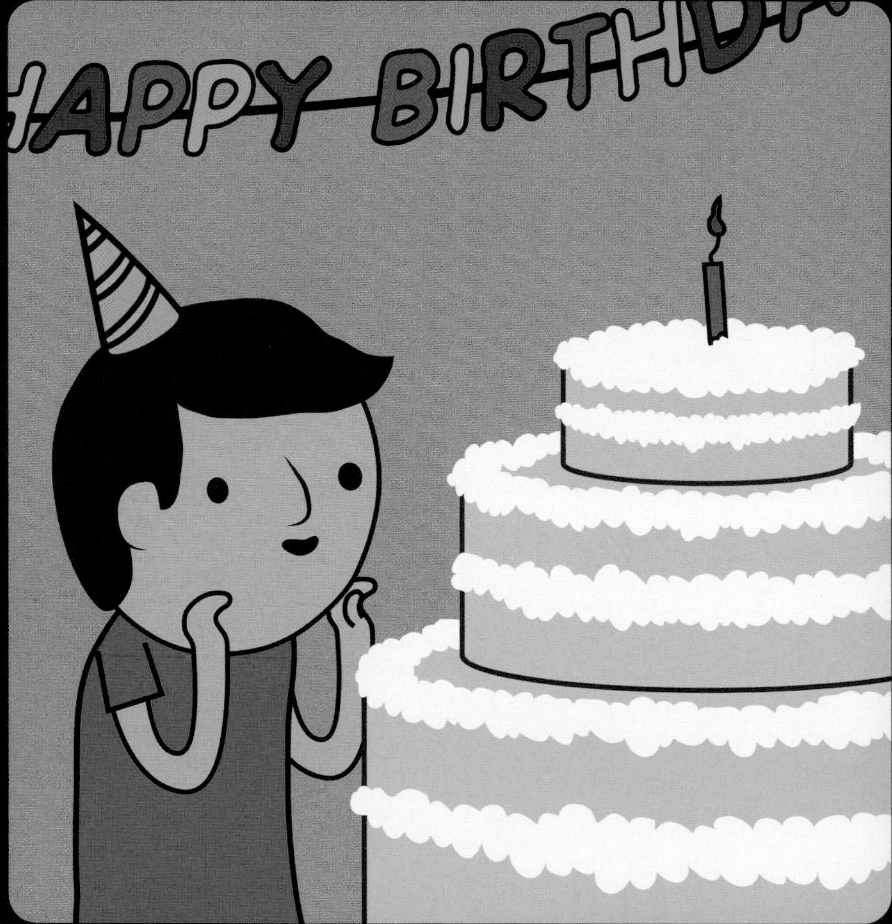
HAPPY BIRTHD

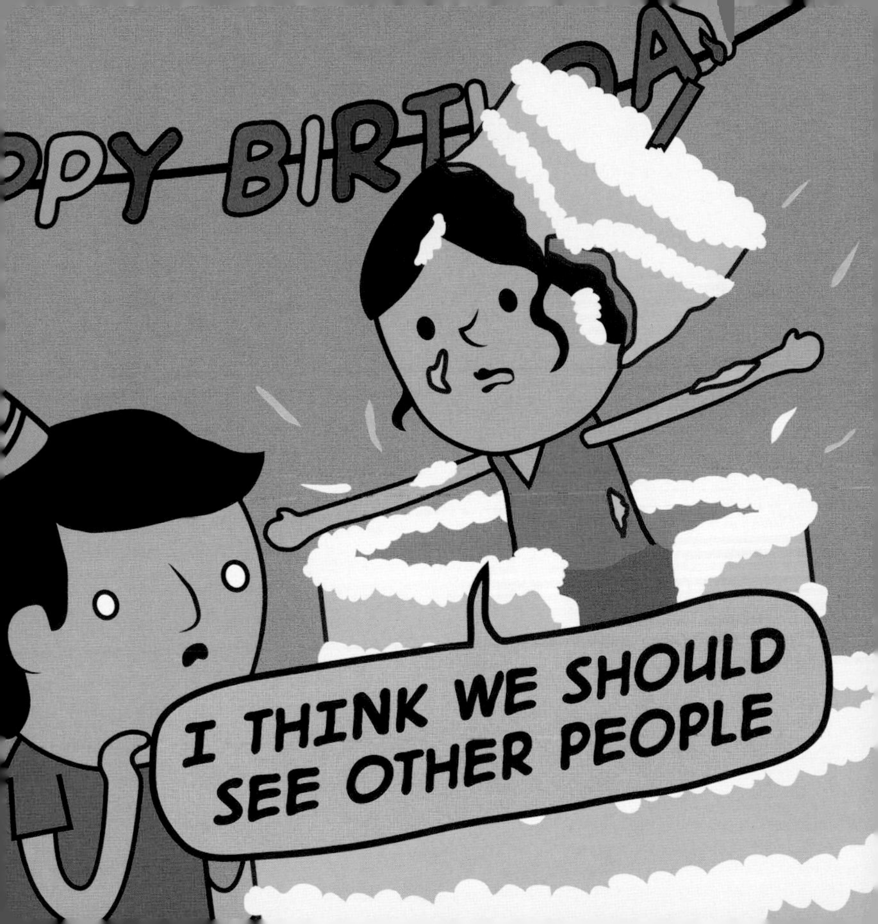
PPY BIRTHDA
I THINK WE SHOULD SEE OTHER PEOPLE

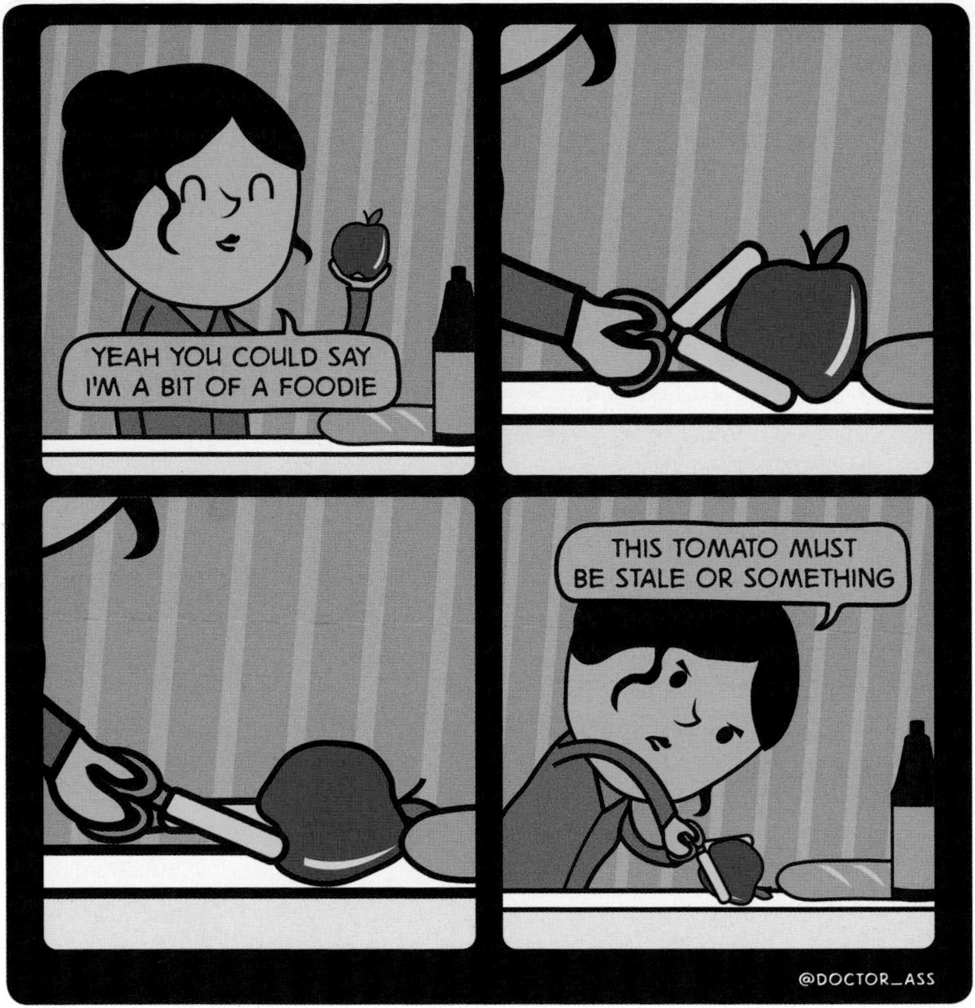
YEAH YOU COULD SAY I'M A BIT OF A FOODIE
THIS TOMATO MUST BE STALE OR SOMETHING
@DOCTOR_ASS

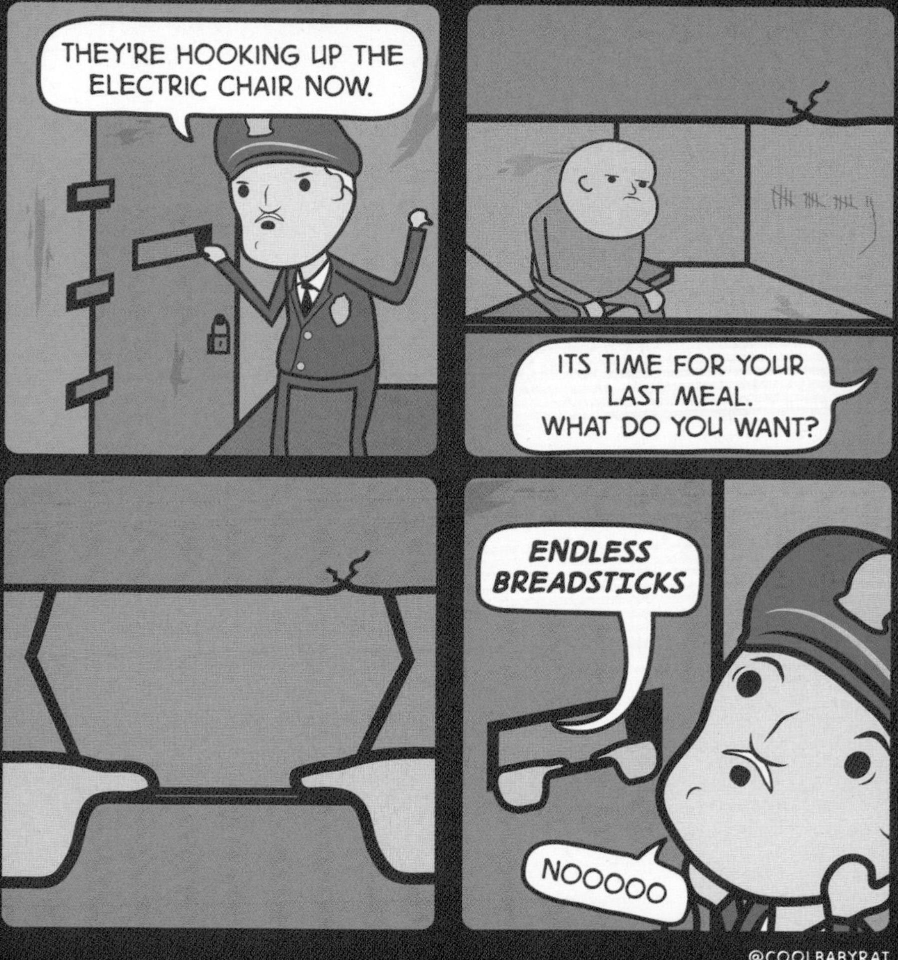

THEY'RE HOOKING UP THE ELECTRIC CHAIR NOW.
ITS TIME FOR YOUR LAST MEAL. WHAT DO YOU WANT?
ENDLESS BREADSTICKS
NOOOOO
@COOLBABYRAT

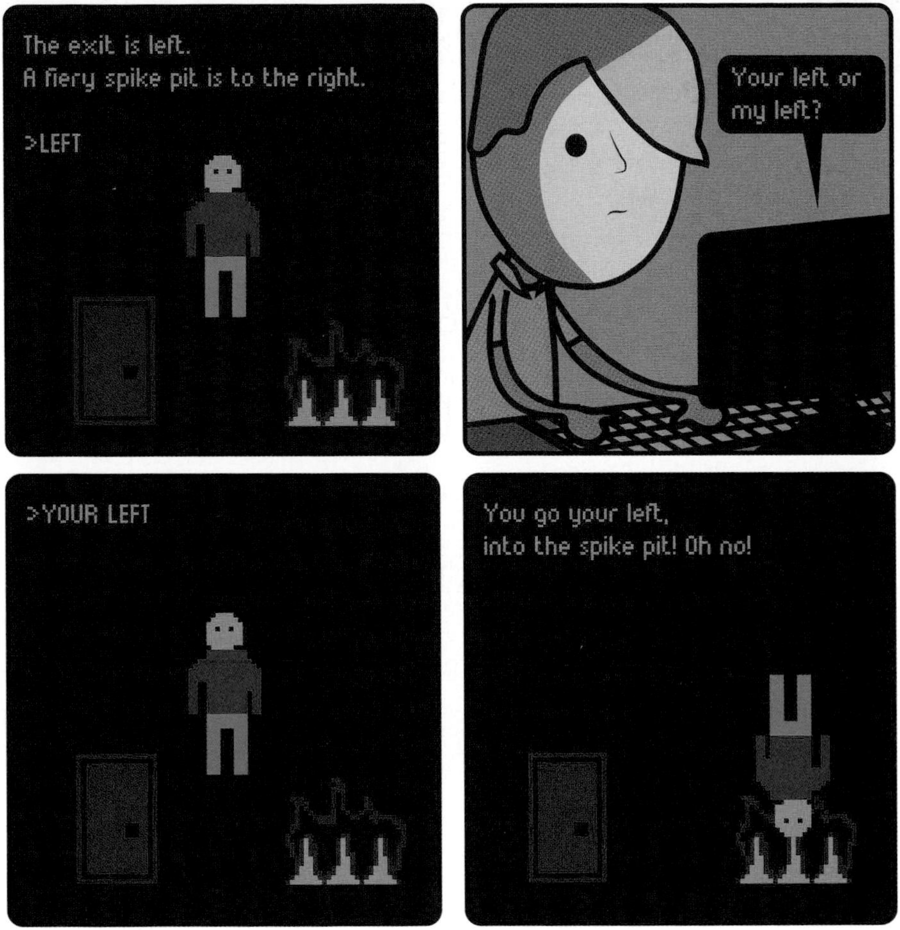
The exit is left.
A fiery spike pit is to the right.
>LEFT
Your left or my left?
>YOUR LEFT
You go your left,
into the spike pit! Oh no!

@WEBBEDSPACE

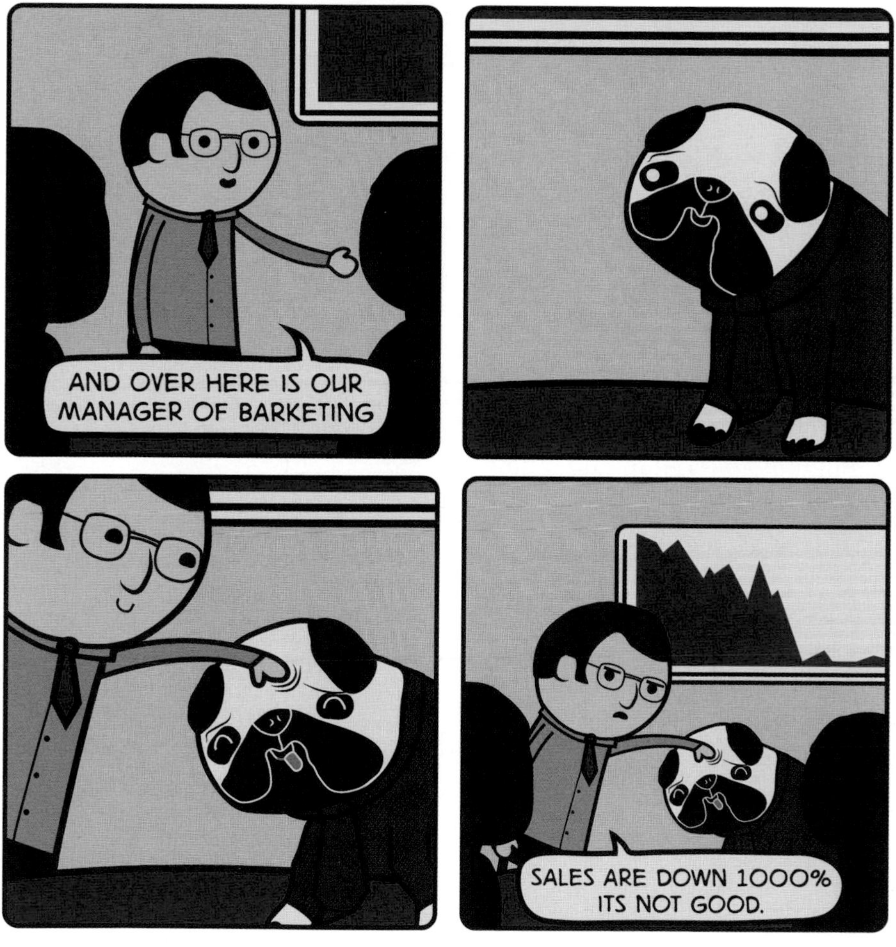
AND OVER HERE IS OUR MANAGER OF BARKETING
SALES ARE DOWN 1000% ITS NOT GOOD.

@FUCPK

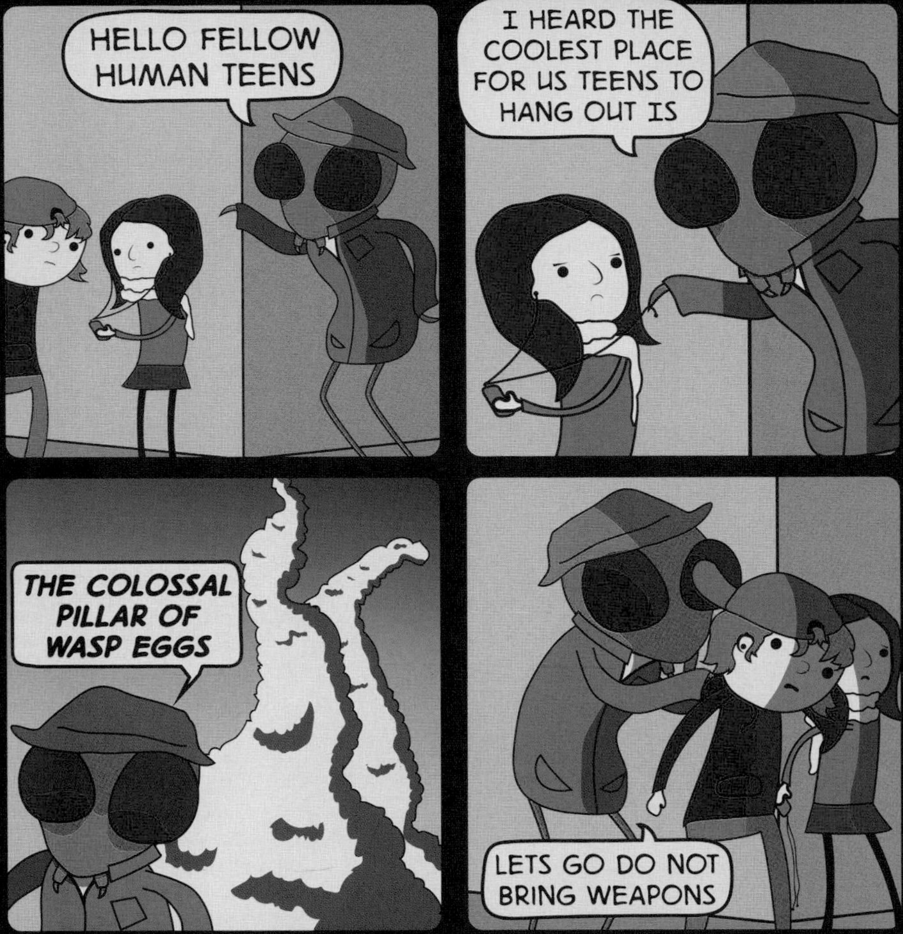
HELLO FELLOW HUMAN TEENS
I HEARD THE COOLEST PLACE FOR US TEENS TO HANG OUT IS
THE COLOSSAL PILLAR OF WASP EGGS
LETS GO DO NOT BRING WEAPONS

@PISSCOP

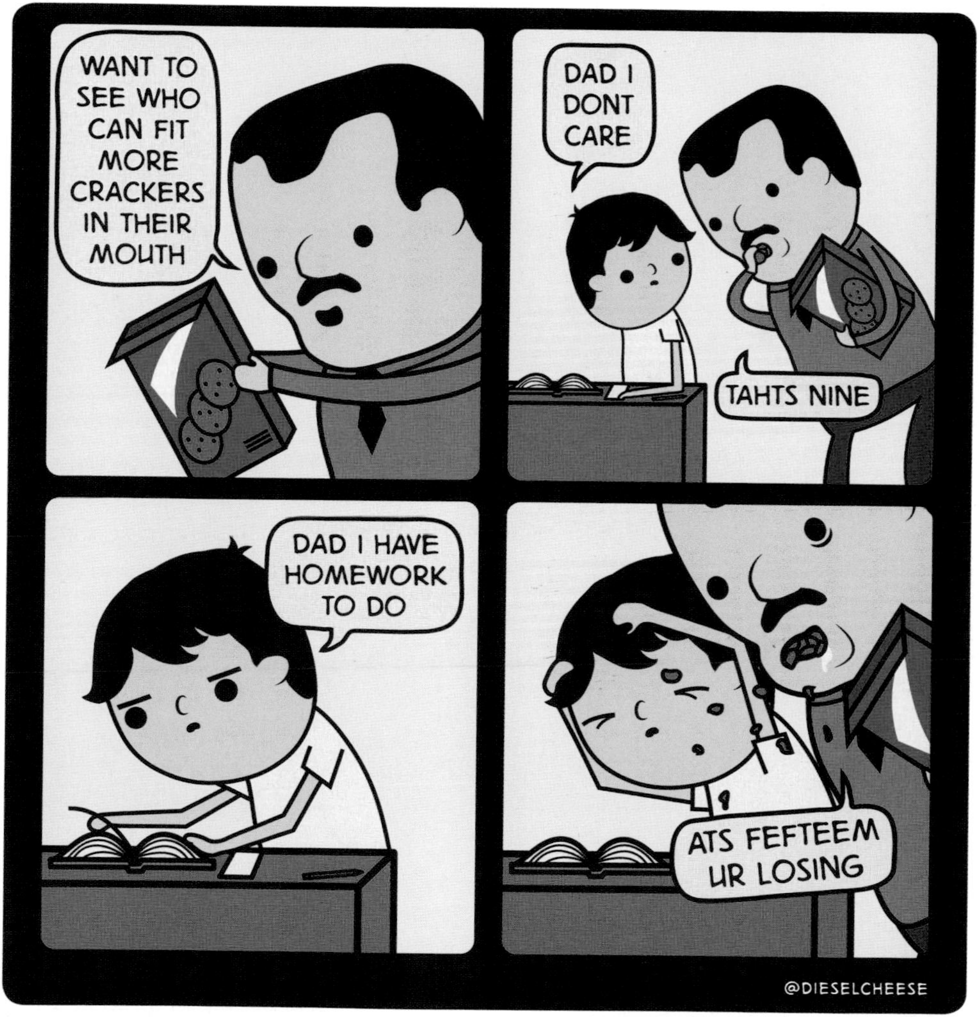
WANT TO SEE WHO CAN FIT MORE CRACKERS IN THEIR MOUTH
DAD I DONT CARE
TAHTS NINE
DAD I HAVE HOMEWORK TO DO
ATS FEFTEEM UR LOSING
@DIESELCHEESE

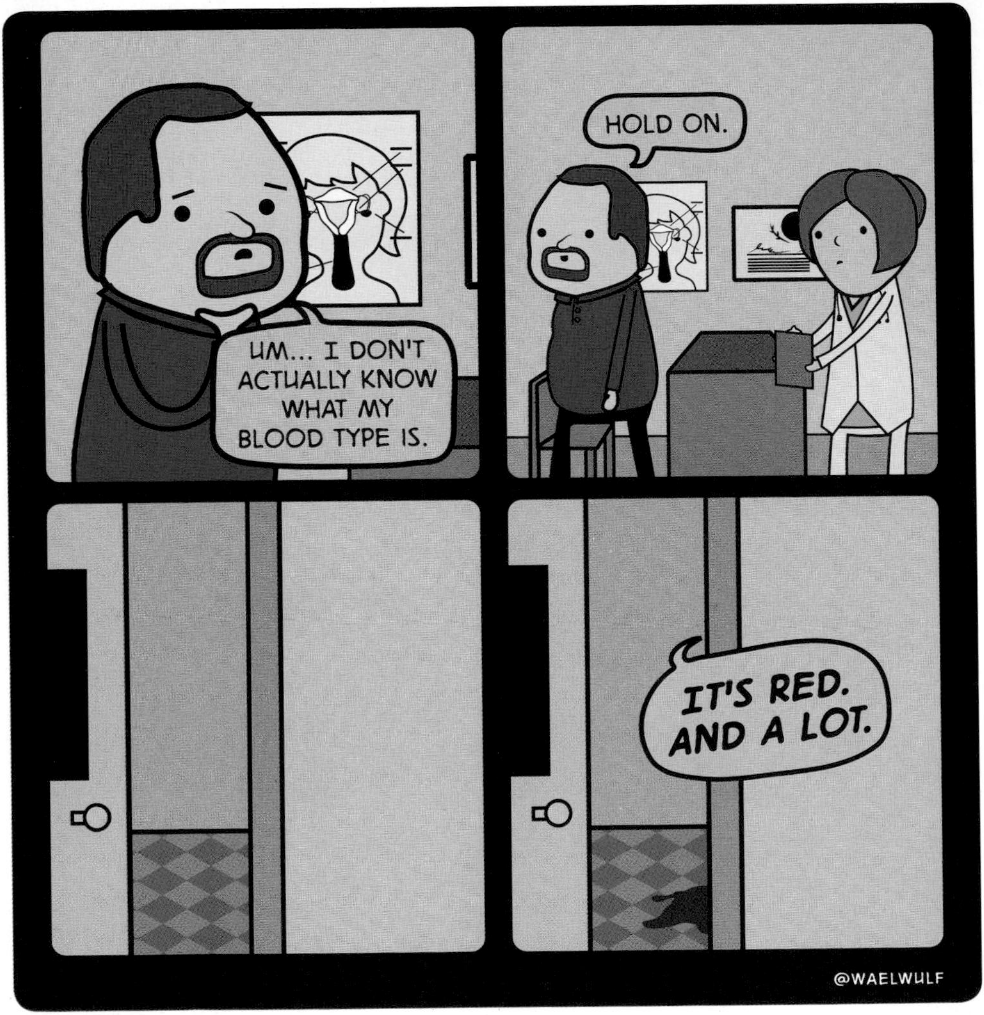
UM... I DON'T ACTUALLY KNOW WHAT MY BLOOD TYPE IS.
HOLD ON.
IT'S RED. AND A LOT.
@WAELWULF

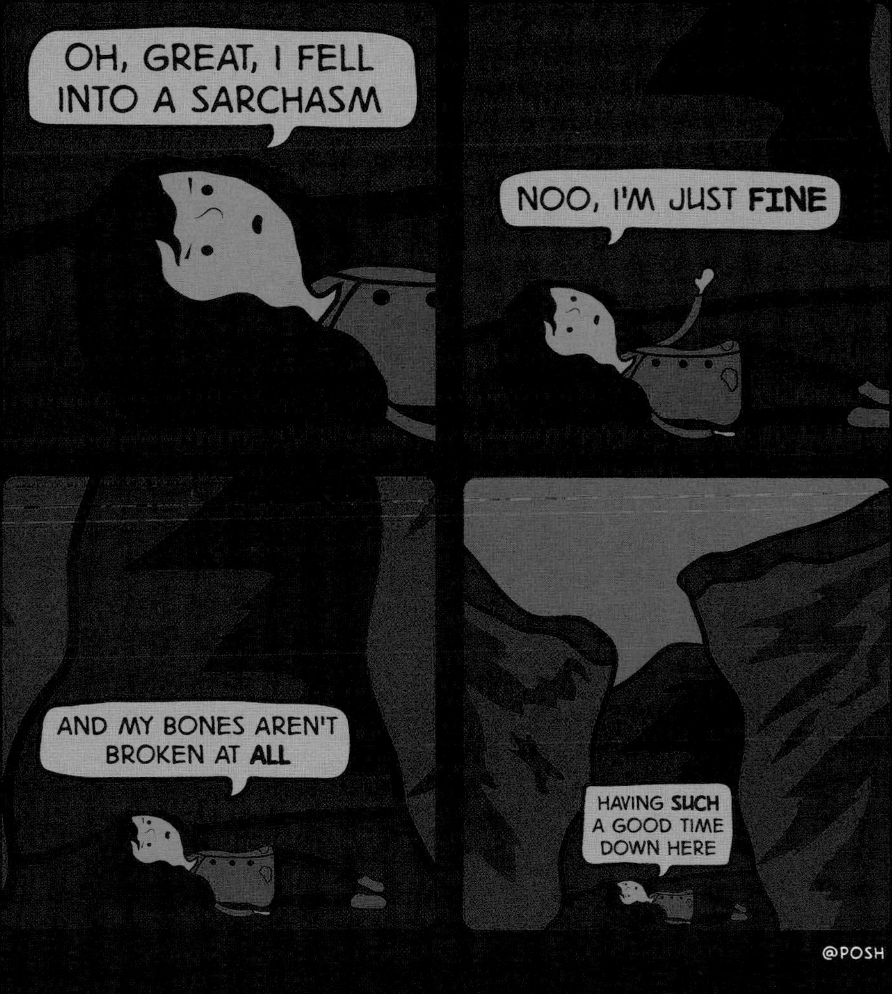
OH, GREAT, I FELL INTO A SARCHASM
NOO, I'M JUST **FINE**
AND MY BONES AREN'T BROKEN AT **ALL**
HAVING **SUCH** A GOOD TIME DOWN HERE
@POSH

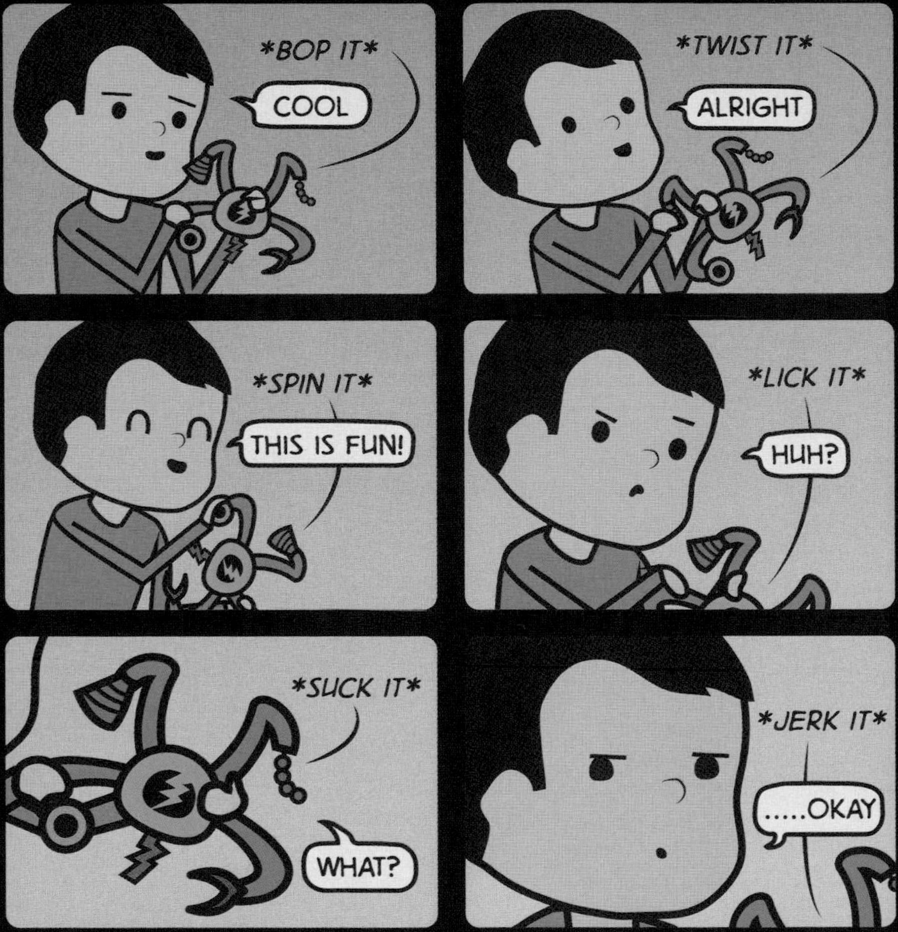
BOP IT
COOL
TWIST IT
ALRIGHT
SPIN IT
THIS IS FUN!
LICK IT
HUH?
SUCK IT
WHAT?
JERK IT
.....OKAY

@BRANDONELZBY

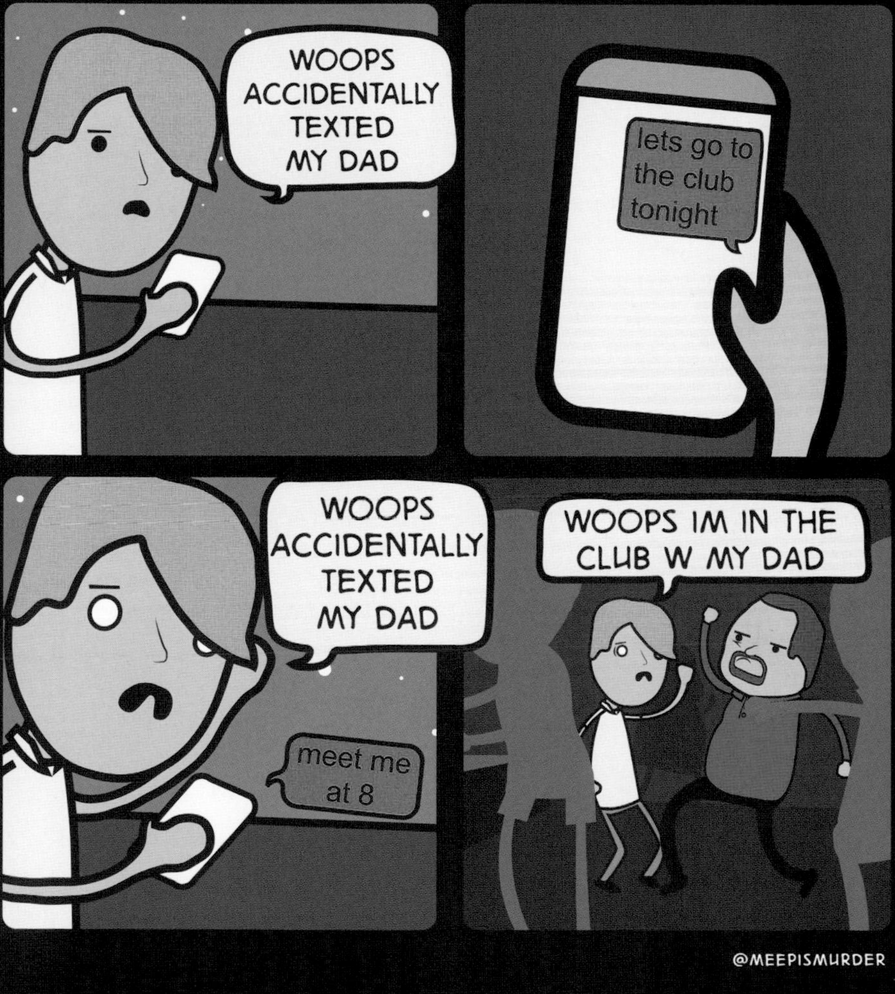
WOOPS ACCIDENTALLY TEXTED MY DAD
lets go to the club tonight
WOOPS ACCIDENTALLY TEXTED MY DAD
meet me at 8
WOOPS IM IN THE CLUB W MY DAD
@MEEPISMURDER

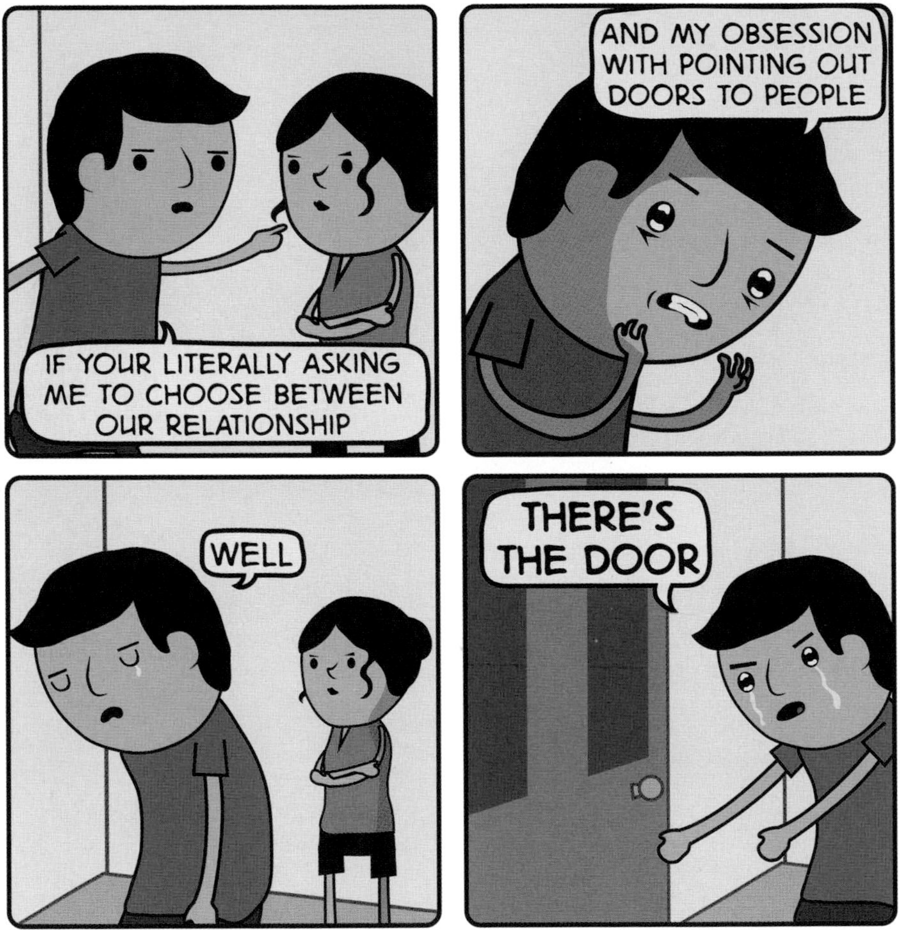
IF YOUR LITERALLY ASKING ME TO CHOOSE BETWEEN OUR RELATIONSHIP
AND MY OBSESSION WITH POINTING OUT DOORS TO PEOPLE
WELL
THERE'S THE DOOR

@INGMARBIRDMAN

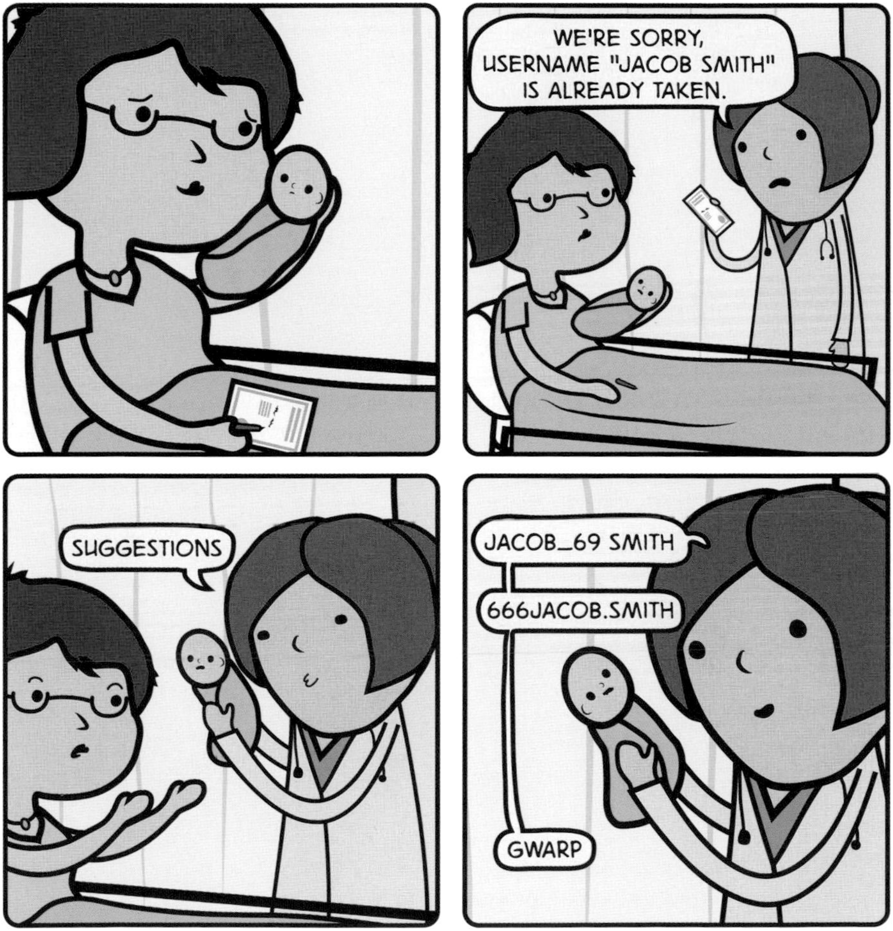

WE'RE SORRY, USERNAME "JACOB SMITH" IS ALREADY TAKEN.
SUGGESTIONS
JACOB_69 SMITH
666JACOB.SMITH
GWARP

@BURGERKRANG

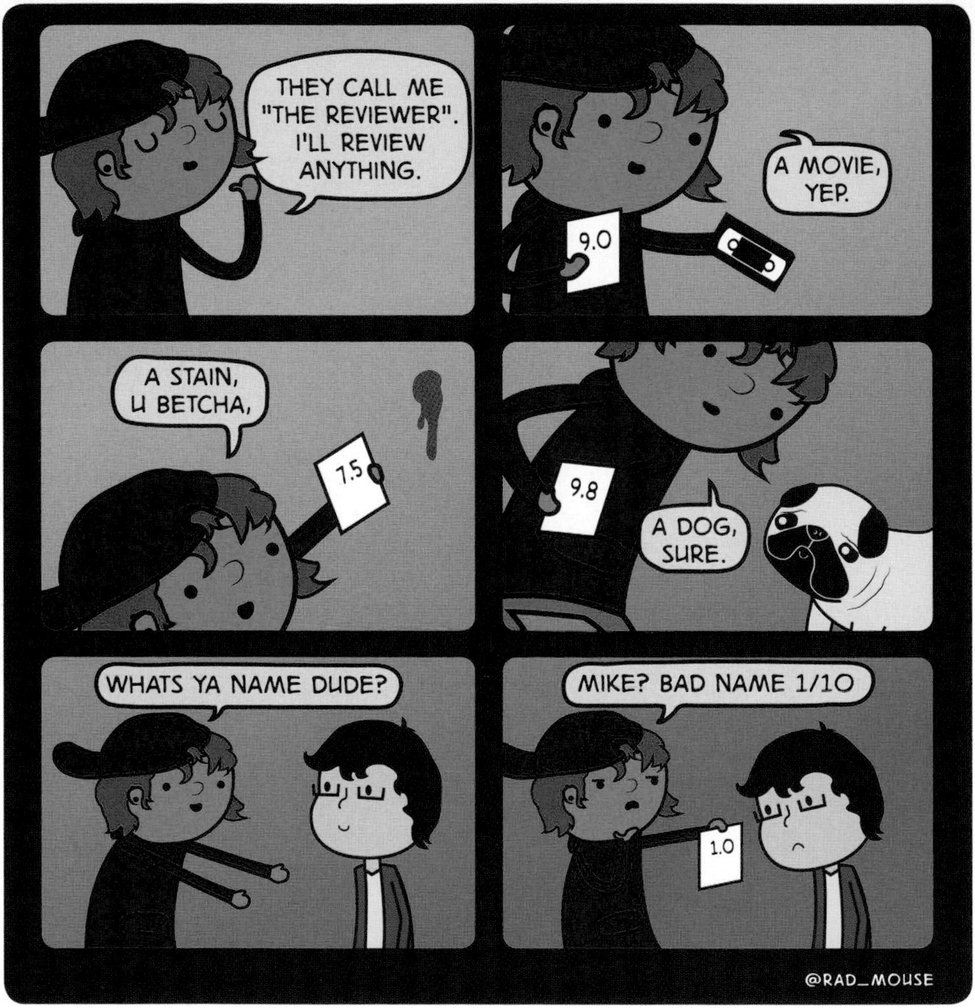
THEY CALL ME "THE REVIEWER". I'LL REVIEW ANYTHING.
A MOVIE, YEP.
9.0
A STAIN, U BETCHA,
7.5
A DOG, SURE.
9.8
WHATS YA NAME DUDE?
MIKE? BAD NAME 1/10
1.0
@RAD_MOUSE

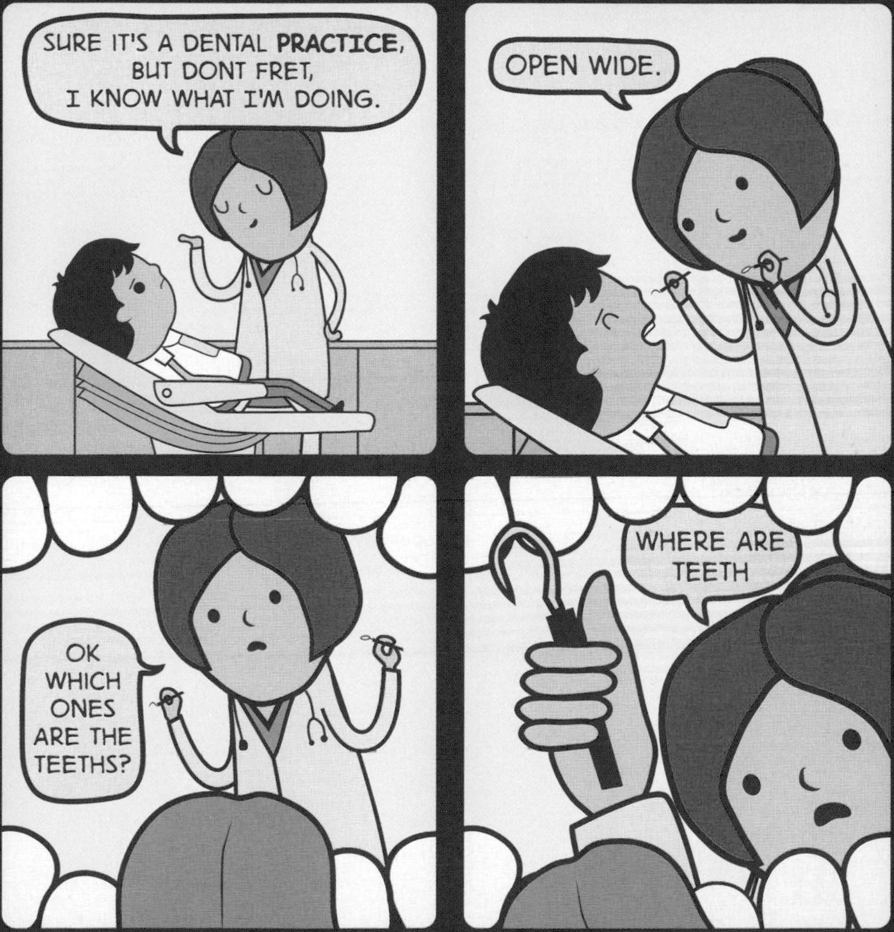
SURE IT'S A DENTAL **PRACTICE**, BUT DONT FRET, I KNOW WHAT I'M DOING.
OPEN WIDE.
OK WHICH ONES ARE THE TEETHS?
WHERE ARE TEETH

@LENNOXTRUMAN

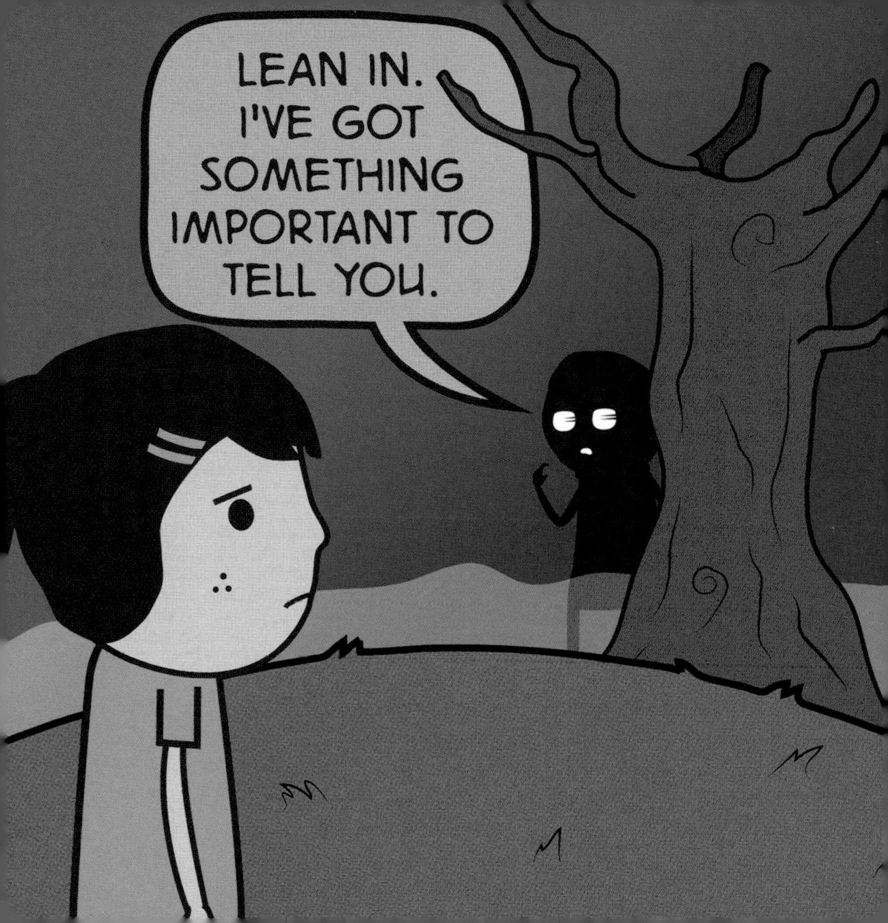
LEAN IN. I'VE GOT SOMETHING IMPORTANT TO TELL YOU.

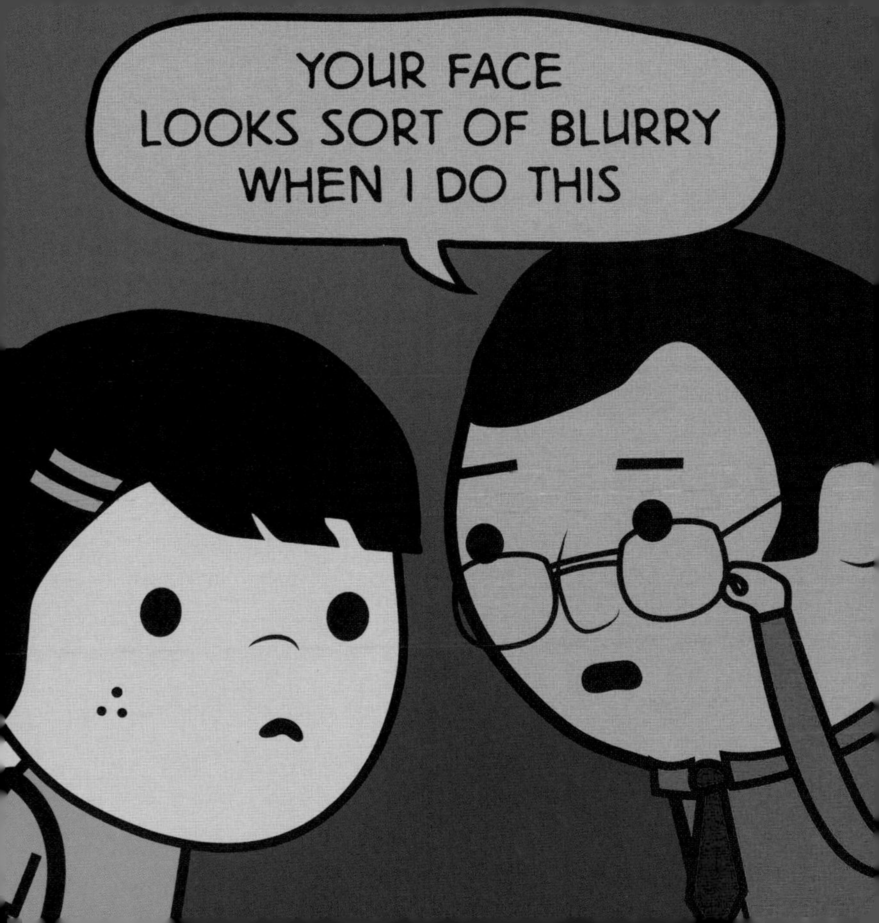
YOUR FACE LOOKS SORT OF BLURRY WHEN I DO THIS

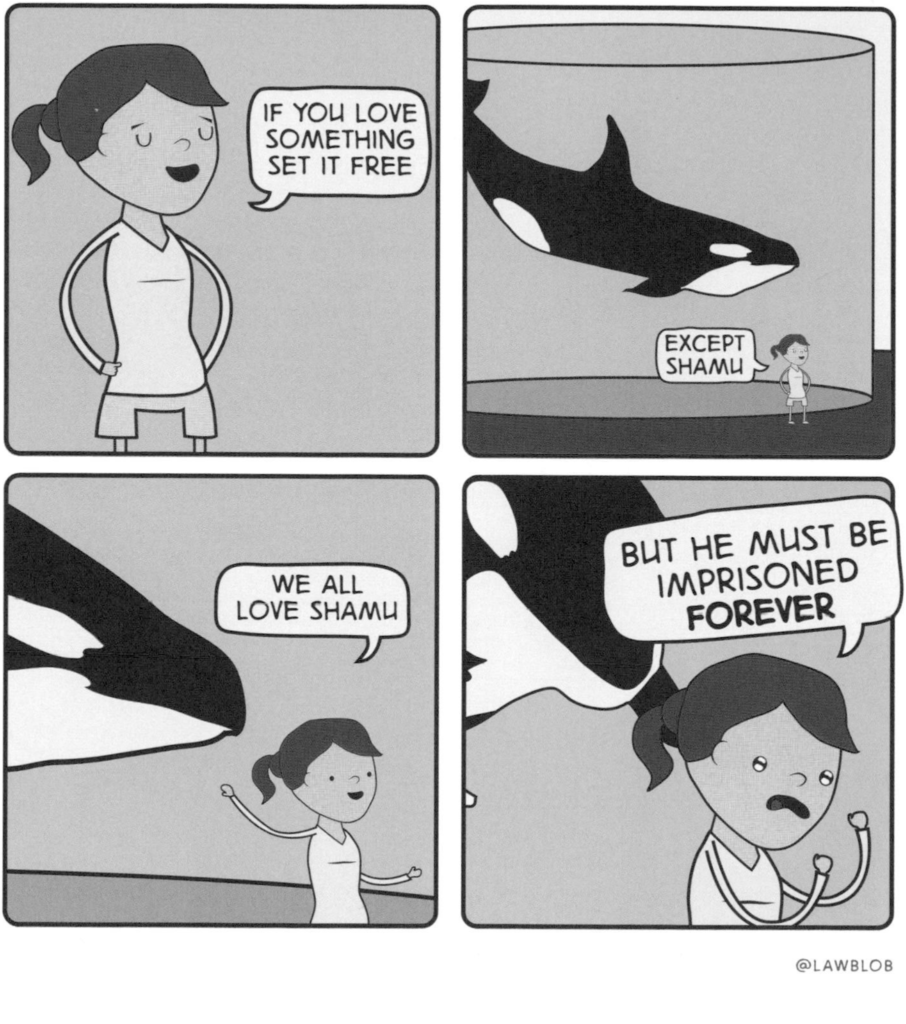
IF YOU LOVE SOMETHING SET IT FREE
EXCEPT SHAMU
WE ALL LOVE SHAMU
BUT HE MUST BE IMPRISONED **FOREVER**

@LAWBLOB

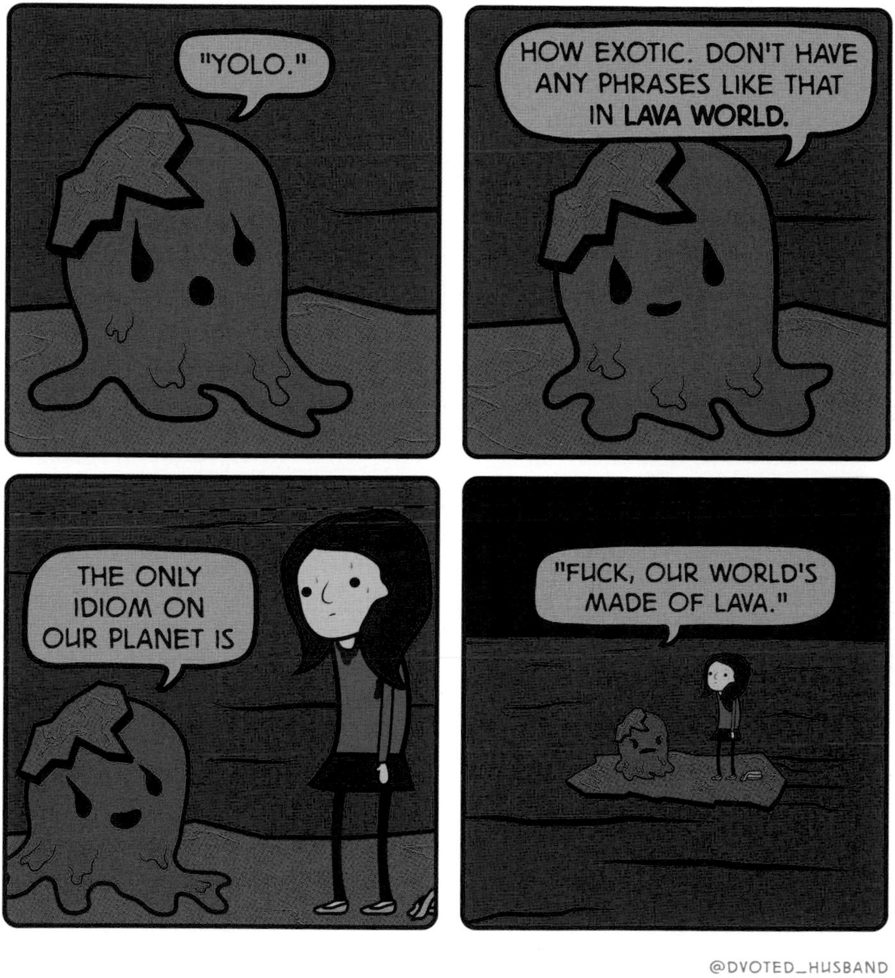
"YOLO."
HOW EXOTIC. DON'T HAVE ANY PHRASES LIKE THAT IN LAVA WORLD.
THE ONLY IDIOM ON OUR PLANET IS
"FUCK, OUR WORLD'S MADE OF LAVA."
@DVOTED_HUSBAND

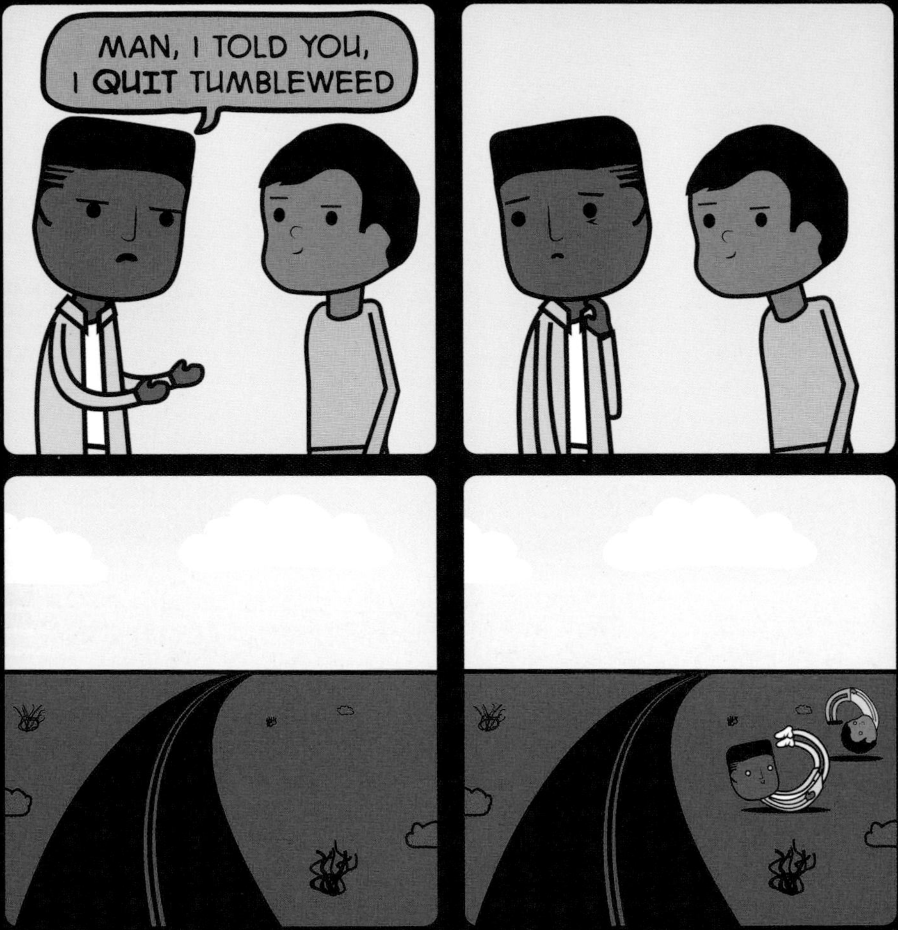
MAN, I TOLD YOU, I QUIT TUMBLEWEED

@VINCENESS

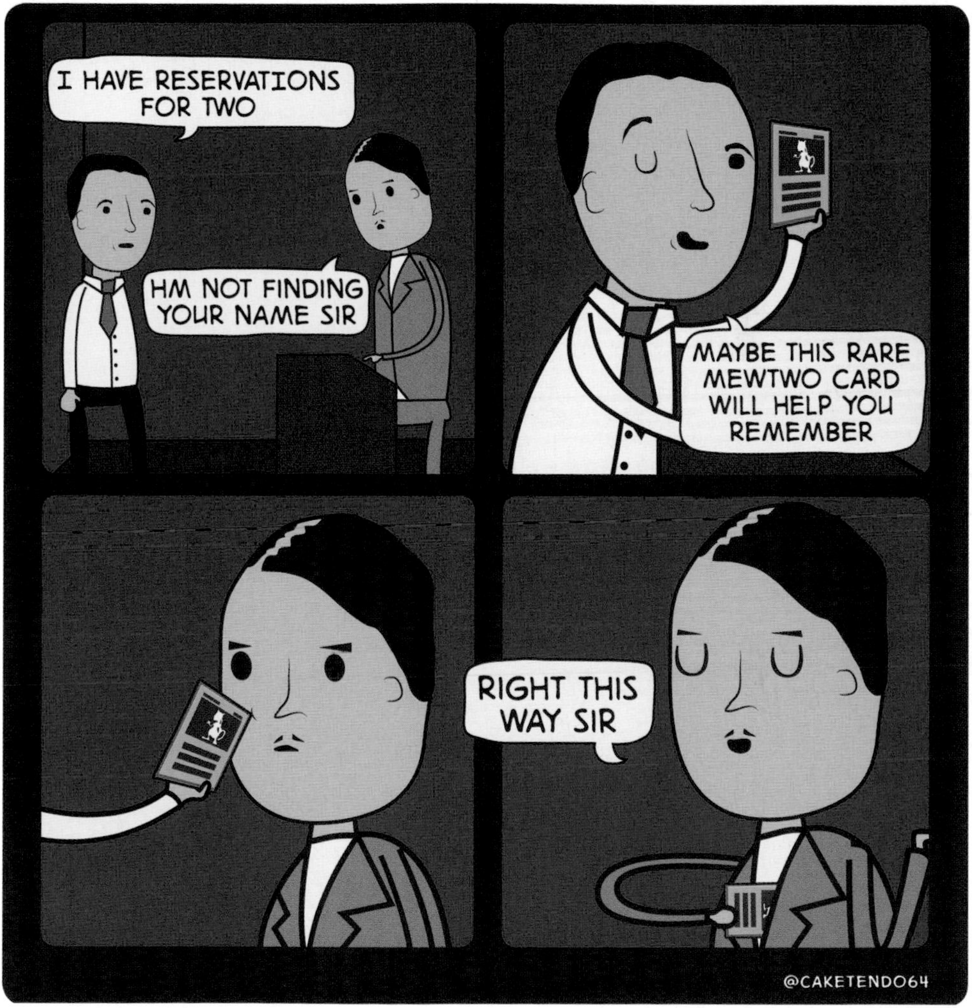
I HAVE RESERVATIONS FOR TWO
HM NOT FINDING YOUR NAME SIR
MAYBE THIS RARE MEWTWO CARD WILL HELP YOU REMEMBER
RIGHT THIS WAY SIR
@CAKETENDO64

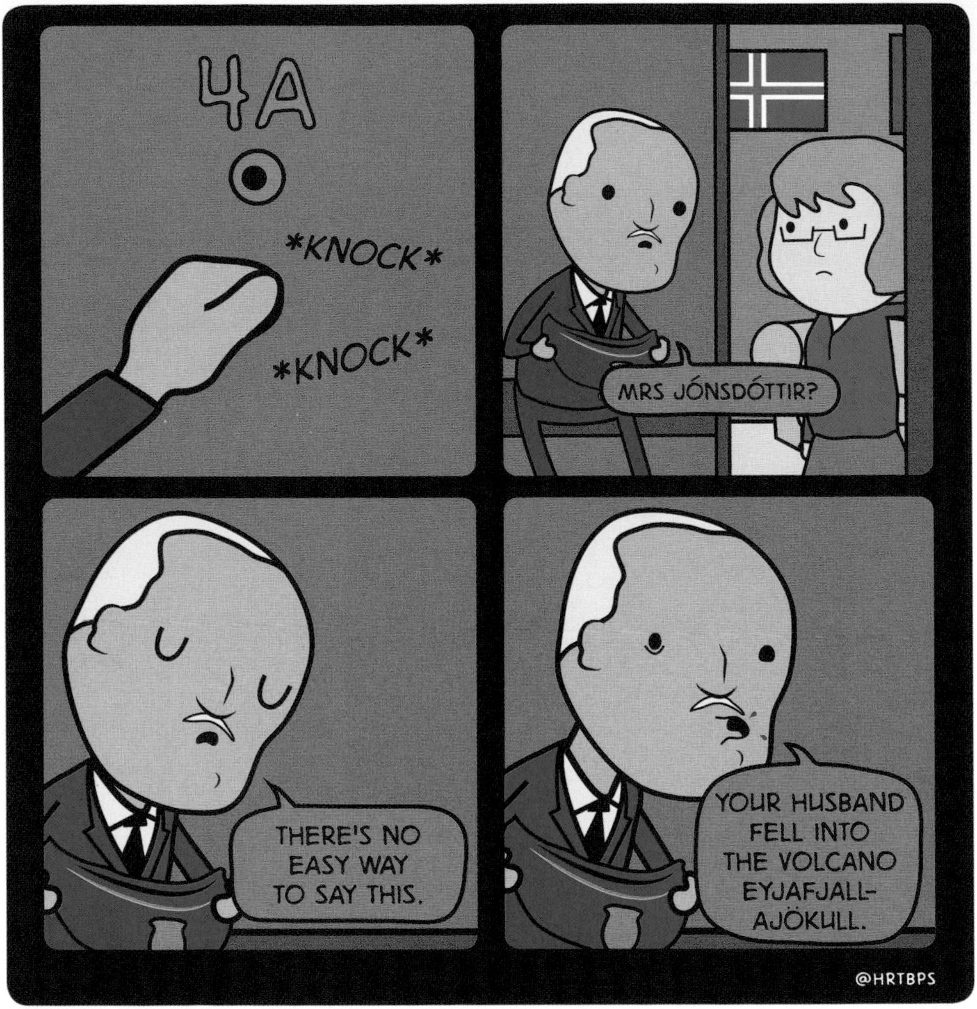
4A
KNOCK
KNOCK
MRS JÓNSDÓTTIR?
THERE'S NO EASY WAY TO SAY THIS.
YOUR HUSBAND FELL INTO THE VOLCANO EYJAFJALL-AJÖKULL.
@HRTBPS

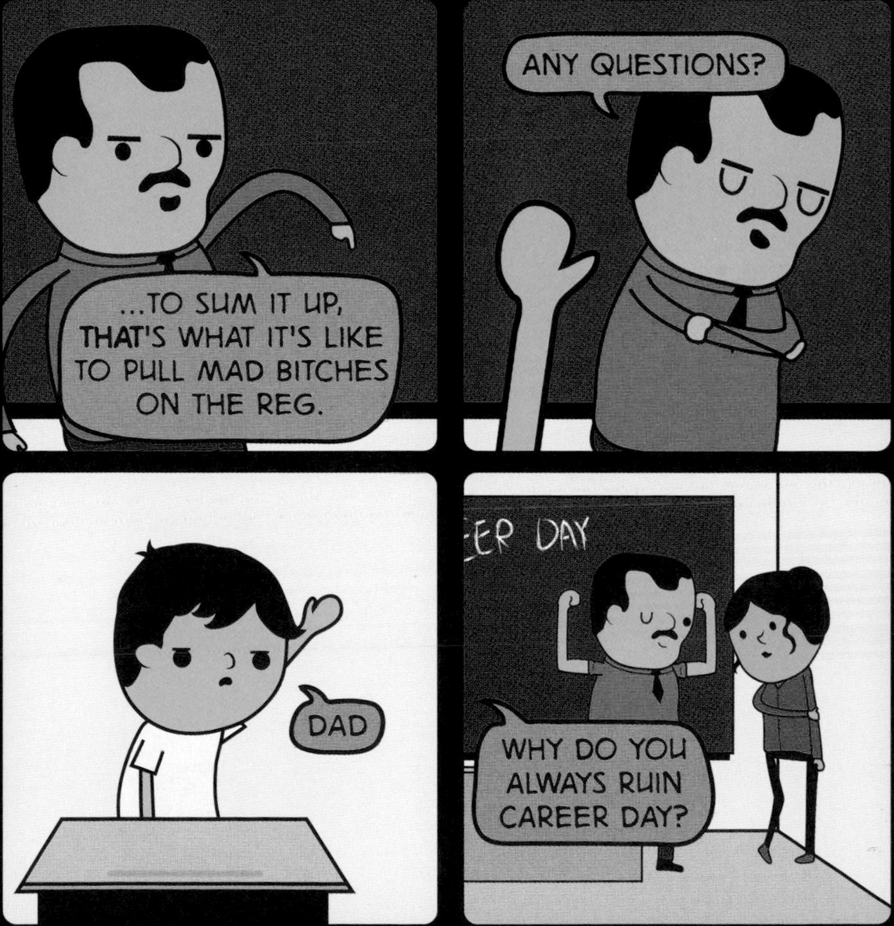
...TO SUM IT UP, THAT'S WHAT IT'S LIKE TO PULL MAD BITCHES ON THE REG.
ANY QUESTIONS?
DAD
ER DAY
WHY DO YOU ALWAYS RUIN CAREER DAY?

@SCREWCUMBER

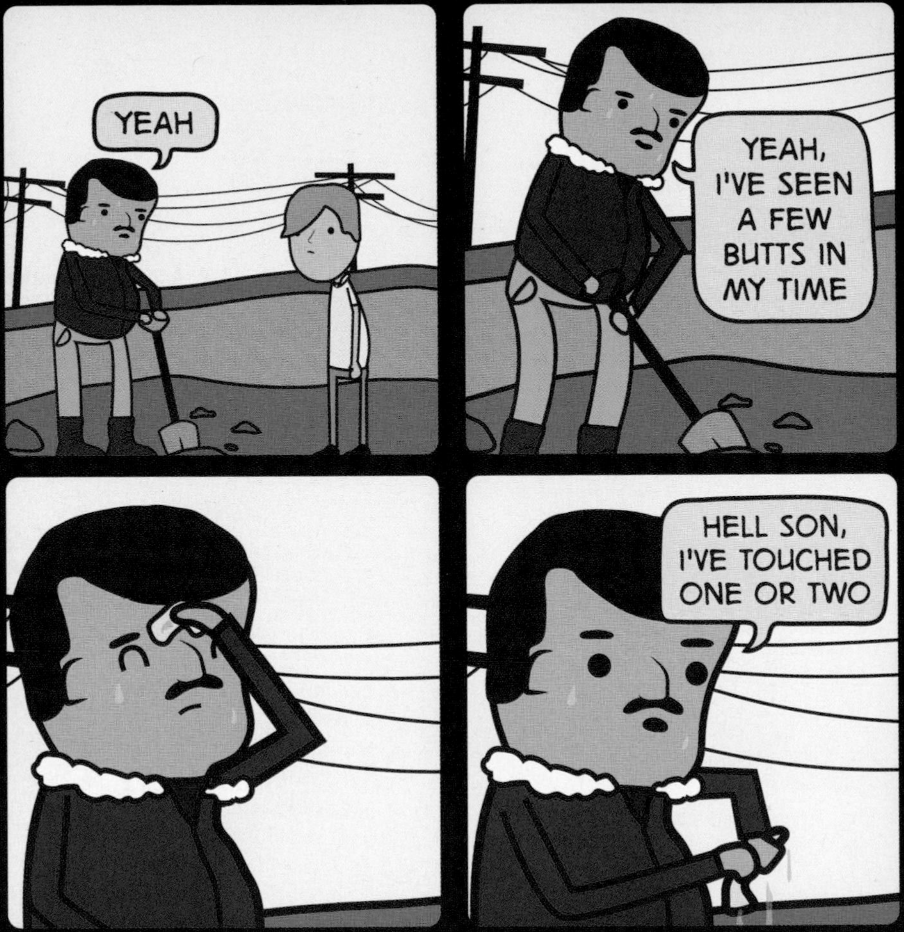
YEAH
YEAH, I'VE SEEN A FEW BUTTS IN MY TIME
HELL SON, I'VE TOUCHED ONE OR TWO

@DEBBIE_HAIRY

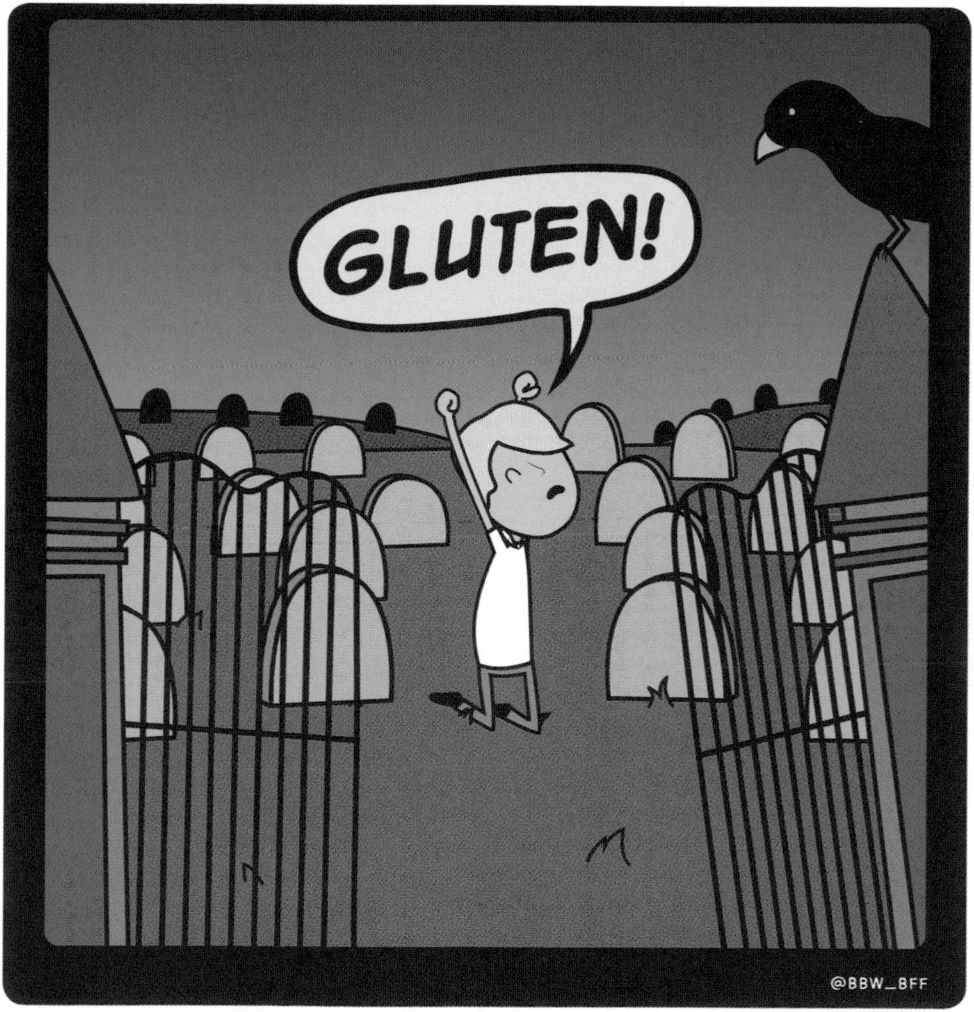
GLUTEN!
@BBW_BFF

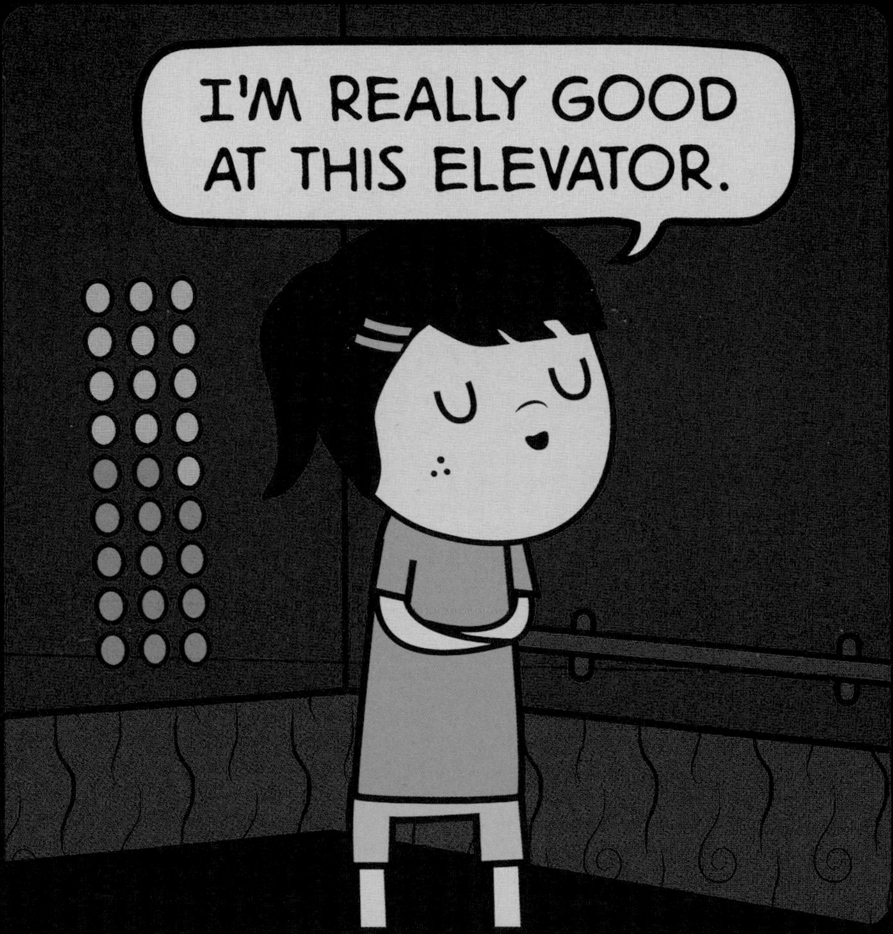
I'M REALLY GOOD AT THIS ELEVATOR.

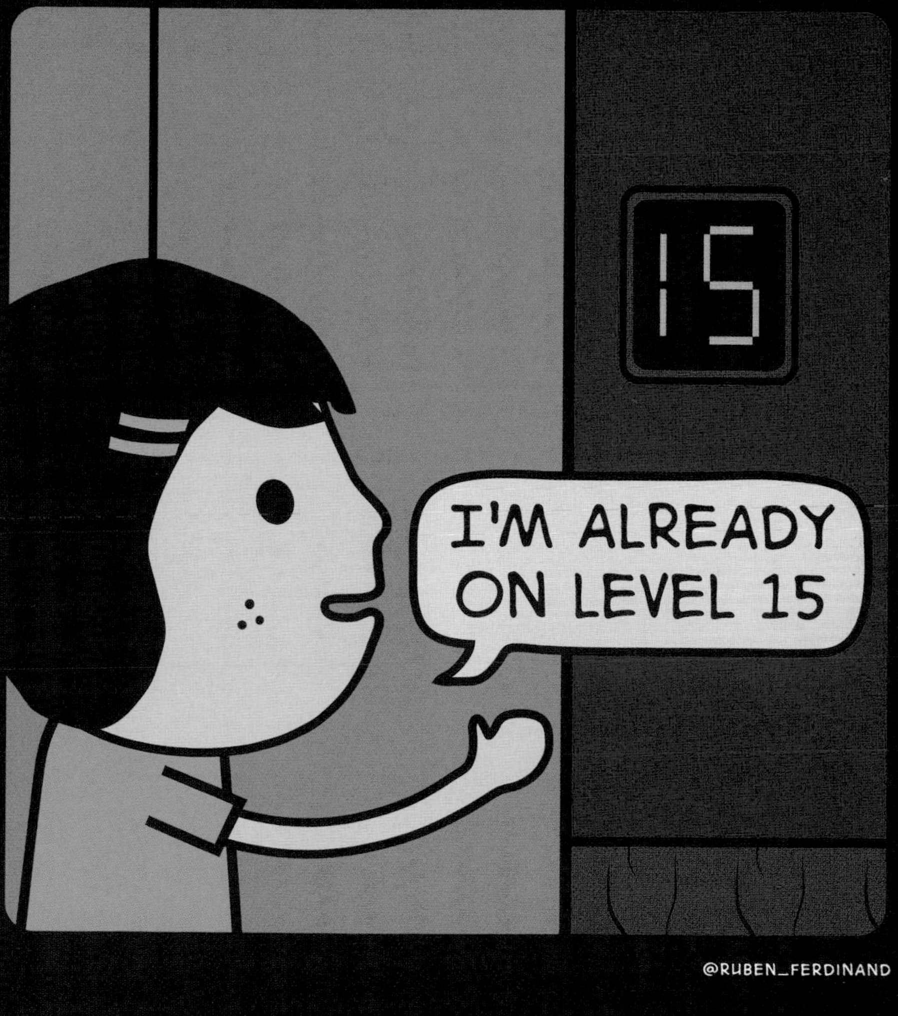
15
I'M ALREADY ON LEVEL 15
@RUBEN_FERDINAND

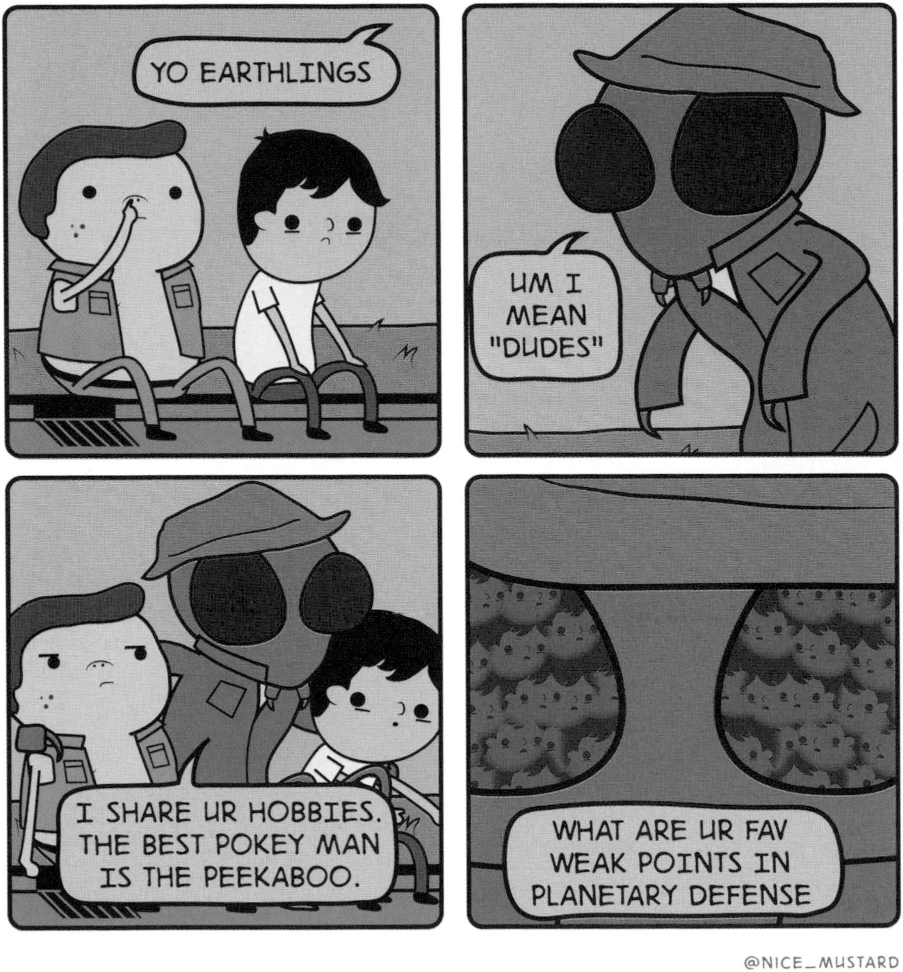
YO EARTHLINGS
UM I MEAN "DUDES"
I SHARE UR HOBBIES. THE BEST POKEY MAN IS THE PEEKABOO.
WHAT ARE UR FAV WEAK POINTS IN PLANETARY DEFENSE
@NICE_MUSTARD

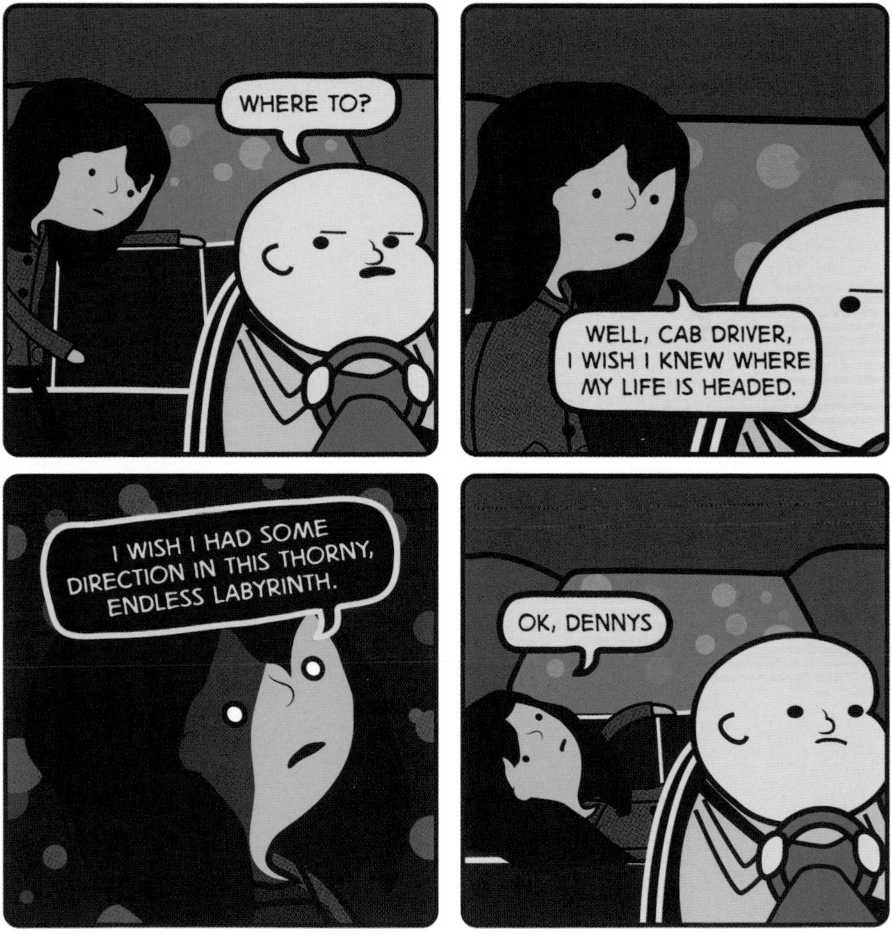
WHERE TO?
WELL, CAB DRIVER, I WISH I KNEW WHERE MY LIFE IS HEADED.
I WISH I HAD SOME DIRECTION IN THIS THORNY, ENDLESS LABYRINTH.
OK, DENNYS

@SADDESTTIGER

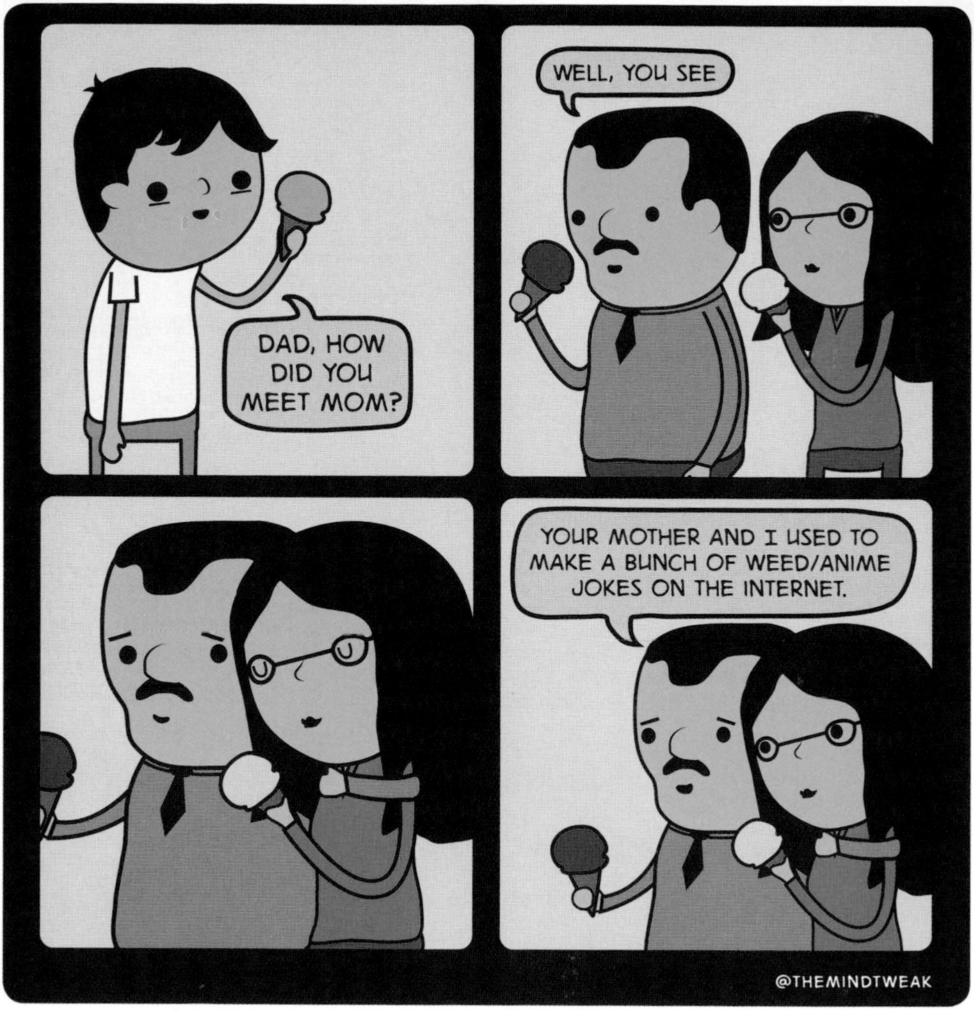
DAD, HOW DID YOU MEET MOM?
WELL, YOU SEE
YOUR MOTHER AND I USED TO MAKE A BUNCH OF WEED/ANIME JOKES ON THE INTERNET.
@THEMINDTWEAK

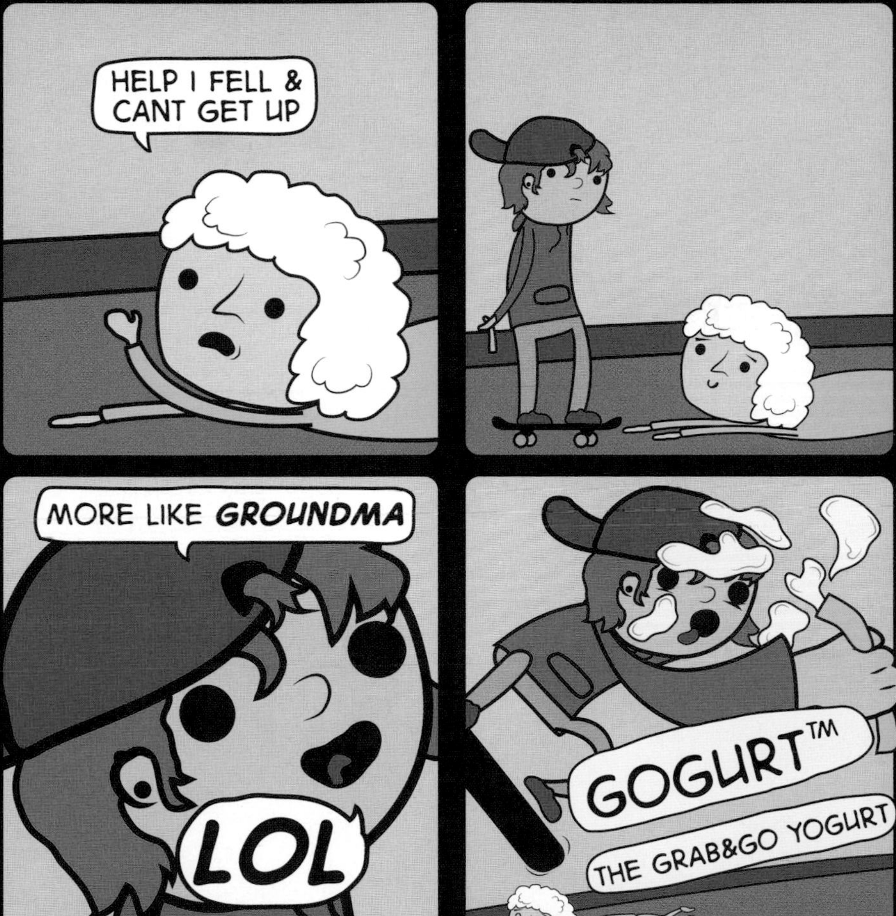
HELP I FELL & CANT GET UP
MORE LIKE GROUNDMA
LOL
GOGURT™
THE GRAB&GO YOGURT

@RAD_MILK

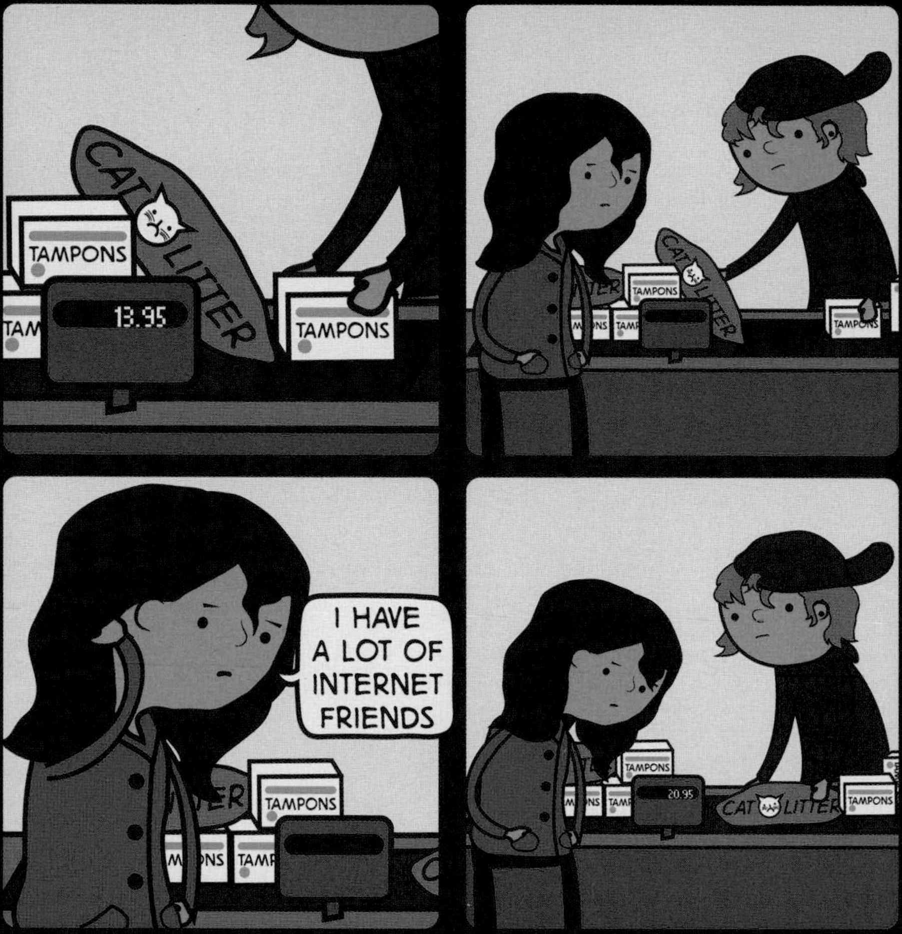
CAT LITTER
TAMPONS
13.95
TAMPONS
TAMPONS
I HAVE A LOT OF INTERNET FRIENDS
TAMPONS
TAMPONS
20.95
CAT LITTER
TAMPONS

@IAMENIDCOLESLAW

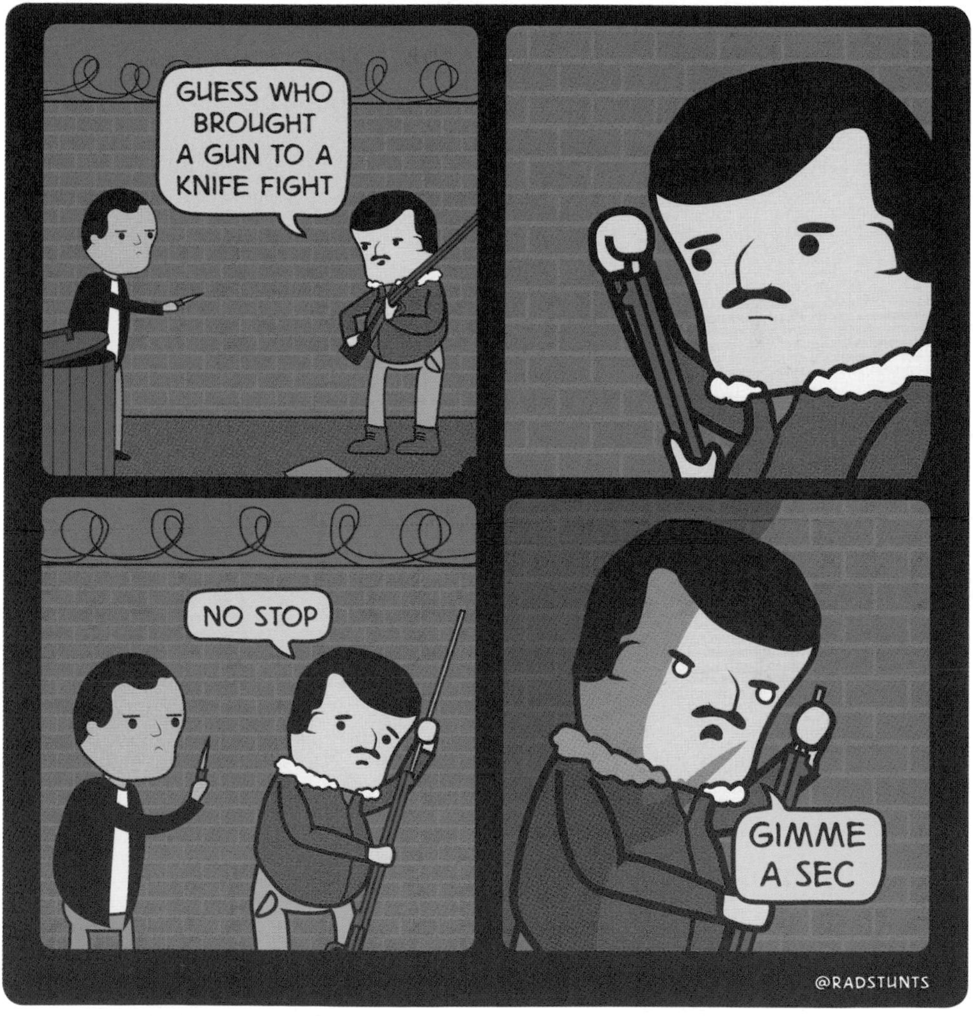
GUESS WHO BROUGHT A GUN TO A KNIFE FIGHT
NO STOP
GIMME A SEC
@RADSTUNTS

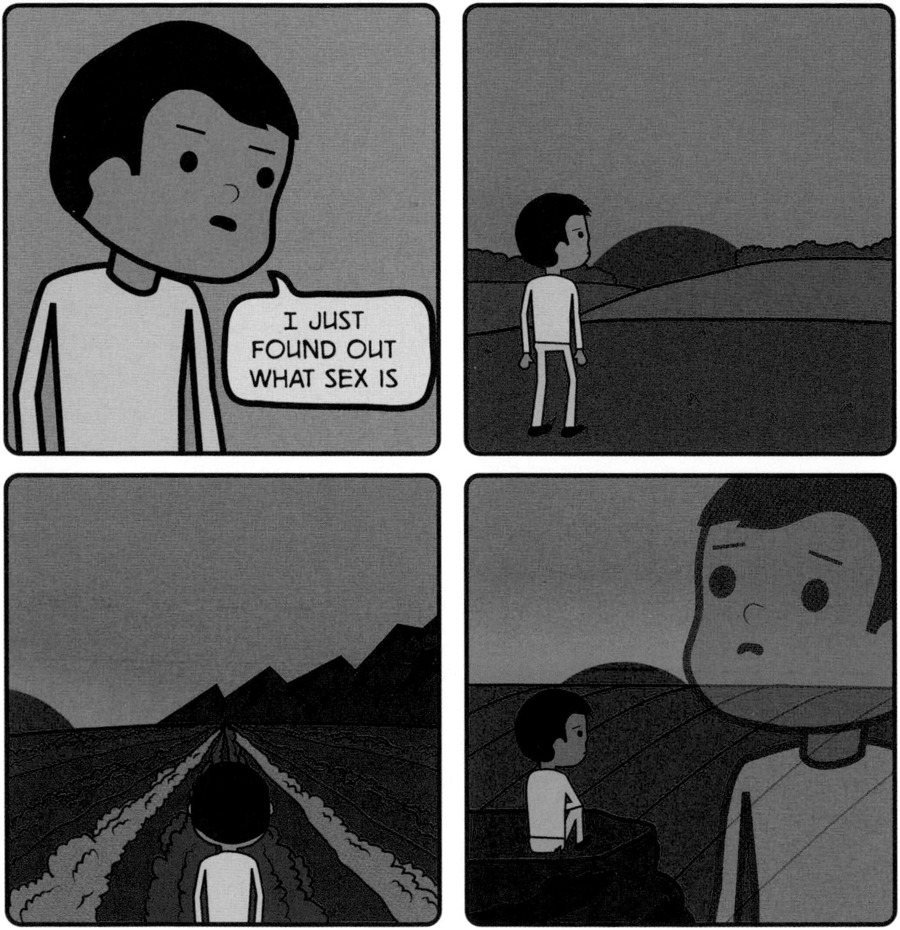
I JUST FOUND OUT WHAT SEX IS

@SHY_BONER

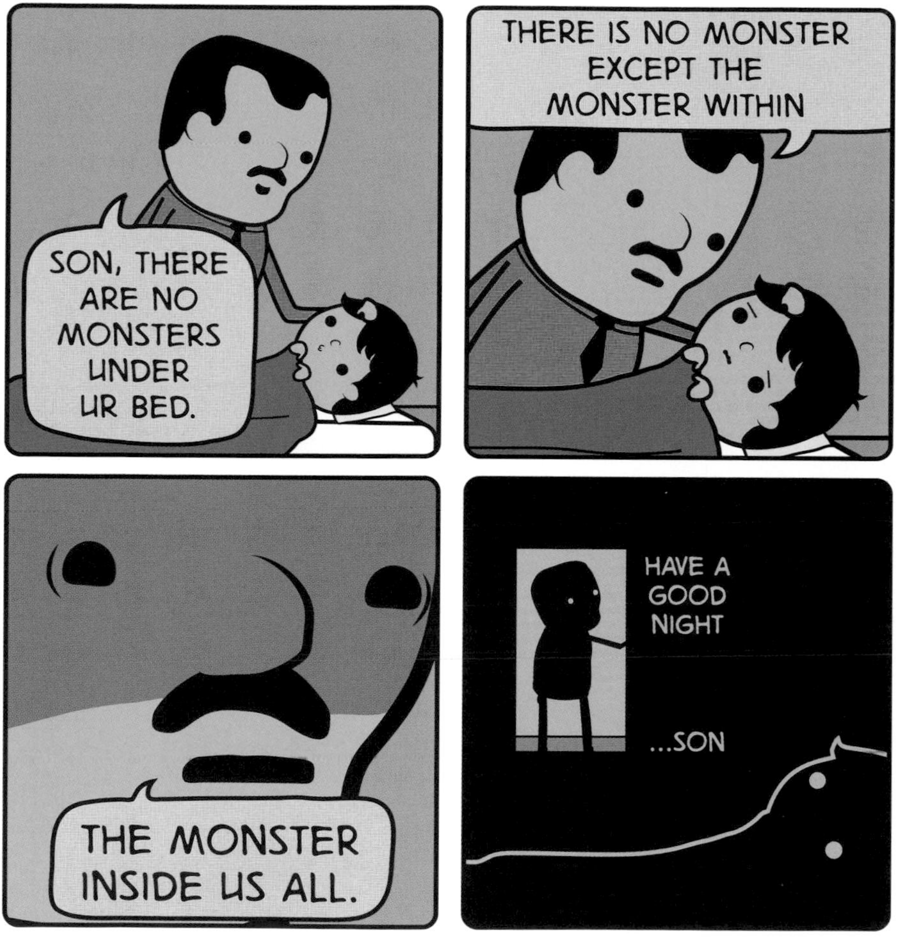
SON, THERE ARE NO MONSTERS UNDER UR BED.
THERE IS NO MONSTER EXCEPT THE MONSTER WITHIN
THE MONSTER INSIDE US ALL.
HAVE A GOOD NIGHT
...SON

@TORMNY_PICKEALS

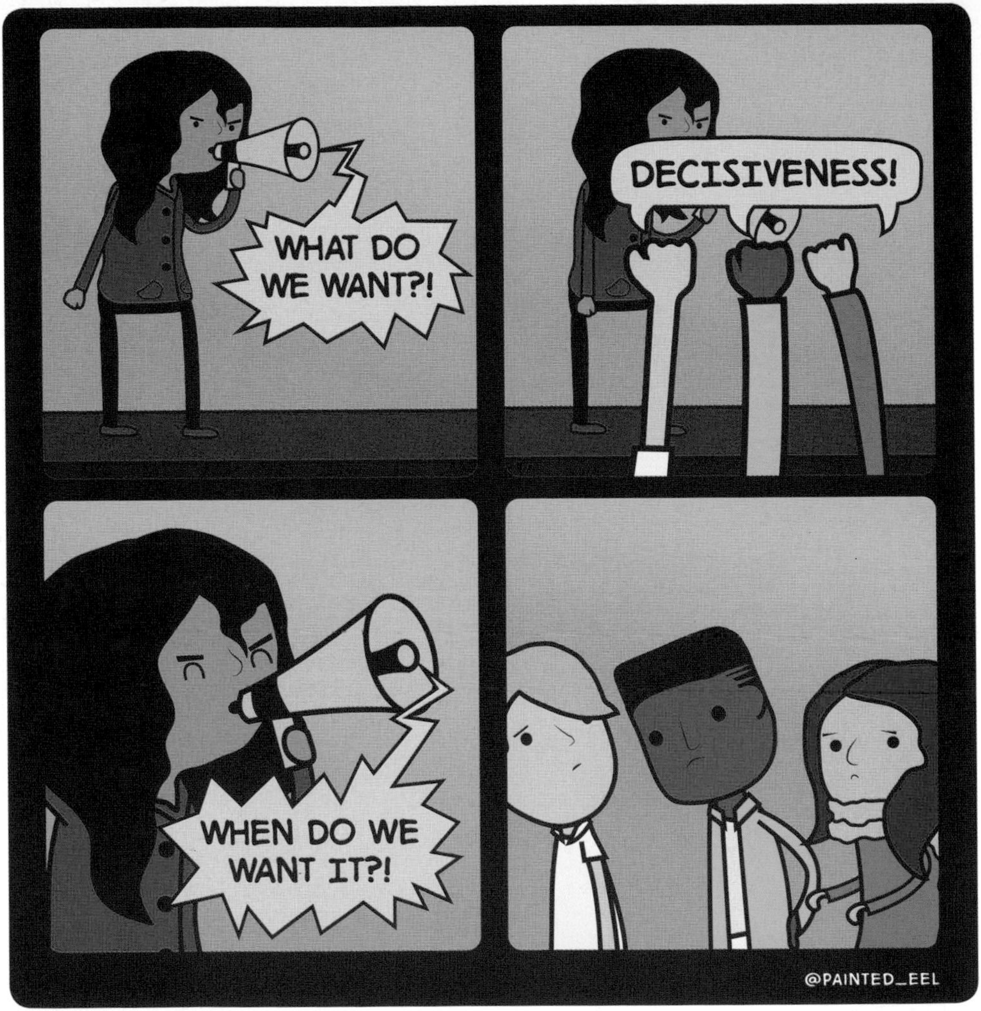
WHAT DO WE WANT?!
DECISIVENESS!
WHEN DO WE WANT IT?!
@PAINTED_EEL

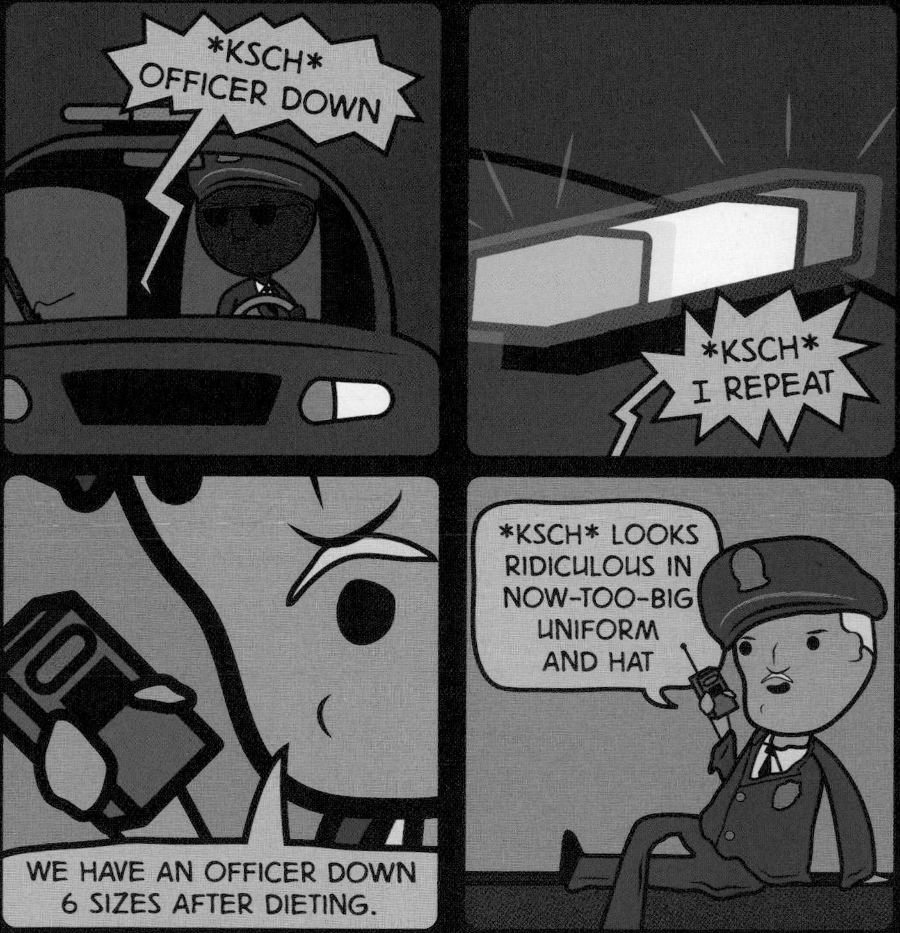
KSCH OFFICER DOWN
KSCH I REPEAT
WE HAVE AN OFFICER DOWN 6 SIZES AFTER DIETING.
KSCH LOOKS RIDICULOUS IN NOW-TOO-BIG UNIFORM AND HAT

@2TONBUG

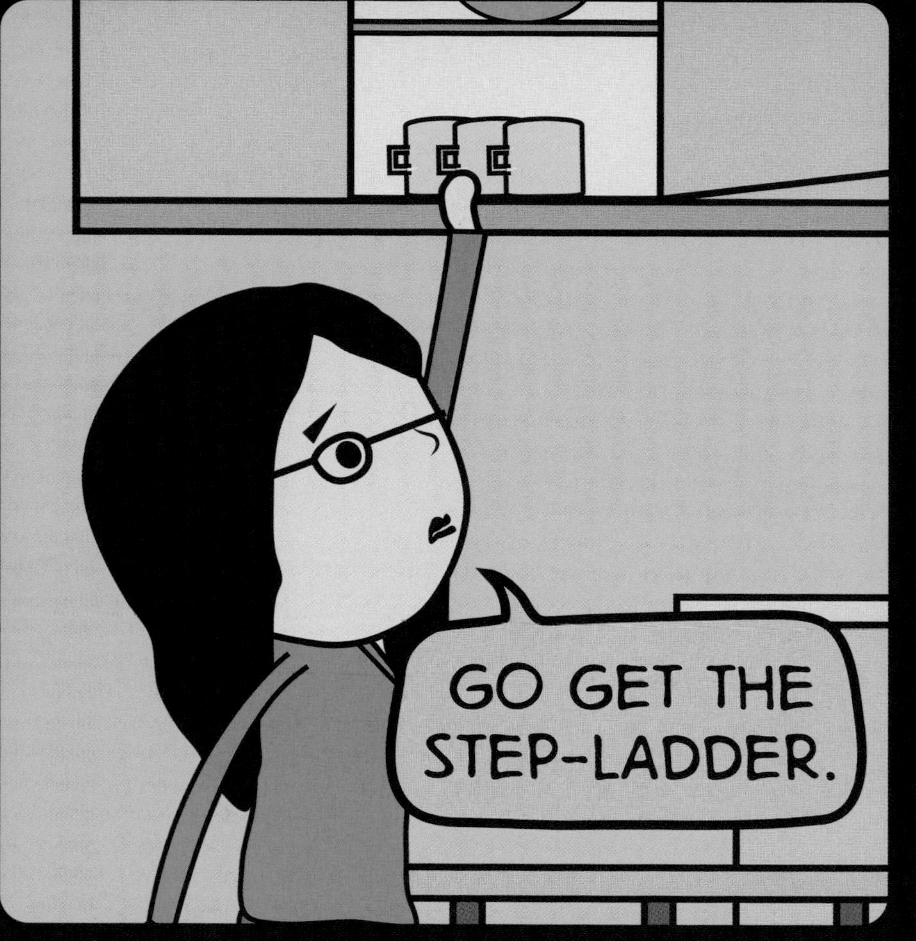
GO GET THE STEP-LADDER.

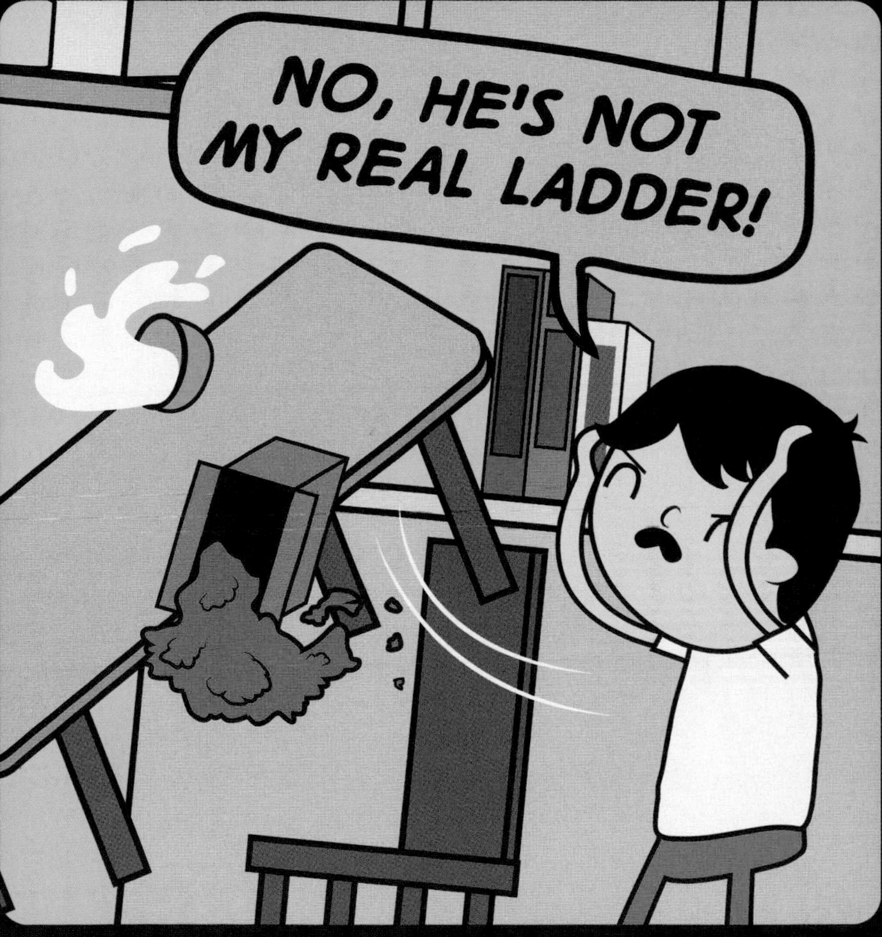
NO, HE'S NOT MY REAL LADDER!

@BROWNBOYBLUES

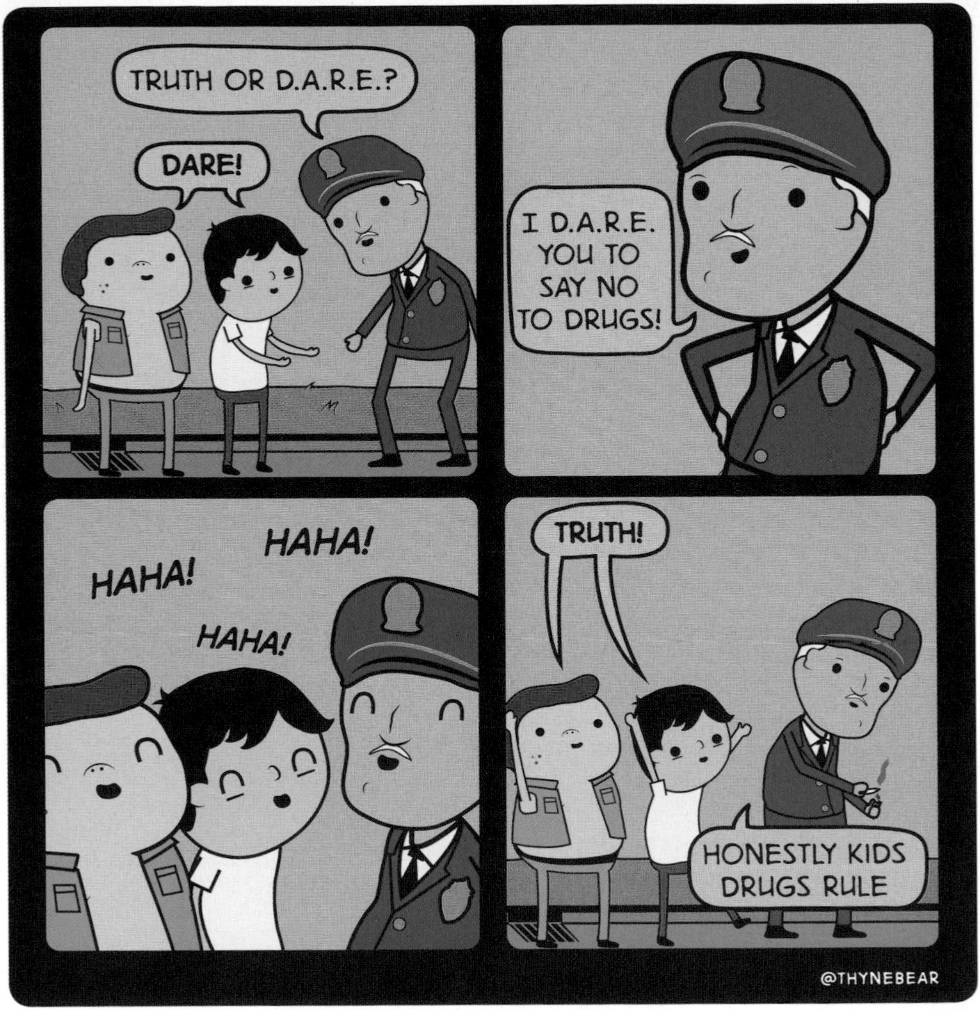
TRUTH OR D.A.R.E.?
DARE!
I D.A.R.E. YOU TO SAY NO TO DRUGS!
HAHA!
HAHA!
HAHA!
TRUTH!
HONESTLY KIDS DRUGS RULE
@THYNEBEAR

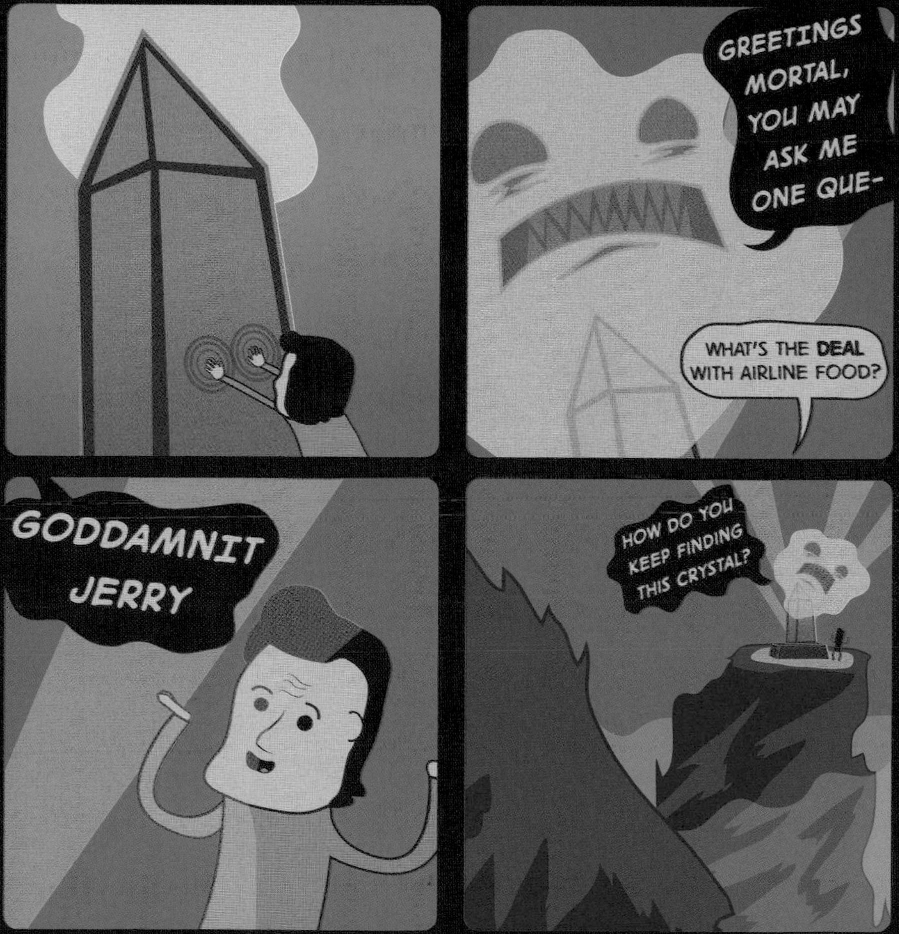
GREETINGS MORTAL, YOU MAY ASK ME ONE QUE-
WHAT'S THE **DEAL** WITH AIRLINE FOOD?
GODDAMNIT JERRY
HOW DO YOU KEEP FINDING THIS CRYSTAL?

@PISSRIFLE

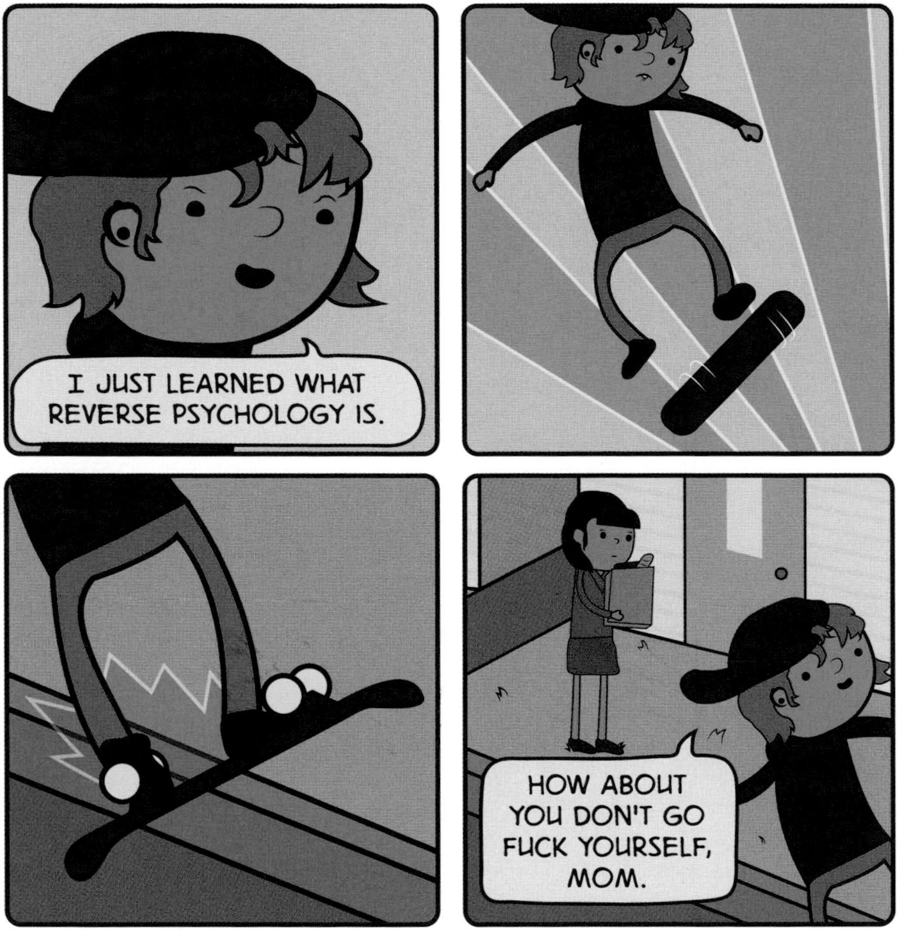
I JUST LEARNED WHAT REVERSE PSYCHOLOGY IS.
HOW ABOUT YOU DON'T GO FUCK YOURSELF, MOM.

@KELLANBC

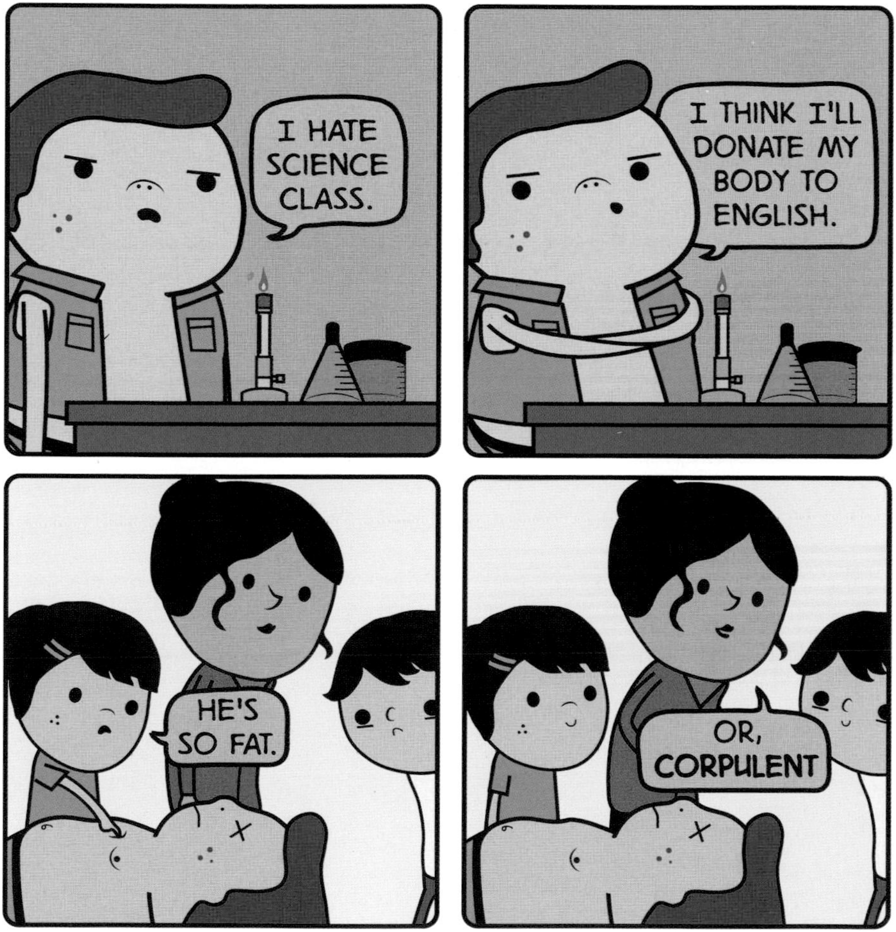
I HATE SCIENCE CLASS.
I THINK I'LL DONATE MY BODY TO ENGLISH.
HE'S SO FAT.
OR, CORPULENT

@SHRUGLORD

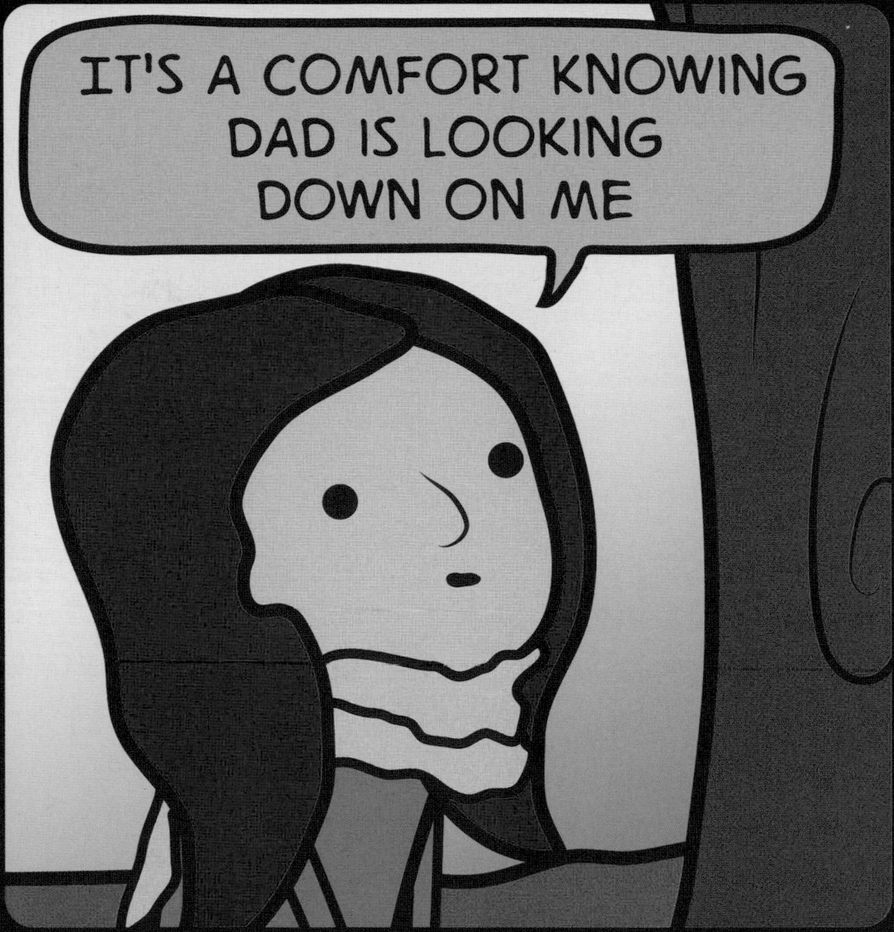
IT'S A COMFORT KNOWING DAD IS LOOKING DOWN ON ME

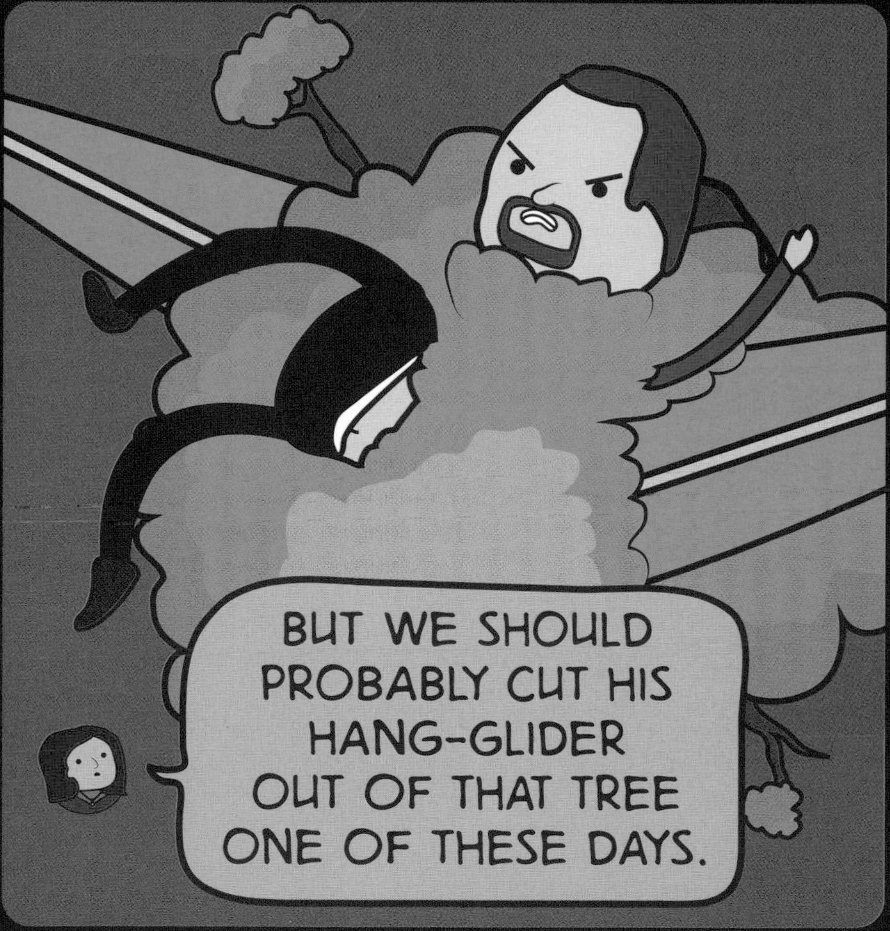
BUT WE SHOULD PROBABLY CUT HIS HANG-GLIDER OUT OF THAT TREE ONE OF THESE DAYS.

@LOSTCATDOG

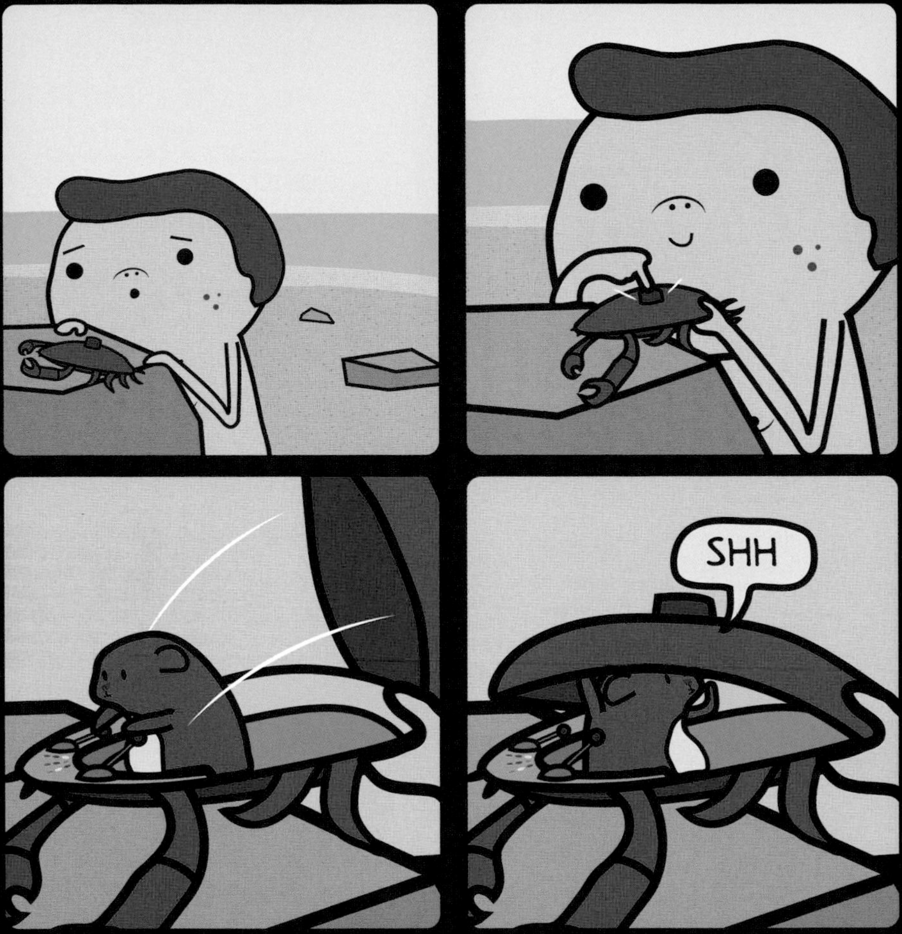
SHH

@MOUTHEATERS

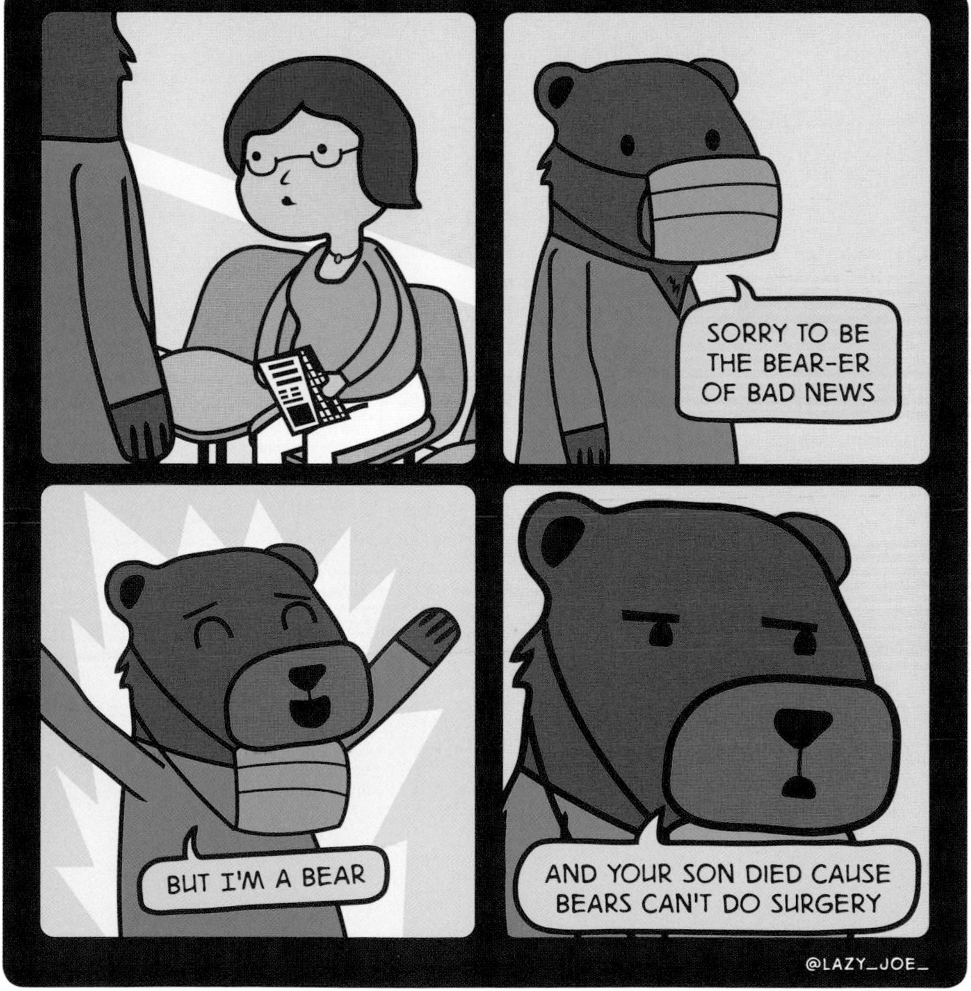
SORRY TO BE THE BEAR-ER OF BAD NEWS
BUT I'M A BEAR
AND YOUR SON DIED CAUSE BEARS CAN'T DO SURGERY
@LAZY_JOE_

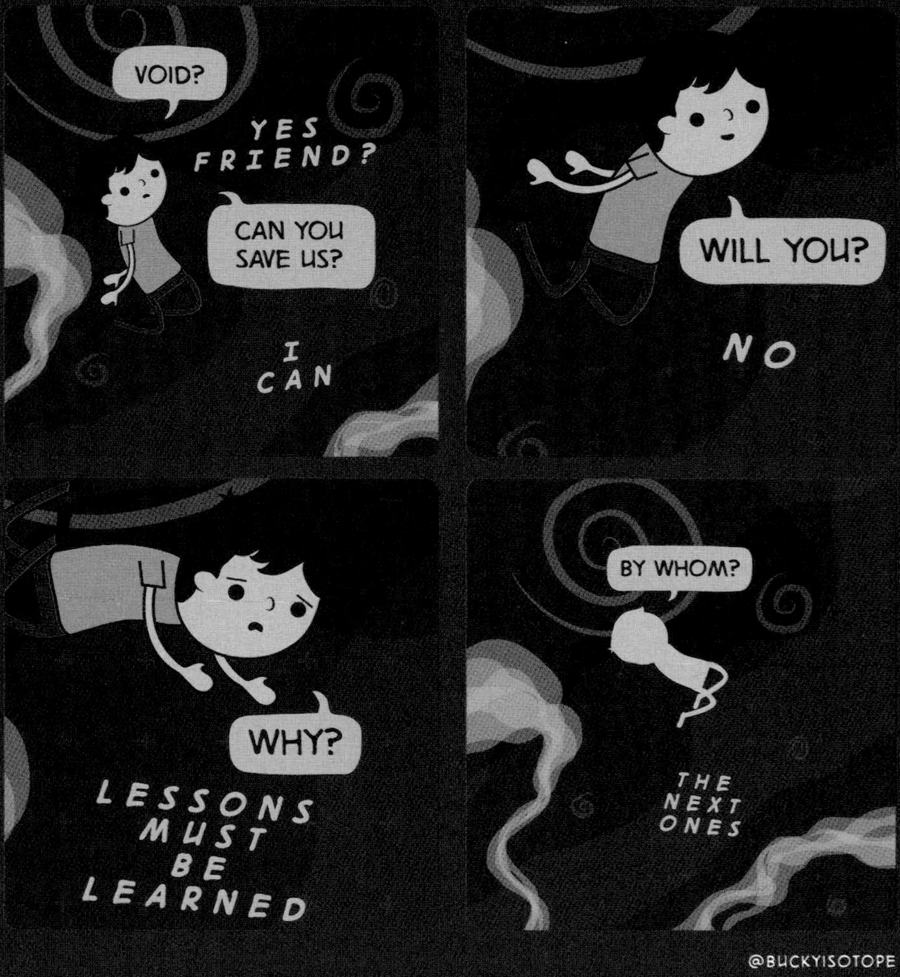
VOID?
YES FRIEND?
CAN YOU SAVE US?
I CAN
WILL YOU?
NO
WHY?
LESSONS MUST BE LEARNED
BY WHOM?
THE NEXT ONES
@BUCKYISOTOPE

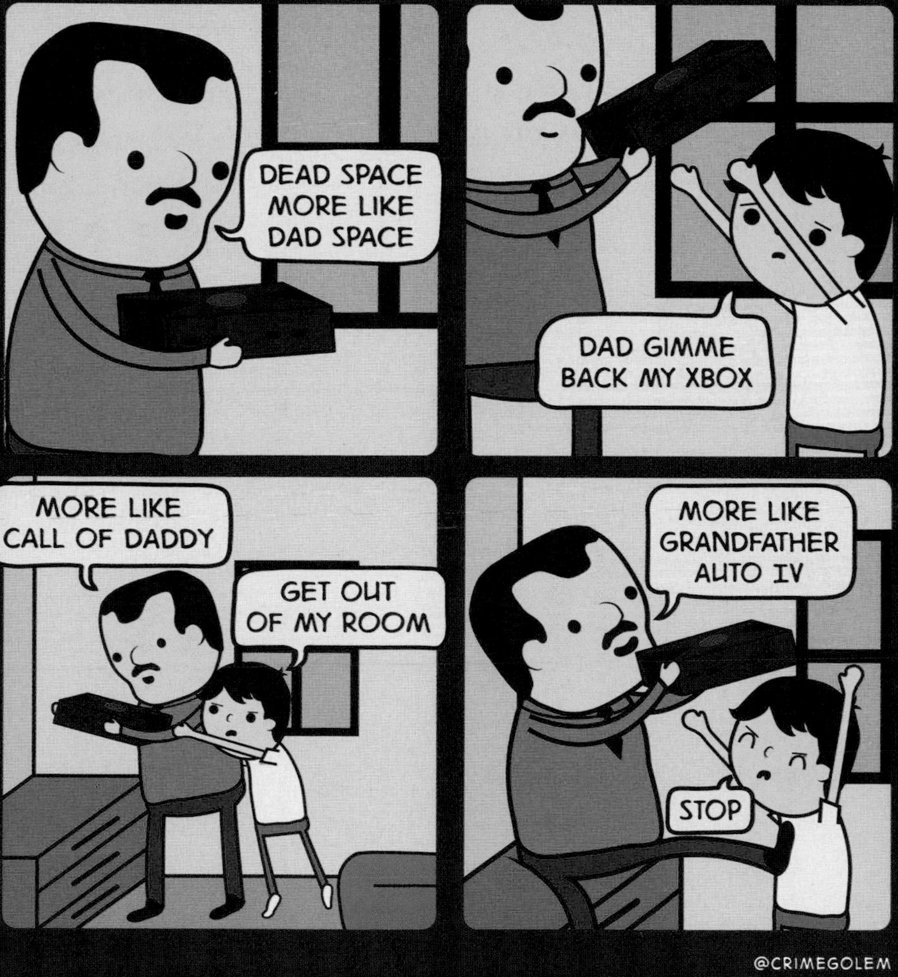
DEAD SPACE MORE LIKE DAD SPACE
DAD GIMME BACK MY XBOX
MORE LIKE CALL OF DADDY
GET OUT OF MY ROOM
MORE LIKE GRANDFATHER AUTO IV
STOP
@CRIMEGOLEM

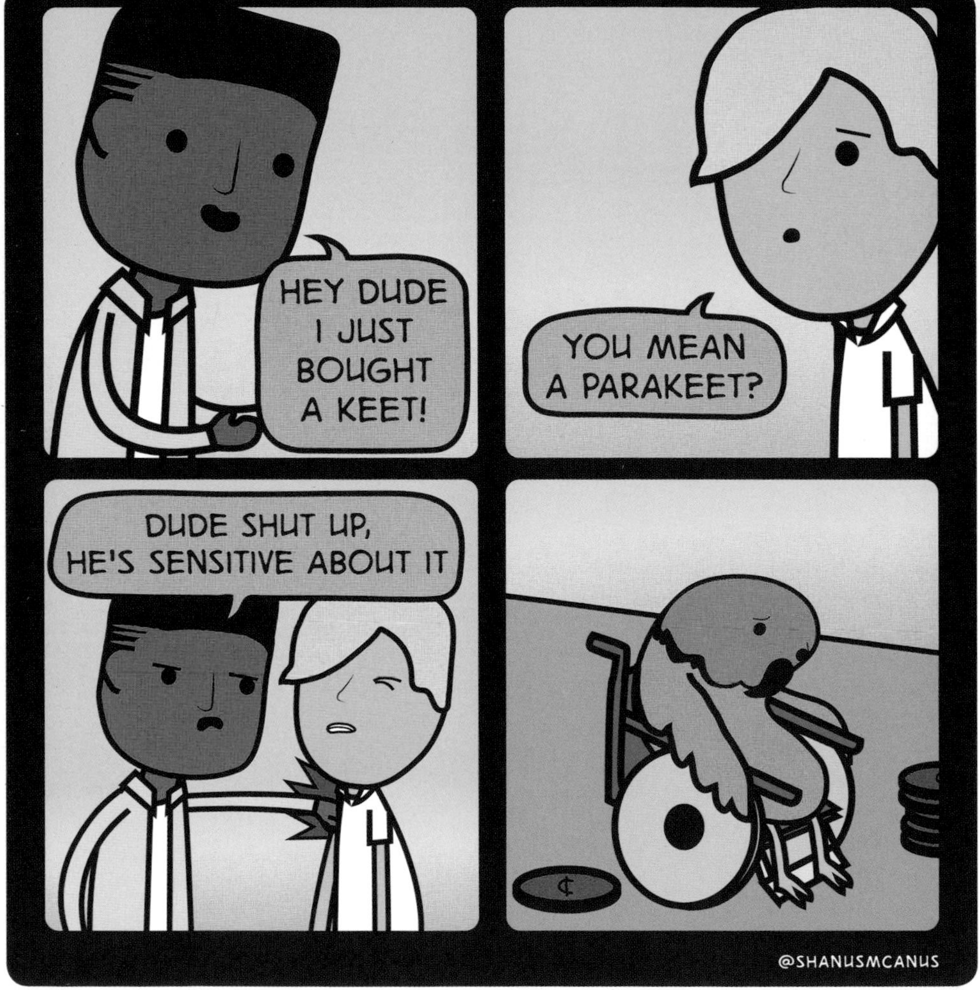
HEY DUDE I JUST BOUGHT A KEET!
YOU MEAN A PARAKEET?
DUDE SHUT UP, HE'S SENSITIVE ABOUT IT
¢
@SHANUSMCANUS

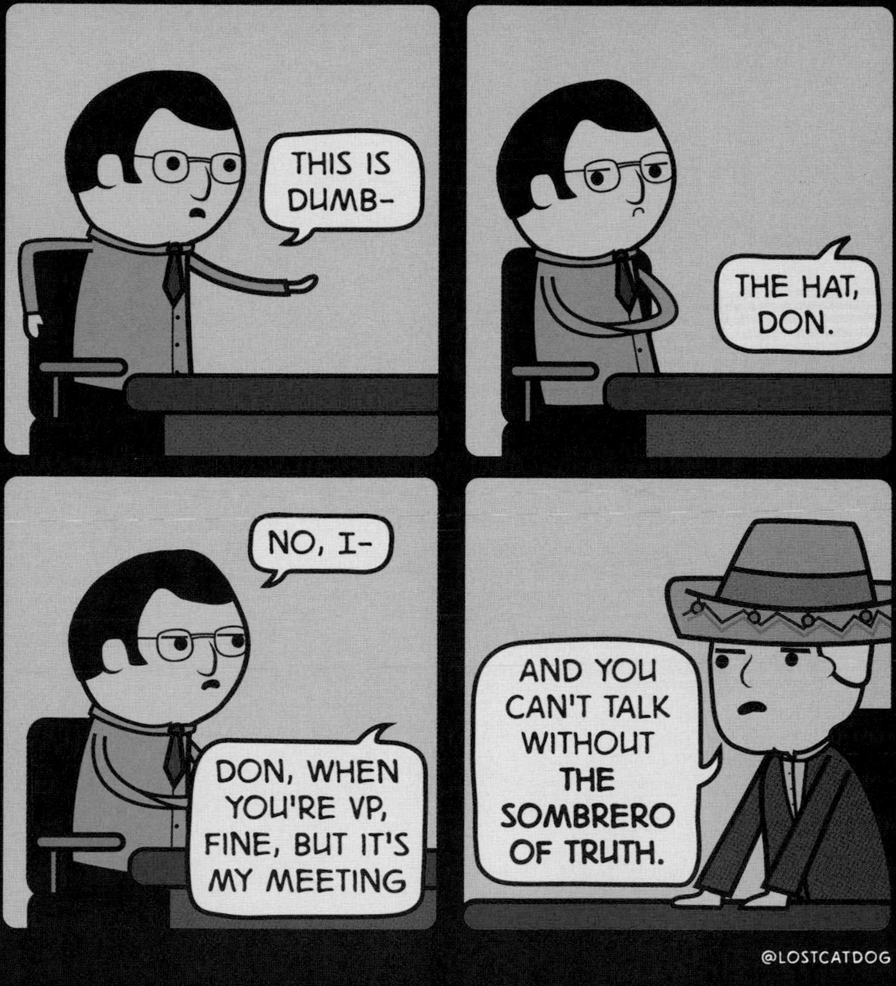

THIS IS DUMB-
THE HAT, DON.
NO, I-
DON, WHEN YOU'RE VP, FINE, BUT IT'S MY MEETING
AND YOU CAN'T TALK WITHOUT THE SOMBRERO OF TRUTH.
@LOSTCATDOG

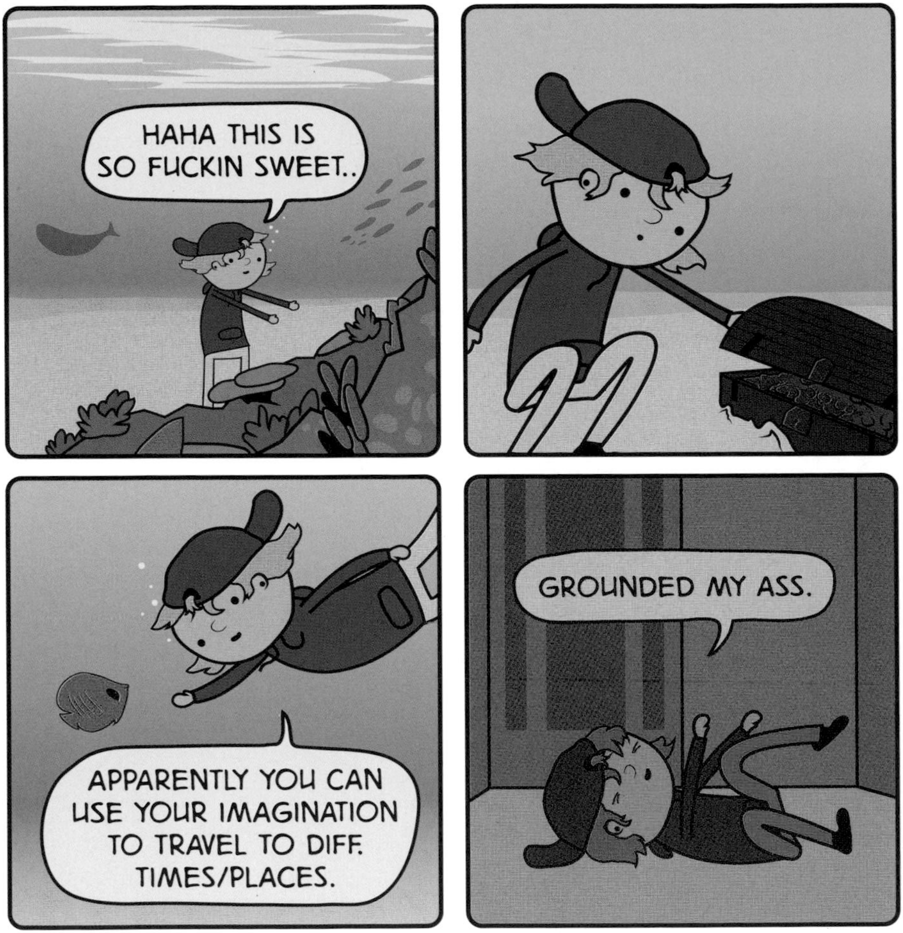
HAHA THIS IS SO FUCKIN SWEET..
APPARENTLY YOU CAN USE YOUR IMAGINATION TO TRAVEL TO DIFF. TIMES/PLACES.
GROUNDED MY ASS.

@DOGBONER

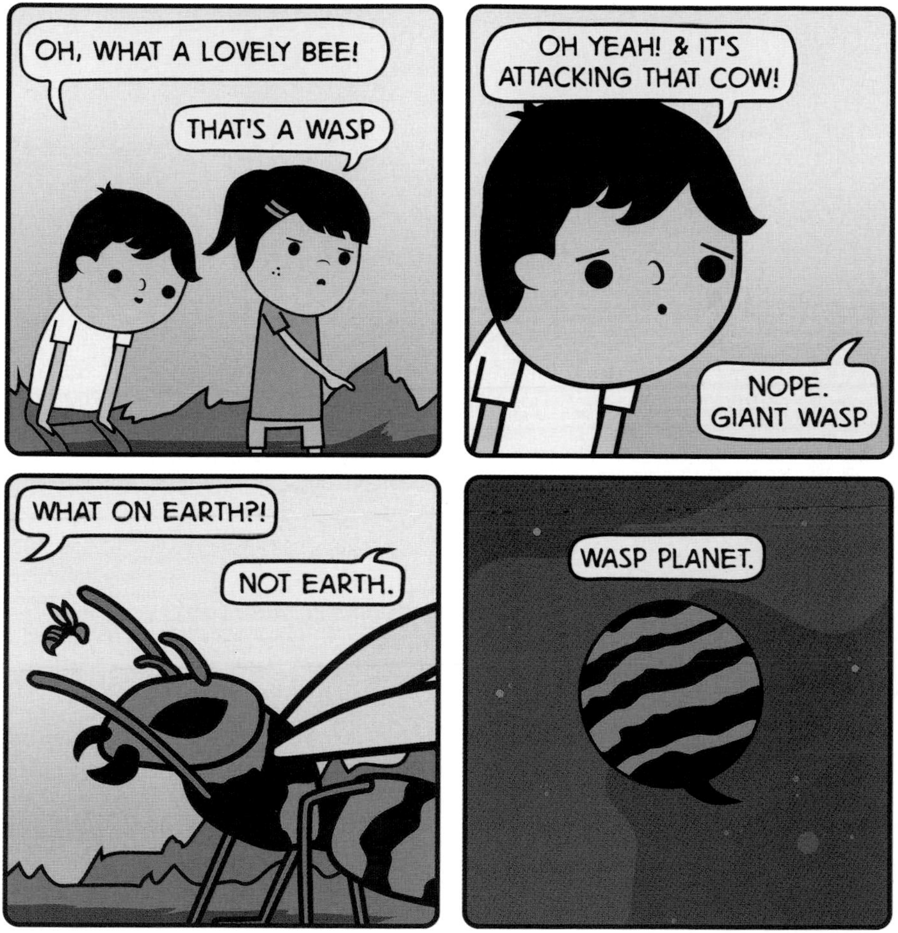
OH, WHAT A LOVELY BEE!
THAT'S A WASP
OH YEAH! & IT'S ATTACKING THAT COW!
NOPE. GIANT WASP
WHAT ON EARTH?!
NOT EARTH.
WASP PLANET.

@HAPPYINVENTOR

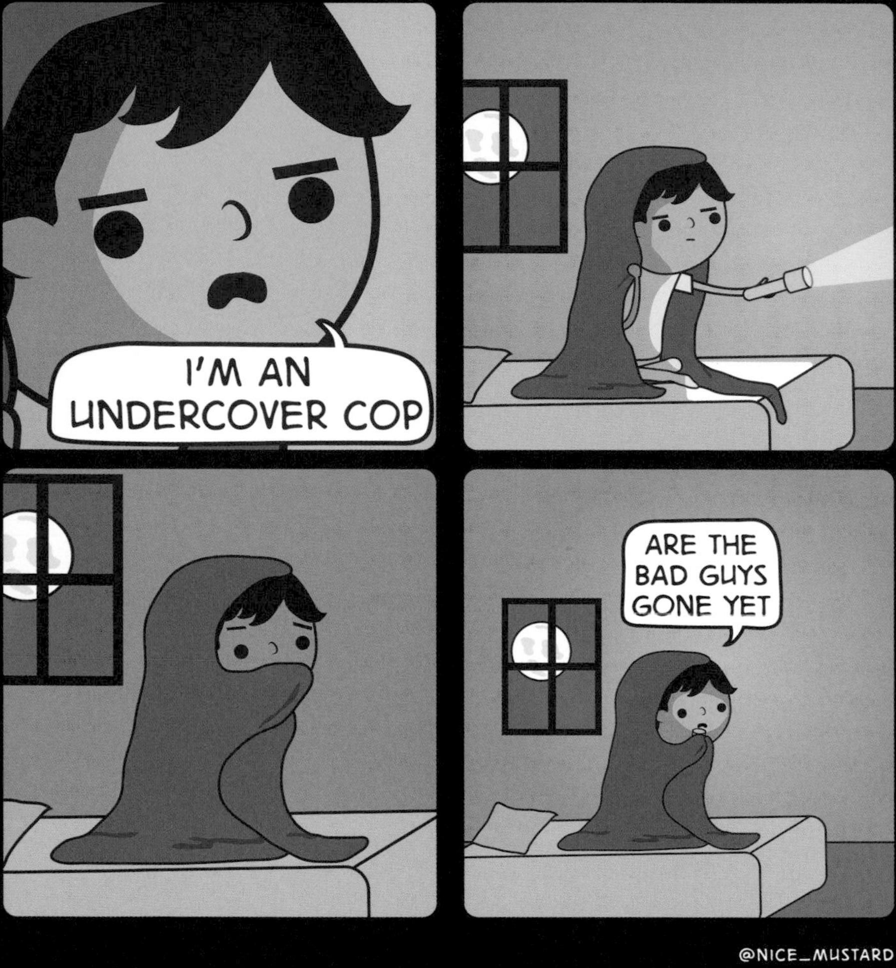
I'M AN UNDERCOVER COP
ARE THE BAD GUYS GONE YET
@NICE_MUSTARD

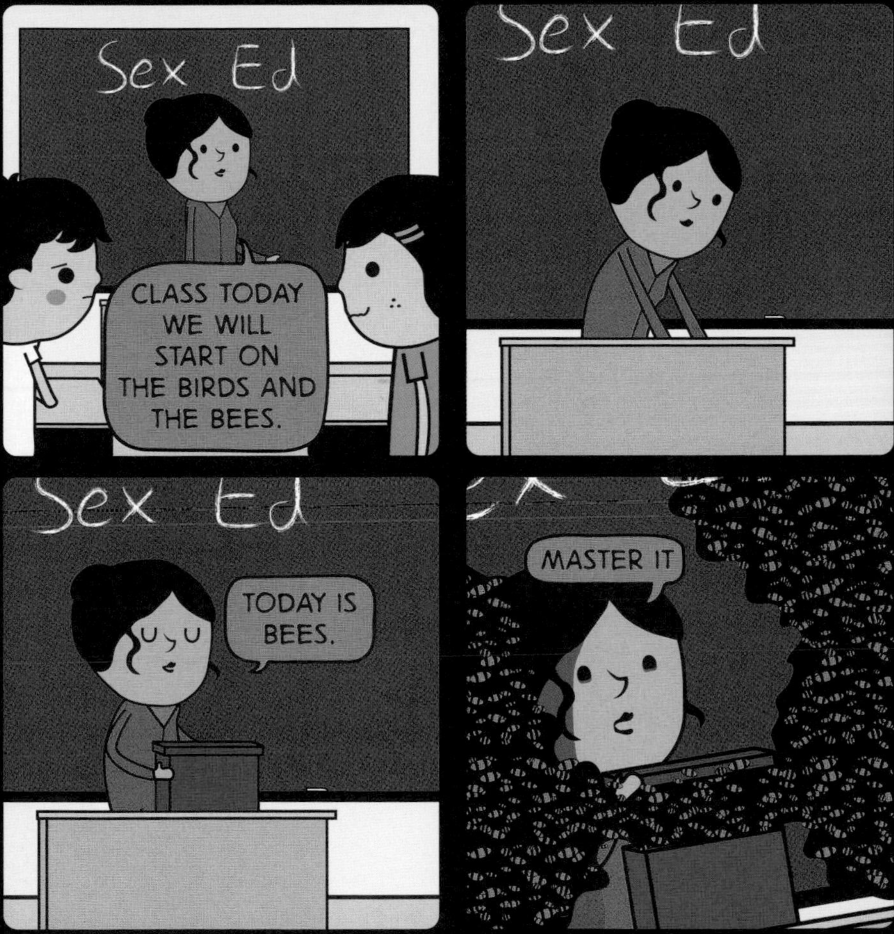
Sex Ed
CLASS TODAY WE WILL START ON THE BIRDS AND THE BEES.
Sex Ed
Sex Ed
TODAY IS BEES.
MASTER IT
@PAJAMABEN_

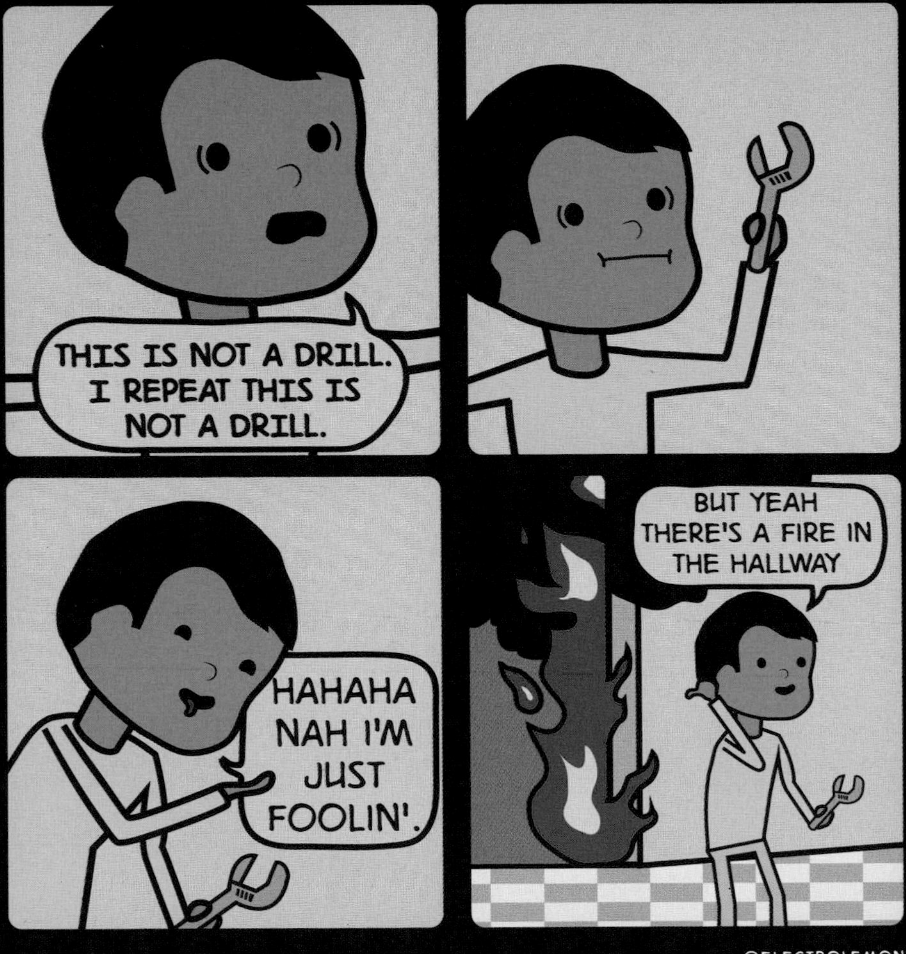
THIS IS NOT A DRILL. I REPEAT THIS IS NOT A DRILL.
HAHAHA NAH I'M JUST FOOLIN'.
BUT YEAH THERE'S A FIRE IN THE HALLWAY
@ELECTROLEMON

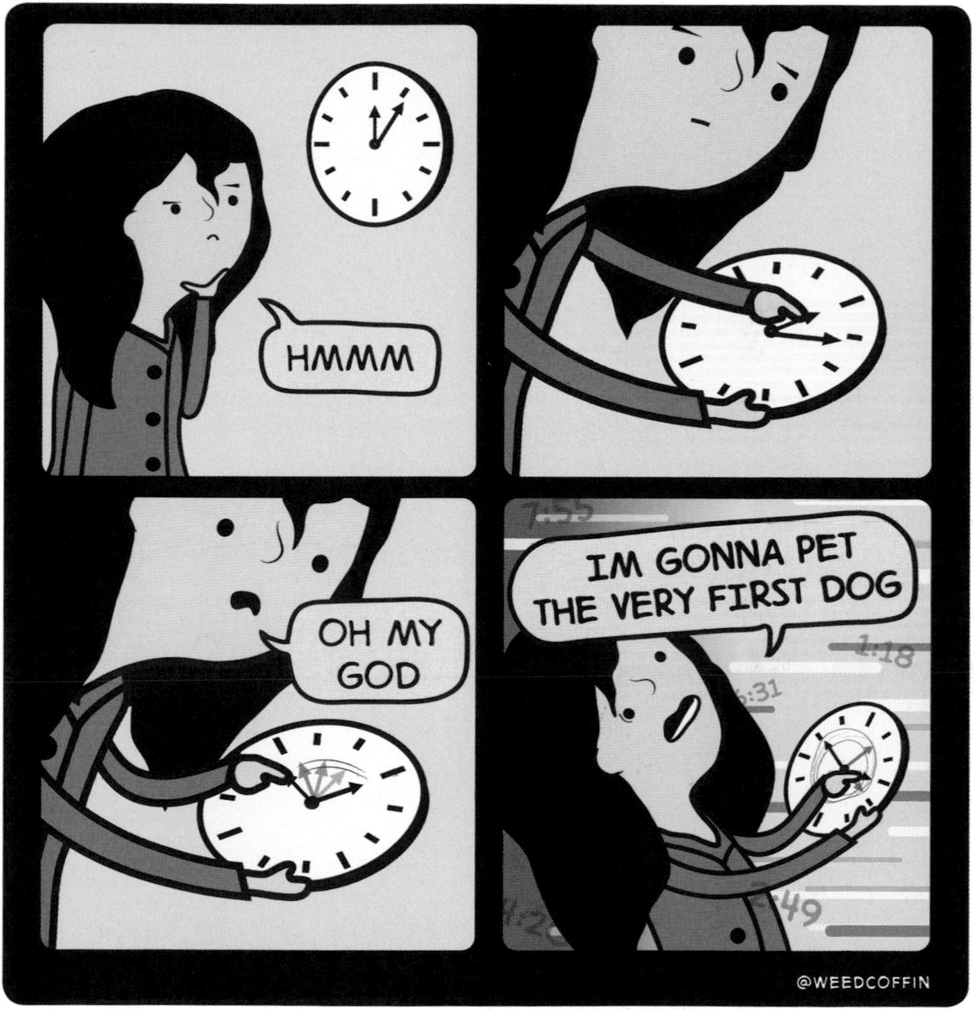
HMMM
OH MY GOD
IM GONNA PET THE VERY FIRST DOG
1:18
:31
7:55
49
@WEEDCOFFIN

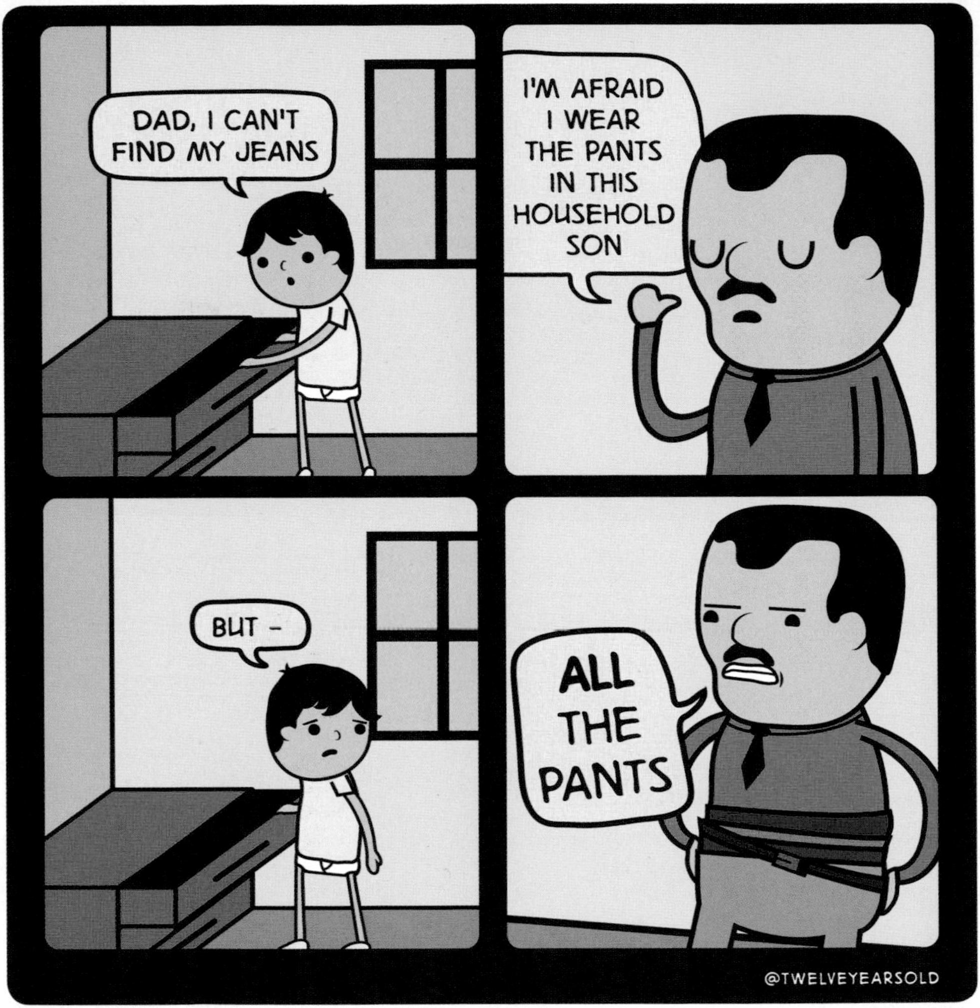
DAD, I CAN'T FIND MY JEANS
I'M AFRAID I WEAR THE PANTS IN THIS HOUSEHOLD SON
BUT -
ALL THE PANTS
@TWELVEYEARSOLD

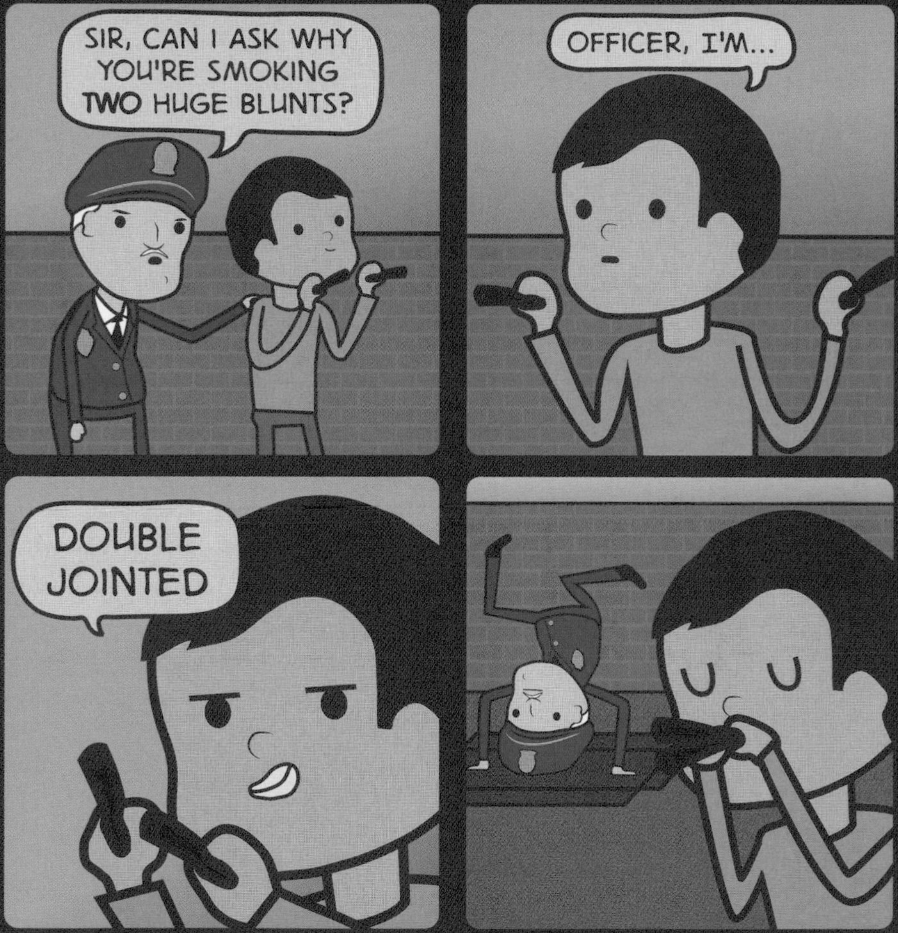
SIR, CAN I ASK WHY YOU'RE SMOKING TWO HUGE BLUNTS?
OFFICER, I'M...
DOUBLE JOINTED
@FRED_DELICIOUS

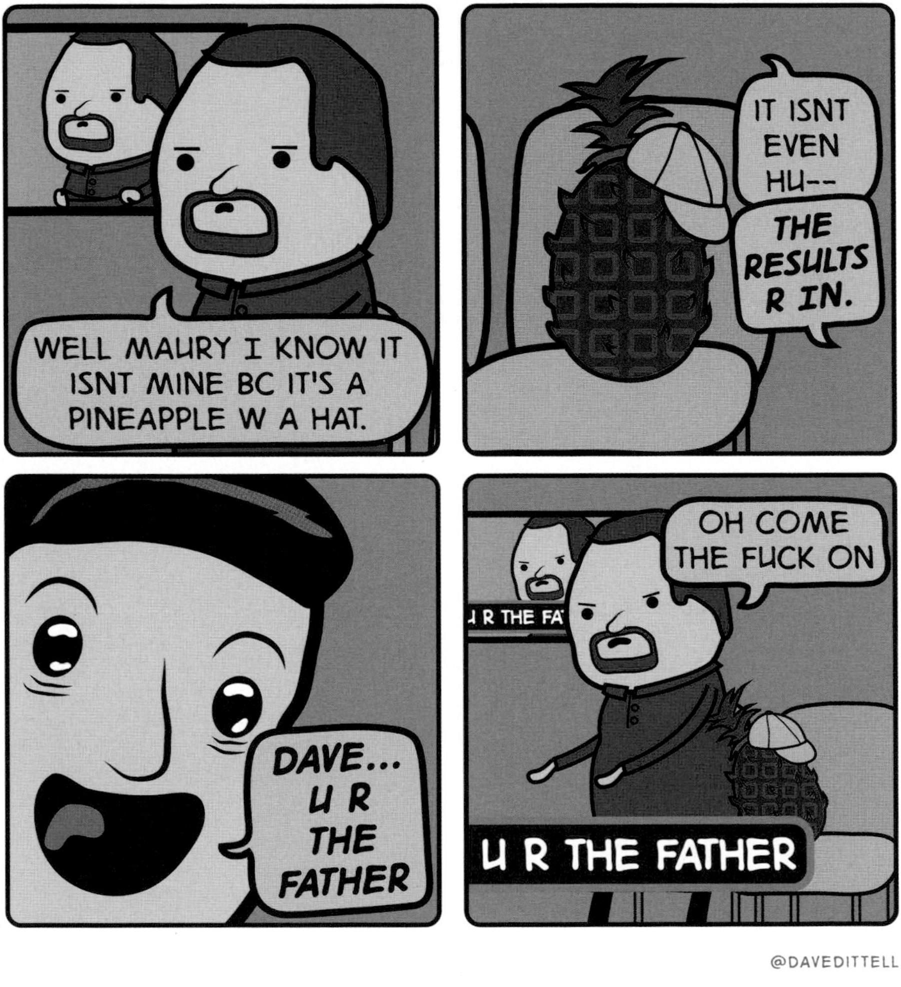
WELL MAURY I KNOW IT ISNT MINE BC IT'S A PINEAPPLE W A HAT.
IT ISNT EVEN HU--
THE RESULTS R IN.
DAVE... U R THE FATHER
OH COME THE FUCK ON
U R THE FATHER

@DAVEDITTELL

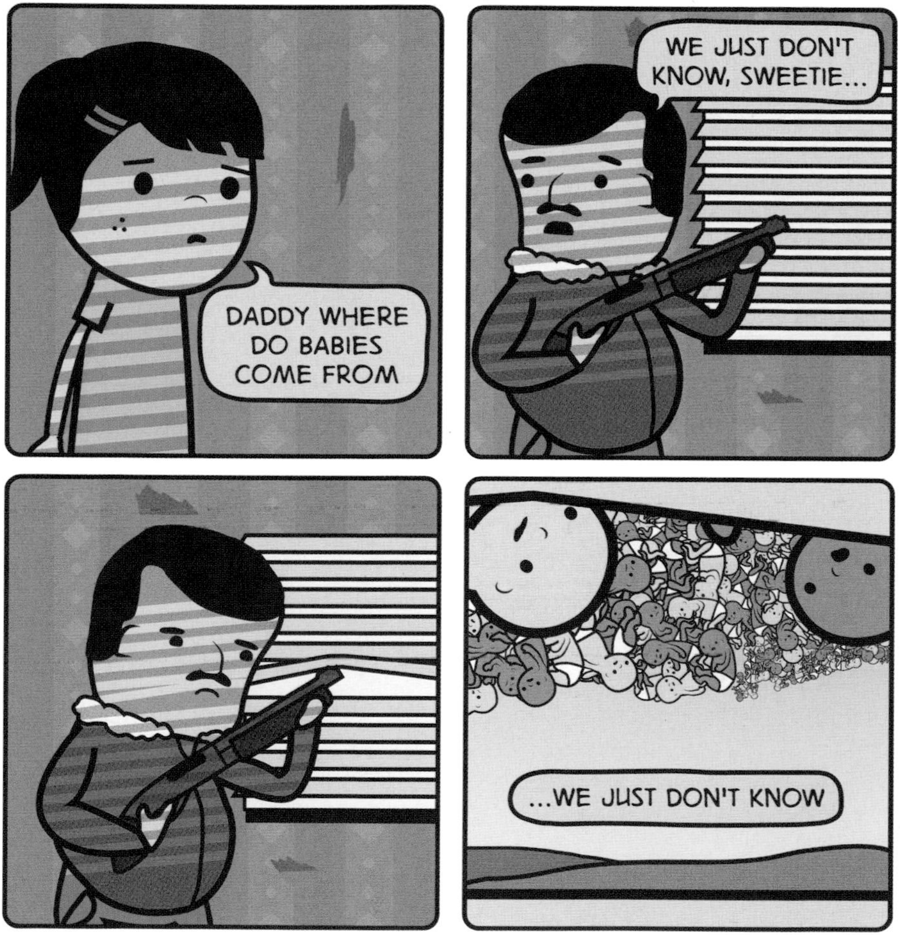
DADDY WHERE DO BABIES COME FROM
WE JUST DON'T KNOW, SWEETIE...
...WE JUST DON'T KNOW

@CRUSHINGBORT

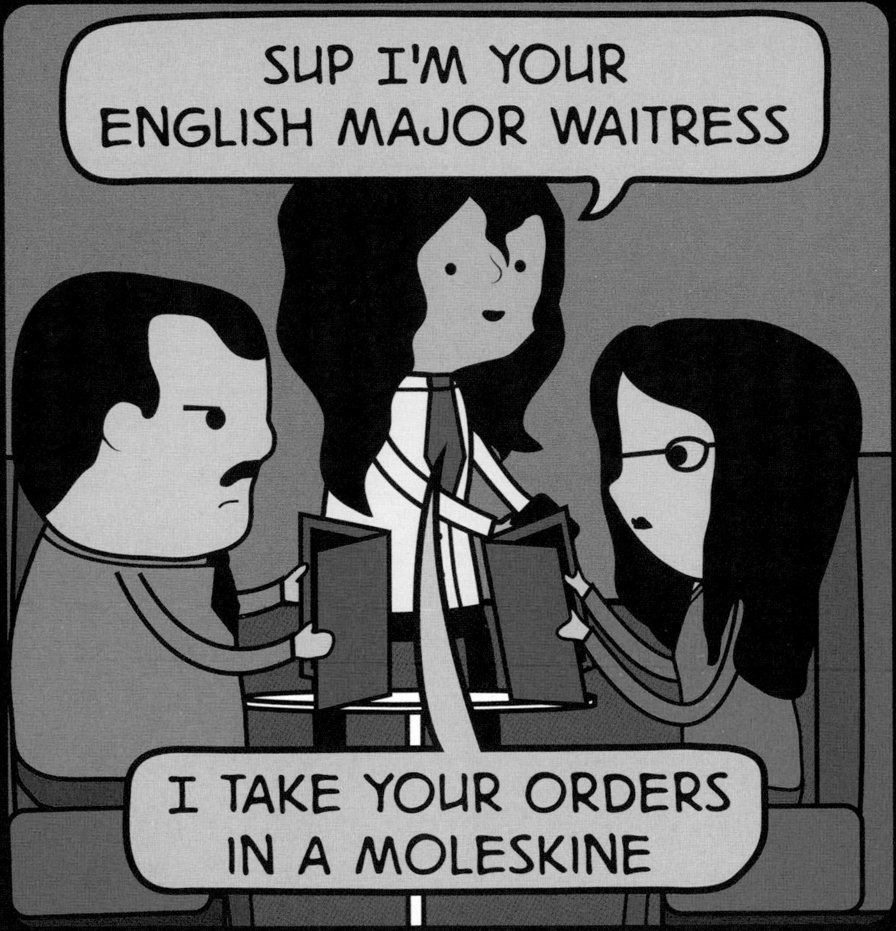
SUP I'M YOUR ENGLISH MAJOR WAITRESS
I TAKE YOUR ORDERS IN A MOLESKINE

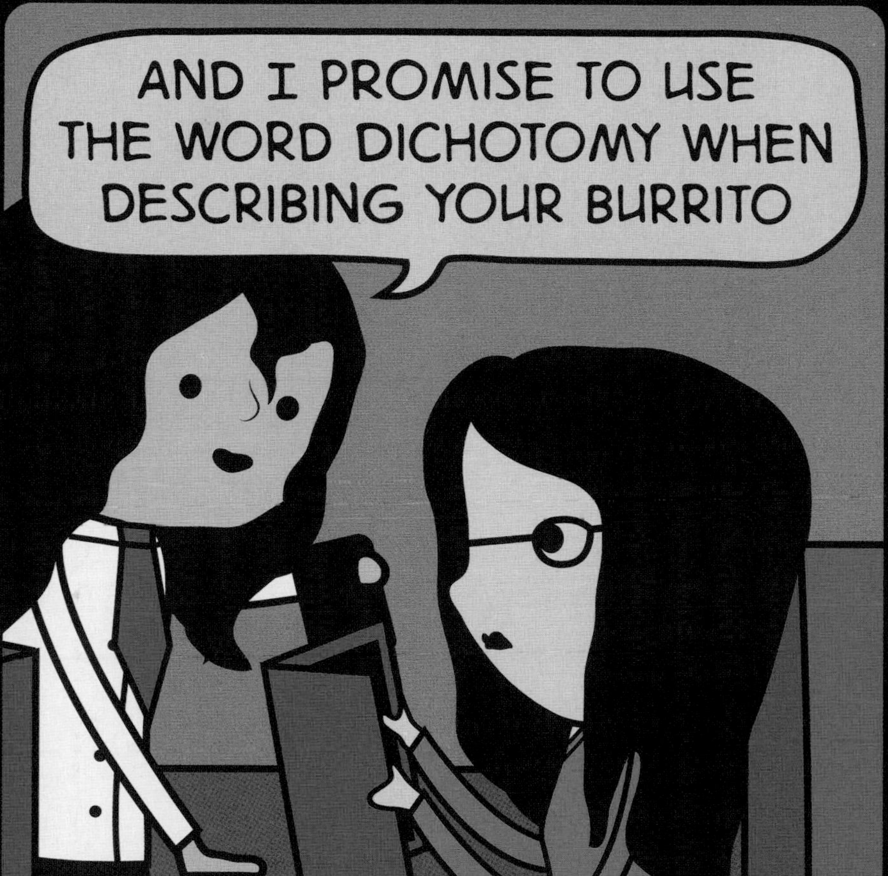
AND I PROMISE TO USE THE WORD DICHOTOMY WHEN DESCRIBING YOUR BURRITO

@RACHELMILLMAN

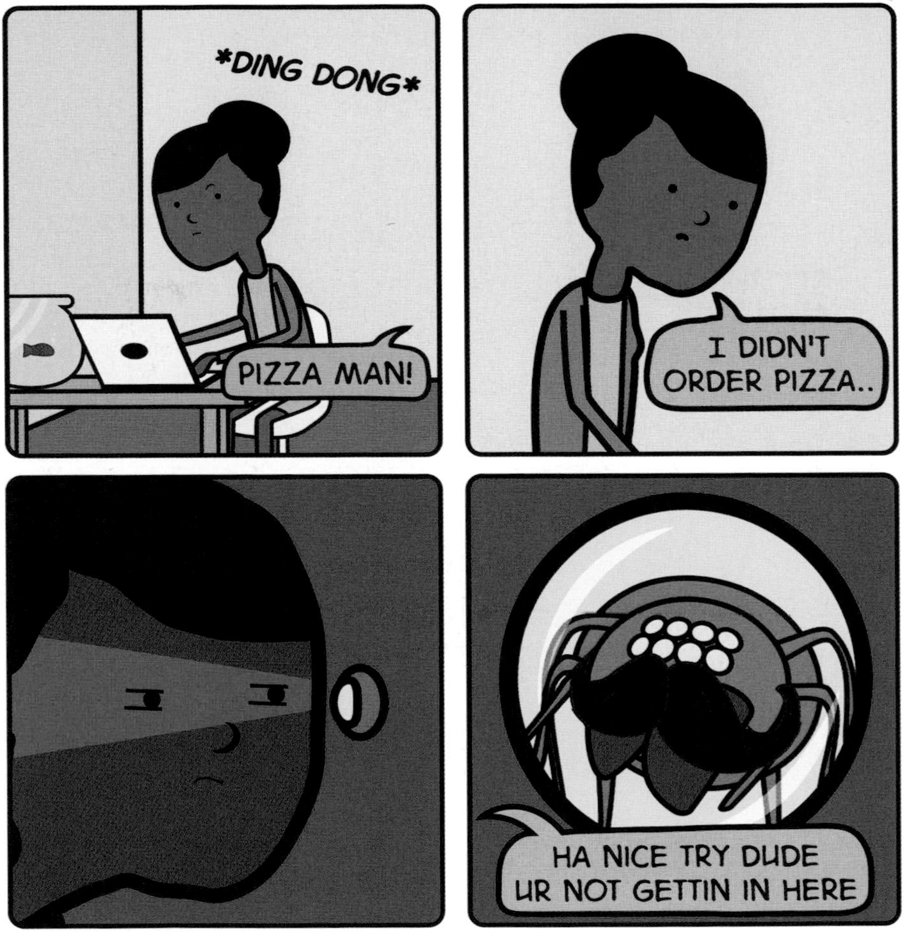
DING DONG
PIZZA MAN!
I DIDN'T ORDER PIZZA..
HA NICE TRY DUDE UR NOT GETTIN IN HERE

@TASTEFACTORY

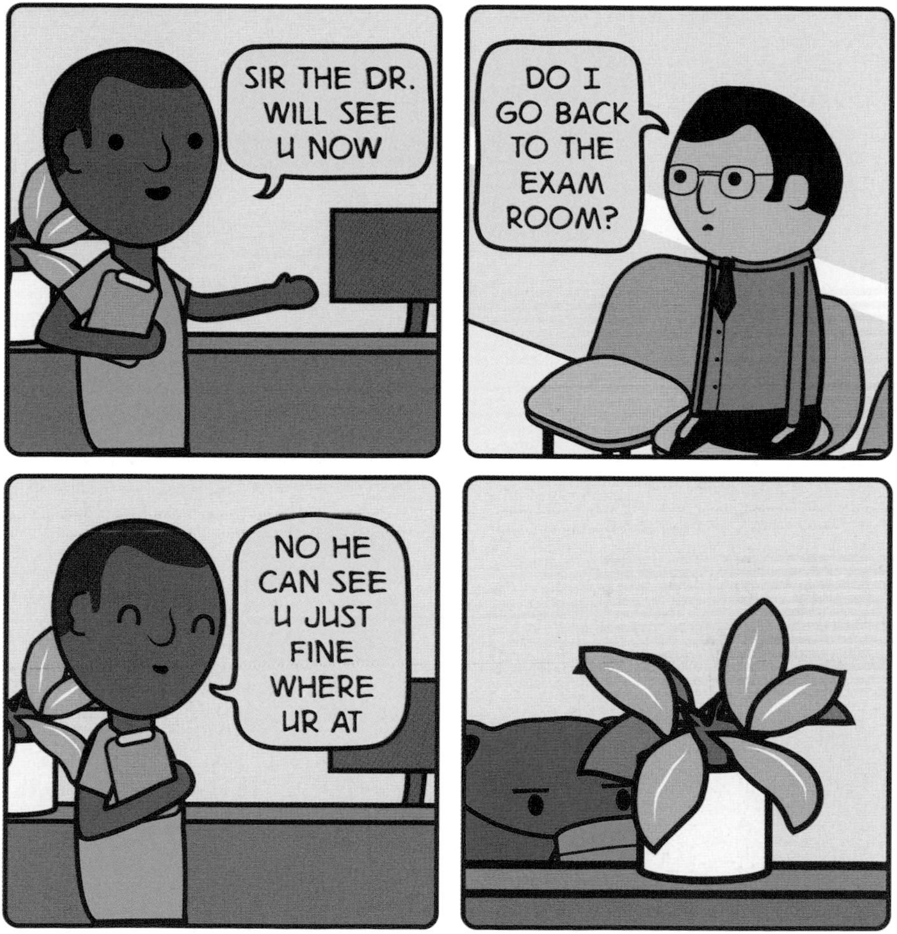
SIR THE DR. WILL SEE U NOW
DO I GO BACK TO THE EXAM ROOM?
NO HE CAN SEE U JUST FINE WHERE UR AT

@FART_BRINGER

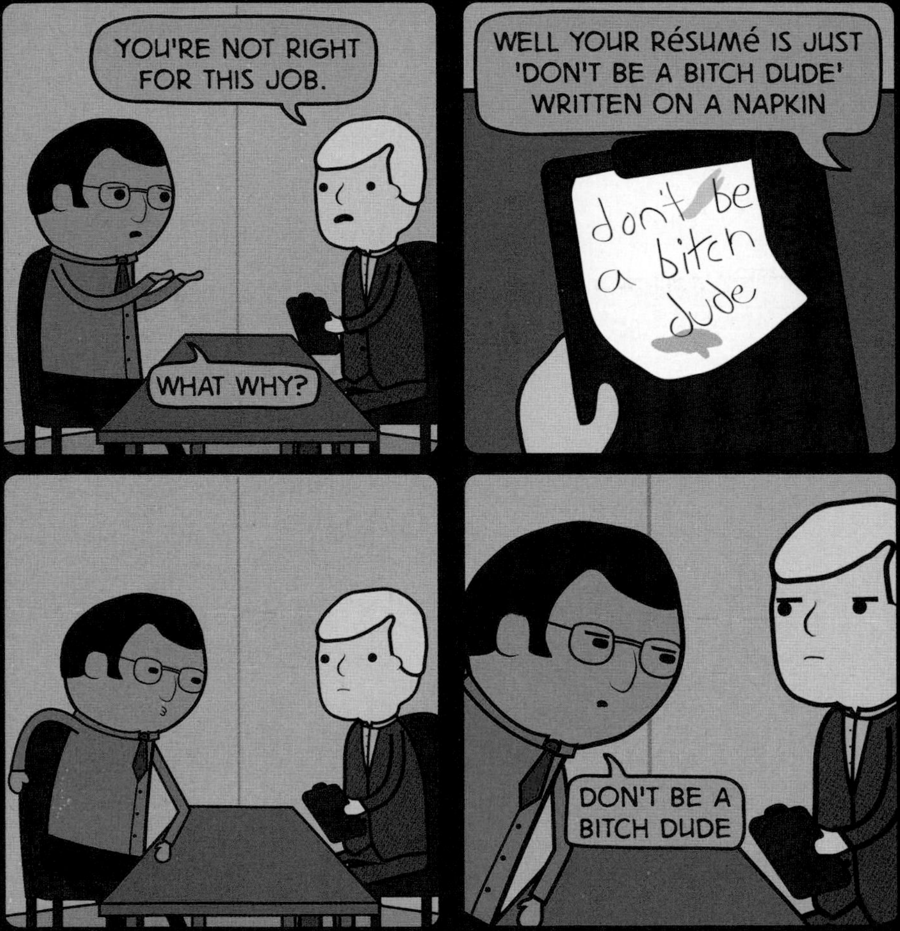
YOU'RE NOT RIGHT FOR THIS JOB.
WHAT WHY?
WELL YOUR RÉSUMÉ IS JUST 'DON'T BE A BITCH DUDE' WRITTEN ON A NAPKIN
don't be a bitch dude
DON'T BE A BITCH DUDE

@SATANSTONGUE

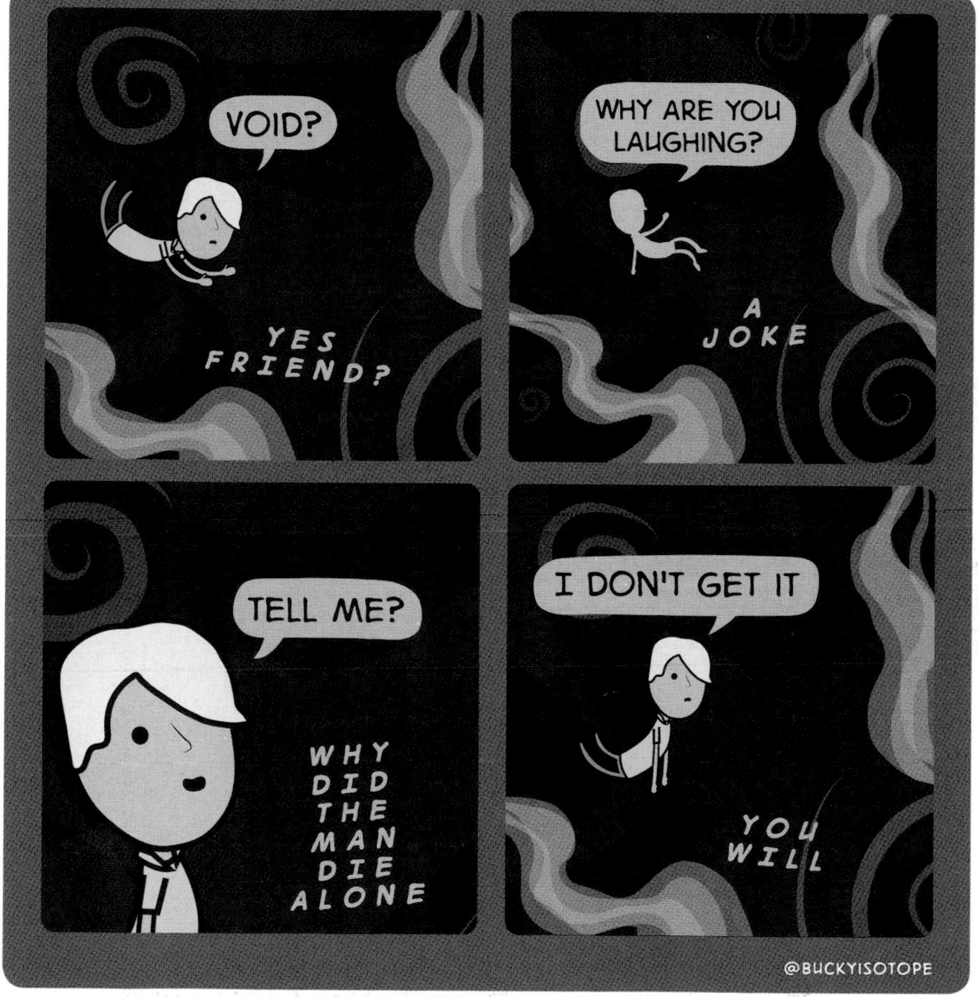
VOID?
YES FRIEND?
WHY ARE YOU LAUGHING?
A JOKE
TELL ME?
WHY DID THE MAN DIE ALONE
I DON'T GET IT
YOU WILL
@BUCKYISOTOPE

ABOUT THE AUTHOR

MIKE ROSENTHAL IS A CARTOONIST, ILLUSTRATOR, IDIOT, AND CREATOR OF *TWITTER: THE COMIC* AND *OUR NEW ELECTRICAL MORALS*. HIS WORK HAS BEEN FEATURED ON CARTOON HANGOVER, COLLEGE HUMOR, SALON, THE ATLANTIC, TECHCRUNCH, AND KOTAKU. HE LIVES IN LOS ANGELES.